Life Application Bible Studies
MATTHEW

APPLICATION® BIBLE STUDIES

Part 1:
Complete text of Matthew with study notes and features from the
Life Application Study Bible

Part 2:
Thirteen lessons for individual or group study

Study questions written and edited by

Rev. Neil S. Wilson
Rev. David R. Veerman
Dr. James C. Galvin
Dr. Bruce B. Barton
Daryl J. Lucas

matthew

New Living
Translation®

Tyndale House Publishers, Inc.
Carol Stream, Illinois

Visit Tyndale's exciting Web site at www.tyndale.com

New Living Translation, NLT, the New Living Translation logo, and *Life Application* are registered trademarks of Tyndale House Publishers, Inc.

Life Application Bible Studies: Matthew

CONTENTS

A NOTE TO READERS

The *Holy Bible*, New Living Translation, was first published in 1996. It quickly became one of the most popular Bible translations in the English-speaking world. While the NLT's influence was rapidly growing, the Bible Translation Committee determined that an additional investment in scholarly review and text refinement could make it even better. So shortly after its initial publication, the committee began an eight-year process with the purpose of increasing the level of the NLT's precision without sacrificing its easy-to-understand quality. This second-generation text was completed in 2004 and is reflected in this edition of the New Living Translation. An additional update with minor changes was subsequently introduced in 2007.

The goal of any Bible translation is to convey the meaning and content of the ancient Hebrew, Aramaic, and Greek texts as accurately as possible to contemporary readers. The challenge for our translators was to create a text that would communicate as clearly and powerfully to today's readers as the original texts did to readers and listeners in the ancient biblical world. The resulting translation is easy to read and understand, while also accurately communicating the meaning and content of the original biblical texts. The NLT is a general-purpose text especially good for study, devotional reading, and reading aloud in worship services.

We believe that the New Living Translation—which combines the latest biblical scholarship with a clear, dynamic writing style—will communicate God's word powerfully to all who read it. We publish it with the prayer that God will use it to speak his timeless truth to the church and the world in a fresh, new way.

The Publishers
October 2007

INTRODUCTION TO THE
NEW LIVING TRANSLATION

Translation Philosophy and Methodology

English Bible translations tend to be governed by one of two general translation theories. The first theory has been called "formal-equivalence," "literal," or "word-for-word" translation. According to this theory, the translator attempts to render each word of the original language into English and seeks to preserve the original syntax and sentence structure as much as possible in translation. The second theory has been called "dynamic-equivalence," "functional-equivalence," or "thought-for-thought" translation. The goal of this translation theory is to produce in English the closest natural equivalent of the message expressed by the original-language text, both in meaning and in style.

Both of these translation theories have their strengths. A formal-equivalence translation preserves aspects of the original text—including ancient idioms, term consistency, and original-language syntax—that are valuable for scholars and professional study. It allows a reader to trace formal elements of the original-language text through the English translation. A dynamic-equivalence translation, on the other hand, focuses on translating the message of the original-language text. It ensures that the meaning of the text is readily apparent to the contemporary reader. This allows the message to come through with immediacy, without requiring the reader to struggle with foreign idioms and awkward syntax. It also facilitates serious study of the text's message and clarity in both devotional and public reading.

The pure application of either of these translation philosophies would create translations at opposite ends of the translation spectrum. But in reality, all translations contain a mixture of these two philosophies. A purely formal-equivalence translation would be unintelligible in English, and a purely dynamic-equivalence translation would risk being unfaithful to the original. That is why translations shaped by dynamic-equivalence theory are usually quite literal when the original text is relatively clear, and the translations shaped by formal-equivalence theory are sometimes quite dynamic when the original text is obscure.

The translators of the New Living Translation set out to render the message of the original texts of Scripture into clear, contemporary English. As they did so, they kept the concerns of both formal-equivalence and dynamic-equivalence in mind. On the one hand, they translated as simply and literally as possible when that approach yielded an accurate, clear, and natural English text. Many words and phrases were rendered literally and consistently into English, preserving essential literary and rhetorical devices, ancient metaphors, and word choices that give structure to the text and provide echoes of meaning from one passage to the next.

On the other hand, the translators rendered the message more dynamically when the literal rendering was hard to understand, was misleading, or yielded archaic or foreign wording. They clarified difficult metaphors and terms to aid in the reader's understanding. The translators first struggled with the meaning of the words and phrases in the ancient context; then they rendered the message into clear, natural English. Their goal was to be both faithful to the ancient texts and eminently readable. The result is a translation that is both exegetically accurate and idiomatically powerful.

Translation Process and Team

To produce an accurate translation of the Bible into contemporary English, the translation team needed the skills necessary to enter into the thought patterns of the ancient authors and then to render their ideas, connotations, and effects into clear, contemporary English.

To begin this process, qualified biblical scholars were needed to interpret the meaning of the original text and to check it against our base English translation. In order to guard against personal and theological biases, the scholars needed to represent a diverse group of evangelicals who would employ the best exegetical tools. Then to work alongside the scholars, skilled English stylists were needed to shape the text into clear, contemporary English.

With these concerns in mind, the Bible Translation Committee recruited teams of scholars that represented a broad spectrum of denominations, theological perspectives, and backgrounds within the worldwide evangelical community. Each book of the Bible was assigned to three different scholars with proven expertise in the book or group of books to be reviewed. Each of these scholars made a thorough review of a base translation and submitted suggested revisions to the appropriate Senior Translator. The Senior Translator then reviewed and summarized these suggestions and proposed a first-draft revision of the base text. This draft served as the basis for several additional phases of exegetical and stylistic committee review. Then the Bible Translation Committee jointly reviewed and approved every verse of the final translation.

Throughout the translation and editing process, the Senior Translators and their scholar teams were given a chance to review the editing done by the team of stylists. This ensured that exegetical errors would not be introduced late in the process and that the entire Bible Translation Committee was happy with the final result. By choosing a team of qualified scholars and skilled stylists and by setting up a process that allowed their interaction throughout the process, the New Living Translation has been refined to preserve the essential formal elements of the original biblical texts, while also creating a clear, understandable English text.

The New Living Translation was first published in 1996. Shortly after its initial publication, the Bible Translation Committee began a process of further committee review and translation refinement. The purpose of this continued revision was to increase the level of precision without sacrificing the text's easy-to-understand quality. This second-edition text was completed in 2004, and an additional update with minor changes was subsequently introduced in 2007. This printing of the New Living Translation reflects the updated 2007 text.

Written to Be Read Aloud
It is evident in Scripture that the biblical documents were written to be read aloud, often in public worship (see Nehemiah 8; Luke 4:16-20; 1 Timothy 4:13; Revelation 1:3). It is still the case today that more people will hear the Bible read aloud in church than are likely to read it for themselves. Therefore, a new translation must communicate with clarity and power when it is read publicly. Clarity was a primary goal for the NLT translators, not only to facilitate private reading and understanding, but also to ensure that it would be excellent for public reading and make an immediate and powerful impact on any listener.

The Texts behind the New Living Translation
The Old Testament translators used the Masoretic Text of the Hebrew Bible as represented in *Biblia Hebraica Stuttgartensia* (1977), with its extensive system of textual notes; this is an update of Rudolf Kittel's *Biblia Hebraica* (Stuttgart, 1937). The translators also further compared the Dead Sea Scrolls, the Septuagint and other Greek manuscripts, the Samaritan Pentateuch, the Syriac Peshitta, the Latin Vulgate, and any other versions or manuscripts that shed light on the meaning of difficult passages.

The New Testament translators used the two standard editions of the Greek New Testament: the *Greek New Testament*, published by the United Bible Societies (UBS, fourth revised edition, 1993), and *Novum Testamentum Graece*, edited by Nestle and Aland (NA, twenty-seventh edition, 1993). These two editions, which have the same text but differ in punctuation and textual notes, represent, for the most part, the best in modern textual scholarship. However, in cases where strong textual or other scholarly evidence supported the decision, the translators sometimes chose to differ from the UBS and NA Greek texts and followed variant readings found in other ancient witnesses. Significant textual variants of this sort are always noted in the textual notes of the New Living Translation.

Translation Issues
The translators have made a conscious effort to provide a text that can be easily understood by the typical reader of modern English. To this end, we sought to use only vocabulary and

language structures in common use today. We avoided using language likely to become quickly dated or that reflects only a narrow subdialect of English, with the goal of making the New Living Translation as broadly useful and timeless as possible.

But our concern for readability goes beyond the concerns of vocabulary and sentence structure. We are also concerned about historical and cultural barriers to understanding the Bible, and we have sought to translate terms shrouded in history and culture in ways that can be immediately understood. To this end:

- We have converted ancient weights and measures (for example, "ephah" [a unit of dry volume] or "cubit" [a unit of length]) to modern English (American) equivalents, since the ancient measures are not generally meaningful to today's readers. Then in the textual footnotes we offer the literal Hebrew, Aramaic, or Greek measures, along with modern metric equivalents.
- Instead of translating ancient currency values literally, we have expressed them in common terms that communicate the message. For example, in the Old Testament, "ten shekels of silver" becomes "ten pieces of silver" to convey the intended message. In the New Testament, we have often translated the "denarius" as "the normal daily wage" to facilitate understanding. Then a footnote offers: "Greek *a denarius*, the payment for a full day's wage." In general, we give a clear English rendering and then state the literal Hebrew, Aramaic, or Greek in a textual footnote.
- Since the names of Hebrew months are unknown to most contemporary readers, and since the Hebrew lunar calendar fluctuates from year to year in relation to the solar calendar used today, we have looked for clear ways to communicate the time of year the Hebrew months (such as Abib) refer to. When an expanded or interpretive rendering is given in the text, a textual note gives the literal rendering. Where it is possible to define a specific ancient date in terms of our modern calendar, we use modern dates in the text. A textual footnote then gives the literal Hebrew date and states the rationale for our rendering. For example, Ezra 6:15 pinpoints the date when the postexilic Temple was completed in Jerusalem: "the third day of the month Adar." This was during the sixth year of King Darius's reign (that is, 515 B.C.). We have translated that date as March 12, with a footnote giving the Hebrew and identifying the year as 515 B.C.
- Since ancient references to the time of day differ from our modern methods of denoting time, we have used renderings that are instantly understandable to the modern reader. Accordingly, we have rendered specific times of day by using approximate equivalents in terms of our common "o'clock" system. On occasion, translations such as "at dawn the next morning" or "as the sun was setting" have been used when the biblical reference is more general.
- When the meaning of a proper name (or a wordplay inherent in a proper name) is relevant to the message of the text, its meaning is often illuminated with a textual footnote. For example, in Exodus 2:10 the text reads: "The princess named him Moses, for she explained, 'I lifted him out of the water.'" The accompanying footnote reads: "*Moses* sounds like a Hebrew term that means 'to lift out.'"

  Sometimes, when the actual meaning of a name is clear, that meaning is included in parentheses within the text itself. For example, the text at Genesis 16:11 reads: "You are to name him Ishmael *(which means 'God hears')*, for the LORD has heard your cry of distress." Since the original hearers and readers would have instantly understood the meaning of the name "Ishmael," we have provided modern readers with the same information so they can experience the text in a similar way.
- Many words and phrases carry a great deal of cultural meaning that was obvious to the original readers but needs explanation in our own culture. For example, the phrase "they beat their breasts" (Luke 23:48) in ancient times meant that people were very upset, often in mourning. In our translation we chose to translate this phrase dynamically for clarity: "They went home *in deep sorrow.*" Then we included a footnote with the literal Greek, which reads: "Greek *went home beating their breasts.*" In other similar cases, however, we have sometimes chosen to illuminate the existing literal expression to make it immediately understandable. For example, here we might have expanded the literal Greek phrase to read: "They went home

beating their breasts *in sorrow."* If we had done this, we would not have included a textual footnote, since the literal Greek clearly appears in translation.

- Metaphorical language is sometimes difficult for contemporary readers to understand, so at times we have chosen to translate or illuminate the meaning of a metaphor. For example, the ancient poet writes, "Your neck is *like* the tower of David" (Song of Songs 4:4). We have rendered it "Your neck is *as beautiful as* the tower of David" to clarify the intended positive meaning of the simile. Another example comes in Ecclesiastes 12:3, which can be literally rendered: "Remember him . . . when the grinding women cease because they are few, and the women who look through the windows see dimly." We have rendered it: "Remember him before your teeth—your few remaining servants—stop grinding; and before your eyes—the women looking through the windows—see dimly." We clarified such metaphors only when we believed a typical reader might be confused by the literal text.

- When the content of the original language text is poetic in character, we have rendered it in English poetic form. We sought to break lines in ways that clarify and highlight the relationships between phrases of the text. Hebrew poetry often uses parallelism, a literary form where a second phrase (or in some instances a third or fourth) echoes the initial phrase in some way. In Hebrew parallelism, the subsequent parallel phrases continue, while also furthering and sharpening, the thought expressed in the initial line or phrase. Whenever possible, we sought to represent these parallel phrases in natural poetic English.

- The Greek term *hoi Ioudaioi* is literally translated "the Jews" in many English translations. In the Gospel of John, however, this term doesn't always refer to the Jewish people generally. In some contexts, it refers more particularly to the Jewish religious leaders. We have attempted to capture the meaning in these different contexts by using terms such as "the people" (with a footnote: Greek *the Jewish people*) or "the religious leaders," where appropriate.

- One challenge we faced was how to translate accurately the ancient biblical text that was originally written in a context where male-oriented terms were used to refer to humanity generally. We needed to respect the nature of the ancient context while also trying to make the translation clear to a modern audience that tends to read male-oriented language as applying only to males. Often the original text, though using masculine nouns and pronouns, clearly intends that the message be applied to both men and women. A typical example is found in the New Testament letters, where the believers are called "brothers" (*adelphoi*). Yet it is clear from the content of these letters that they were addressed to all the believers—male and female. Thus, we have usually translated this Greek word as "brothers and sisters" in order to represent the historical situation more accurately.

  We have also been sensitive to passages where the text applies generally to human beings or to the human condition. In some instances we have used plural pronouns (they, them) in place of the masculine singular (he, him). For example, a traditional rendering of Proverbs 22:6 is: "Train up a child in the way he should go, and when he is old he will not turn from it." We have rendered it: "Direct your children onto the right path, and when they are older, they will not leave it." At times, we have also replaced third person pronouns with the second person to ensure clarity. A traditional rendering of Proverbs 26:27 is: "He who digs a pit will fall into it, and he who rolls a stone, it will come back on him." We have rendered it: "If you set a trap for others, you will get caught in it yourself. If you roll a boulder down on others, it will crush you instead."

  We should emphasize, however, that all masculine nouns and pronouns used to represent God (for example, "Father") have been maintained without exception. All decisions of this kind have been driven by the concern to reflect accurately the intended meaning of the original texts of Scripture.

Lexical Consistency in Terminology

For the sake of clarity, we have translated certain original-language terms consistently, especially within synoptic passages and for commonly repeated rhetorical phrases, and within

certain word categories such as divine names and non-theological technical terminology (e.g., liturgical, legal, cultural, zoological, and botanical terms). For theological terms, we have allowed a greater semantic range of acceptable English words or phrases for a single Hebrew or Greek word. We have avoided some theological terms that are not readily understood by many modern readers. For example, we avoided using words such as "justification" and "sanctification," which are carryovers from Latin translations. In place of these words, we have provided renderings such as "made right with God" and "made holy."

The Spelling of Proper Names

Many individuals in the Bible, especially the Old Testament, are known by more than one name (e.g., Uzziah/Azariah). For the sake of clarity, we have tried to use a single spelling for any one individual, footnoting the literal spelling whenever we differ from it. This is especially helpful in delineating the kings of Israel and Judah. King Joash/Jehoash of Israel has been consistently called Jehoash, while King Joash/Jehoash of Judah is called Joash. A similar distinction has been used to distinguish between Joram/Jehoram of Israel and Joram/Jehoram of Judah. All such decisions were made with the goal of clarifying the text for the reader. When the ancient biblical writers clearly had a theological purpose in their choice of a variant name (e.g., Esh-baal/Ishbosheth), the different names have been maintained with an explanatory footnote.

For the names Jacob and Israel, which are used interchangeably for both the individual patriarch and the nation, we generally render it "Israel" when it refers to the nation and "Jacob" when it refers to the individual. When our rendering of the name differs from the underlying Hebrew text, we provide a textual footnote, which includes this explanation: "The names 'Jacob' and 'Israel' are often interchanged throughout the Old Testament, referring sometimes to the individual patriarch and sometimes to the nation."

The Rendering of Divine Names

All appearances of *'el, 'elohim,* or *'eloah* have been translated "God," except where the context demands the translation "god(s)." We have generally rendered the tetragrammaton (YHWH) consistently as "the LORD," utilizing a form with small capitals that is common among English translations. This will distinguish it from the name *'adonai,* which we render "Lord." When *'adonai* and YHWH appear together, we have rendered it "Sovereign LORD." This also distinguishes *'adonai YHWH* from cases where YHWH appears with *'elohim,* which is rendered "LORD God." When YH (the short form of YHWH) and YHWH appear together, we have rendered it "LORD GOD." When YHWH appears with the term *tseba'oth,* we have rendered it "LORD of Heaven's Armies" to translate the meaning of the name. In a few cases, we have utilized the transliteration, *Yahweh,* when the personal character of the name is being invoked in contrast to another divine name or the name of some other god (for example, see Exodus 3:15; 6:2-3).

In the New Testament, the Greek word *christos* has been translated as "Messiah" when the context assumes a Jewish audience. When a Gentile audience can be assumed, *christos* has been translated as "Christ." The Greek word *kurios* is consistently translated "Lord," except that it is translated "LORD" wherever the New Testament text explicitly quotes from the Old Testament, and the text there has it in small capitals.

Textual Footnotes

The New Living Translation provides several kinds of textual footnotes, all designated in the text with an asterisk:

- When for the sake of clarity the NLT renders a difficult or potentially confusing phrase dynamically, we generally give the literal rendering in a textual footnote. This allows the reader to see the literal source of our dynamic rendering and how our translation relates to other more literal translations. These notes are prefaced with "Hebrew," "Aramaic," or "Greek," identifying the language of the underlying source text. For example, in Acts 2:42 we translated the literal "breaking of bread" (from the Greek) as "the Lord's Supper" to clarify that this verse refers to the ceremonial practice of the church rather than just an ordinary meal. Then we attached a footnote to "the Lord's Supper," which reads: "Greek *the breaking of bread.*"

- Textual footnotes are also used to show alternative renderings, prefaced with the word "Or." These normally occur for passages where an aspect of the meaning is debated. On occasion, we also provide notes on words or phrases that represent a departure from long-standing tradition. These notes are prefaced with "Tradition-ally rendered." For example, the footnote to the translation "serious skin disease" at Leviticus 13:2 says: "Traditionally rendered *leprosy.* The Hebrew word used throughout this passage is used to describe various skin diseases."
- When our translators follow a textual variant that differs significantly from our stan-dard Hebrew or Greek texts (listed earlier), we document that difference with a foot-note. We also footnote cases when the NLT excludes a passage that is included in the Greek text known as the *Textus Receptus* (and familiar to readers through its transla-tion in the King James Version). In such cases, we offer a translation of the excluded text in a footnote, even though it is generally recognized as a later addition to the Greek text and not part of the original Greek New Testament.
- All Old Testament passages that are quoted in the New Testament are identified by a textual footnote at the New Testament location. When the New Testament clearly quotes from the Greek translation of the Old Testament, and when it differs signifi-cantly in wording from the Hebrew text, we also place a textual footnote at the Old Testament location. This note includes a rendering of the Greek version, along with a cross-reference to the New Testament passage(s) where it is cited (for example, see notes on Proverbs 3:12; Psalms 8:2; 53:3).
- Some textual footnotes provide cultural and historical information on places, things, and people in the Bible that are probably obscure to modern readers. Such notes should aid the reader in understanding the message of the text. For example, in Acts 12:1, "King Herod" is named in this translation as "King Herod Agrippa" and is iden-tified in a footnote as being "the nephew of Herod Antipas and a grandson of Herod the Great."
- When the meaning of a proper name (or a wordplay inherent in a proper name) is relevant to the meaning of the text, it is either illuminated with a textual footnote or included within parentheses in the text itself. For example, the footnote concerning the name "Eve" at Genesis 3:20 reads: "*Eve* sounds like a Hebrew term that means 'to give life.' " This wordplay in the Hebrew illuminates the meaning of the text, which goes on to say that Eve "would be the mother of all who live."

As we submit this translation for publication, we recognize that any translation of the Scrip-tures is subject to limitations and imperfections. Anyone who has attempted to communi-cate the richness of God's Word into another language will realize it is impossible to make a perfect translation. Recognizing these limitations, we sought God's guidance and wisdom throughout this project. Now we pray that he will accept our efforts and use this translation for the benefit of the church and of all people.

We pray that the New Living Translation will overcome some of the barriers of history, cul-ture, and language that have kept people from reading and understanding God's Word. We hope that readers unfamiliar with the Bible will find the words clear and easy to understand and that readers well versed in the Scriptures will gain a fresh perspective. We pray that readers will gain insight and wisdom for living, but most of all that they will meet the God of the Bible and be forever changed by knowing him.

The Bible Translation Committee
October 2007

WHY THE
LIFE APPLICATION STUDY BIBLE
IS UNIQUE

Have you ever opened your Bible and asked the following:

- What does this passage really mean?
- How does it apply to my life?
- Why does some of the Bible seem irrelevant?
- What do these ancient cultures have to do with today?
- I love God; why can't I understand what he is saying to me through his word?
- What's going on in the lives of these Bible people?

Many Christians do not read the Bible regularly. Why? Because in the pressures of daily living they cannot find a connection between the timeless principles of Scripture and the ever-present problems of day-by-day living.

God urges us to apply his word (Isaiah 42:23; 1 Corinthians 10:11; 2 Thessalonians 3:4), but too often we stop at accumulating Bible knowledge. This is why the *Life Application Study Bible* was developed—to show how to put into practice what we have learned.

Applying God's word is a vital part of one's relationship with God; it is the evidence that we are obeying him. The difficulty in applying the Bible is not with the Bible itself, but with the reader's inability to bridge the gap between the past and present, the conceptual and practical. When we don't or can't do this, spiritual dryness, shallowness, and indifference are the results.

The words of Scripture itself cry out to us, "But don't just listen to God's word. You must do what it says. Otherwise, you are only fooling yourselves" (James 1:22). The *Life Application Study Bible* helps us to obey God's word. Developed by an interdenominational team of pastors, scholars, family counselors, and a national organization dedicated to promoting God's word and spreading the gospel, the *Life Application Study Bible* took many years to complete. All the work was reviewed by several renowned theologians under the directorship of Dr. Kenneth Kantzer.

The *Life Application Study Bible* does what a good resource Bible should: It helps you understand the context of a passage, gives important background and historical information, explains difficult words and phrases, and helps you see the interrelationship of Scripture. But it does much more. The *Life Application Study Bible* goes deeper into God's word, helping you discover the timeless truth being communicated, see the relevance for your life, and make a personal application. While some study Bibles attempt application, over 75 percent of this Bible is application oriented. The notes answer the questions "So what?" and "What does this passage mean to me, my family, my friends, my job, my neighborhood, my church, my country?"

Imagine reading a familiar passage of Scripture and gaining fresh insight, as if it were the first time you had ever read it. How much richer your life would be if you left each Bible reading with a new perspective and a small change for the better. A small change every day adds up to a changed life—and that is the very purpose of Scripture.

WHAT IS APPLICATION?

The best way to define application is to first determine what it is *not*. Application is *not* just accumulating knowledge. Accumulating knowledge helps us discover and understand facts and concepts, but it stops there. History is filled with philosophers who knew what the Bible said but failed to apply it to their lives, keeping them from believing and changing. Many think that understanding is the end goal of Bible study, but it is really only the beginning.

Application is *not* just illustration. Illustration only tells us how someone else handled a similar situation. While we may empathize with that person, we still have little direction for our personal situation.

Application is *not* just making a passage "relevant." Making the Bible relevant only helps us to see that the same lessons that were true in Bible times are true today; it does not show us how to apply them to the problems and pressures of our individual lives.

What, then, is application? Application begins by knowing and understanding God's word and its timeless truths. *But you cannot stop there.* If you do, God's word may not change your life, and it may become dull, difficult, tedious, and tiring. A good application focuses the truth of God's word, shows the reader what to do about what is being read, and motivates the reader to respond to what God is teaching. All three are essential to application.

Application is putting into practice what we already know (see Mark 4:24 and Hebrews 5:14) and answering the question "So what?" by confronting us with the right questions and motivating us to take action (see 1 John 2:5-6 and James 2:26). Application is deeply personal—unique for each individual. It makes a relevant truth a personal truth and involves developing a strategy and action plan to live your life in harmony with the Bible. It is the biblical "how to" of life.

You may ask, "How can your application notes be relevant to my life?" Each application note has three parts: (1) an *explanation*, which ties the note directly to the Scripture passage and sets up the truth that is being taught; (2) the *bridge*, which explains the timeless truth and makes it relevant for today; (3) the *application*, which shows you how to take the timeless truth and apply it to your personal situation. No note, by itself, can apply Scripture directly to your life. It can only teach, direct, lead, guide, inspire, recommend, and urge. It can give you the resources and direction you need to apply the Bible, but only you can take these resources and put them into practice.

A good note, therefore should not only give you knowledge and understanding but point you to application. Before you buy any kind of resource study Bible, you should evaluate the notes and ask the following questions: (1) Does the note contain enough information to help me understand the point of the Scripture passage? (2) Does the note assume I know more than I do? (3) Does the note avoid denominational bias? (4) Do the notes touch most of life's experiences? (5) Does the note help me apply God's word?

FEATURES OF THE
LIFE APPLICATION STUDY BIBLE

NOTES

In addition to providing the reader with many application notes, the *Life Application Study Bible* also offers several kinds of explanatory notes, which help the reader understand culture, history, context, difficult-to-understand passages, background, places, theological concepts, and the relationship of various passages in Scripture to other passages.

BOOK INTRODUCTIONS

Each book introduction is divided into several easy-to-find parts:

Timeline. A guide that puts the Bible book into its historical setting. It lists the key events and the dates when they occurred.

Vital Statistics. A list of straight facts about the book—those pieces of information you need to know at a glance.

Overview. A summary of the book with general lessons and applications that can be learned from the book as a whole.

Blueprint. The outline of the book. It is printed in easy-to-understand language and is designed for easy memorization. To the right of each main heading is a key lesson that is taught in that particular section.

Megathemes. A section that gives the main themes of the Bible book, explains their significance, and then tells you why they are still important for us today.

Map. If included, this shows the key places found in that book and retells the story of the book from a geographical point of view.

OUTLINE

The *Life Application Study Bible* has a new, custom-made outline that was designed specifically from an application point of view. Several unique features should be noted:

1. To avoid confusion and to aid memory work, the book outline has only three levels for headings. Main outline heads are marked with a capital letter. Subheads are marked by a number. Minor explanatory heads have no letter or number.

2. Each main outline head marked by a letter also has a brief paragraph below it summarizing the Bible text and offering a general application.

3. Parallel passages are listed where they apply.

PERSONALITY PROFILES

Among the unique features of this Bible are the profiles of key Bible people, including their strengths and weaknesses, greatest accomplishments and mistakes, and key lessons from their lives.

MAPS

The *Life Application Study Bible* has a thorough and comprehensive Bible atlas built right into the book. There are two kinds of maps: a book-introduction map, telling the story of the book, and thumbnail maps in the notes, plotting most geographic movements.

CHARTS AND DIAGRAMS

Many charts and diagrams are included to help the reader better visualize difficult concepts or relationships. Most charts not only present the needed information but show the significance of the information as well.

CROSS-REFERENCES

An updated, exhaustive cross-reference system in the margins of the Bible text helps the reader find related passages quickly.

TEXTUAL NOTES

Directly related to the text of the New Living Translation, the textual notes provide explanations on certain wording in the translation, alternate translations, and information about readings in the ancient manuscripts.

HIGHLIGHTED NOTES

In each Bible study lesson, you will be asked to read specific notes as part of your preparation. These notes have each been highlighted by a bullet (•) so that you can find them easily.

MATTHEW

MATTHEW

VITAL STATISTICS

PURPOSE:
To prove that Jesus is the Messiah, the eternal King

AUTHOR:
Matthew (Levi)

ORIGINAL AUDIENCE:
Matthew wrote especially to the Jews.

DATE WRITTEN:
Approximately A.D. 60–65

SETTING:
Matthew was a Jewish tax collector who became one of Jesus' disciples. This Gospel forms the connecting link between the Old and New Testaments because of its emphasis on the fulfillment of prophecy.

KEY VERSE:
"Don't misunderstand why I have come. I did not come to abolish the law of Moses or the writings of the prophets. No, I came to accomplish their purpose" (5:17).

KEY PEOPLE:
Jesus, Mary, Joseph, John the Baptist, the disciples, the religious leaders, Caiaphas, Pilate, Mary Magdalene

KEY PLACES:
Bethlehem, Jerusalem, Capernaum, Galilee, Judea

SPECIAL FEATURES:
Matthew is filled with messianic language ("Son of David" is used throughout) and Old Testament references (53 quotes and 76 other references). This Gospel was not written as a chronological account; its purpose was to present the clear evidence that Jesus is the Messiah, the Savior.

AS the motorcade slowly winds through the city, thousands pack the sidewalks hoping to catch a glimpse. Marching bands with great fanfare announce the arrival, and protective agents scan the crowd and run alongside the limousine. Pomp, ceremony, protocol—modern symbols of position and evidences of importance—herald the arrival of a head of state. Whether they are leaders by birth or election, we honor and respect them.

The Jews waited for a leader who had been promised centuries before by prophets. They believed that this leader—the Messiah ("anointed one")—would rescue them from their Roman oppressors and establish a new kingdom. As their king, he would rule the world with justice. Many Jews, however, overlooked prophecies that also spoke of this king as a suffering servant who would be rejected and killed. It is no wonder, then, that few recognized Jesus as the Messiah. How could this humble carpenter's son from Nazareth be their king? But Jesus was and is the King of all the earth!

Matthew (Levi) was one of Jesus' 12 disciples. Once he was a despised tax collector, but his life was changed by this man from Galilee. Matthew wrote this Gospel to his fellow Jews to prove that Jesus is the Messiah and to explain God's Kingdom.

Matthew begins his account by giving Jesus' genealogy. He then tells of Jesus' birth and early years, including the family's escape to Egypt from the murderous Herod and their return to Nazareth. Following Jesus' baptism by John (3:16, 17) and his defeat of Satan in the wilderness, Jesus began his public ministry by calling his first disciples and giving the Sermon on the Mount (chapters 5—7). Matthew shows Christ's authority by reporting his miracles of healing the sick and the demon-possessed, and even raising the dead.

Despite opposition from the Pharisees and others in the religious establishment (chapters 12—15), Jesus continued to teach concerning the Kingdom of Heaven (chapters 16—20). During this time, Jesus spoke with his disciples about his imminent death and resurrection (16:21) and revealed his true identity to Peter, James, and John (17:1–5). Near the end of his ministry, Jesus entered Jerusalem in a triumphant procession (21:1–11). But soon opposition mounted, and Jesus knew that his death was near. So he taught his disciples about the future—what they could expect before his return (chapter 24) and how to live until then (chapter 25).

In Matthew's finale (chapters 26—28), he focuses on Jesus' final days on earth—the Last Supper, his prayer in Gethsemane, the betrayal by Judas, the flight of the disciples, Peter's denial, the trials before Caiaphas and Pilate, Jesus' final words on the cross, and his burial in a borrowed tomb. But the story does not end there, for the Messiah rose from the dead—conquering death and then telling his followers to continue his work by making disciples in all nations.

As you read this Gospel, listen to Matthew's clear message: Jesus is the Christ, the King of kings and Lord of lords. Celebrate his victory over evil and death, and make Jesus the Lord of your life.

THE BLUEPRINT

A. BIRTH AND PREPARATION
OF JESUS, THE KING
(1:1—4:11)

The people of Israel were waiting for the Messiah, their king. Matthew begins his book by showing how Jesus Christ was a descendant of David. But Matthew goes on to show that God did not send Jesus to be an earthly king but a heavenly King. His Kingdom would be much greater than David's because it would never end. Even at Jesus' birth, many recognized him as a King. Herod, the ruler, as well as Satan, was afraid of Jesus' kingship and tried to stop him, but others worshiped him and brought royal gifts. We must be willing to recognize Jesus for who he really is and worship him as King of our life.

B. MESSAGE AND MINISTRY OF
JESUS, THE KING (4:12—25:46)
1. Jesus begins his ministry
2. Jesus gives the Sermon on the Mount
3. Jesus performs many miracles
4. Jesus teaches about the Kingdom
5. Jesus encounters differing reactions
to his ministry
6. Jesus faces conflict with the
religious leaders
7. Jesus teaches on the Mount of Olives

Jesus gave the Sermon on the Mount, directions for living in his Kingdom. He also told many parables about the difference between his Kingdom and the kingdoms of earth. Forgiveness, peace, and putting others first are some of the characteristics that make one great in the Kingdom of God. And to be great in God's Kingdom, we must live by God's standards right now. Jesus came to show us how to live as faithful subjects in his Kingdom.

C. DEATH AND RESURRECTION
OF JESUS, THE KING
(26:1—28:20)

Jesus was formally presented to the nation of Israel but was rejected. How strange for the King to be accused, arrested, and crucified. But Jesus demonstrated his power, even over death, through his resurrection and gained access for us into his Kingdom. With all this evidence that Jesus is God's Son, we, too, should accept him as our Lord.

MEGATHEMES

THEME	EXPLANATION	IMPORTANCE
Jesus Christ, the King	Jesus is revealed as the King of kings. His miraculous birth, his life and teaching, his miracles, and his triumph over death show his true identity.	Jesus cannot be equated with any person or power. He is the supreme ruler of time and eternity, heaven and earth, humans and angels. We should give him his rightful place as King of our lives.
The Messiah	Jesus was the Messiah, the one for whom the Jews had waited to deliver them from Roman oppression. Yet, tragically, they didn't recognize him when he came because his kingship was not what they expected. The true purpose of God's anointed deliverer was to die for all people to free them from sin's oppression.	Because Jesus was sent by God, we can trust him with our lives. It is worth everything we have to acknowledge him and give ourselves to him, because he came to be our Messiah, our Savior.
Kingdom of God	Jesus came to earth to begin his Kingdom. His full Kingdom will be realized at his return and will be made up of anyone who has faithfully followed him.	The way to enter God's Kingdom is by faith—believing in Christ to save us from sin and change our lives. We must do the work of his Kingdom now to be prepared for his return.

Teachings	Jesus taught the people through sermons, illustrations, and parables. Through his teachings, he showed the true ingredients of faith and how to guard against a fruitless and hypocritical life.	Jesus' teachings show us how to prepare for life in his eternal Kingdom by living properly right now. He lived what he taught, and we, too, must practice what we preach.
Resurrection	When Jesus rose from the dead, he rose in power as the true King. In his victory over death, he established his credentials as King and his power and authority over evil.	The Resurrection shows Jesus' all-powerful life for us—not even death could stop his plan of offering eternal life. Those who believe in Jesus can hope for a resurrection like his. Our role is to tell his story to all the earth so that everyone may share in his victory.

KEY PLACES IN MATTHEW

Jesus' earthly story begins in the town of Bethlehem in the Roman province of Judea (2:1). A threat to kill the infant king led Joseph to take his family to Egypt (2:14). When they returned, God led them to settle in Nazareth in Galilee (2:22, 23). At about age 30, Jesus was baptized in the Jordan River and was tempted by Satan in the Judean wilderness (3:13; 4:1). Jesus set up his base of operations in Capernaum (4:12, 13) and from there ministered throughout Israel, telling parables, teaching about the Kingdom, and healing the sick. He traveled to the region of the Gadarenes around Gadara and healed two demon-possessed men (8:28ff); fed over 5,000 people with five loaves and two fish on the shores of Galilee near Bethsaida (14:15ff); healed the sick in Gennesaret (14:34ff); ministered to the Gentiles in Tyre and Sidon (15:21ff); visited Caesarea Philippi, where Peter declared him to be the Messiah (16:13ff); and taught in Perea, east of the Jordan (19:1). As he set out on his last visit to Jerusalem, he told the disciples what would happen to him there (20:17ff). He spent some time in Jericho (20:29) and then stayed in Bethany at night as he went back and forth to Jerusalem during his last week (21:17ff). In Jerusalem he would be crucified, but he would rise again.

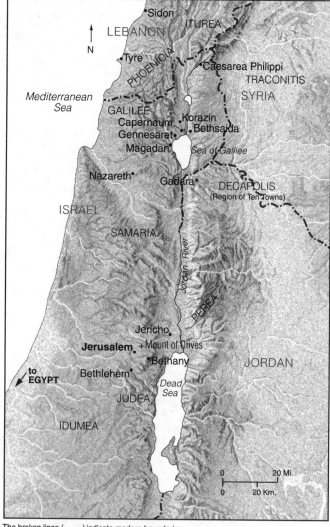

The broken lines (—·—·—) indicate modern boundaries.

A. BIRTH AND PREPARATION OF JESUS, THE KING (1:1—4:11)

Matthew opens his Gospel with a genealogy to prove that Jesus is a descendant of both King David and Abraham, just as the Old Testament had predicted. Jesus' birth didn't go unnoticed, for both shepherds and wise men came to worship him. The Jewish people were waiting for the Messiah to appear. However, after he was born, the Jews didn't recognize him because they were looking for a different kind of king.

The Record of Jesus' Ancestors (3/Luke 3:23-28)

1:1
Gen 22:18
2 Sam 7:12-14
1 Chr 17:11
Pss 89:3-4; 132:11
Isa 9:6; 11:1
Matt 22:42
John 7:42
Rom 1:3
Gal 3:16
Rev 22:16

1:2
Gen 21:3, 12;
25:26; 29:35
1 Chr 1:34

1:3
Gen 38:29-30
Ruth 4:12, 18-19
1 Chr 2:4-5, 9

1:4-5
Ruth 4:13, 17-22
1 Chr 2:10-12, 15
Heb 11:31

1:6
Ruth 4:17, 22
2 Sam 12:24
1 Chr 2:13-15

1:7-10
1 Chr 3:10-14

1 This is a record of the ancestors of Jesus the Messiah, a descendant of David* and of Abraham:

2 Abraham was the father of Isaac.
Isaac was the father of Jacob.
Jacob was the father of Judah and his brothers.
3 Judah was the father of Perez and Zerah (whose mother was Tamar).
Perez was the father of Hezron.
Hezron was the father of Ram.*
4 Ram was the father of Amminadab.
Amminadab was the father of Nahshon.
Nahshon was the father of Salmon.
5 Salmon was the father of Boaz (whose mother was Rahab).
Boaz was the father of Obed (whose mother was Ruth).
Obed was the father of Jesse.
6 Jesse was the father of King David.
David was the father of Solomon (whose mother was Bathsheba, the widow of Uriah).
7 Solomon was the father of Rehoboam.
Rehoboam was the father of Abijah.
Abijah was the father of Asa.*
8 Asa was the father of Jehoshaphat.
Jehoshaphat was the father of Jehoram.*
Jehoram was the father* of Uzziah.
9 Uzziah was the father of Jotham.
Jotham was the father of Ahaz.
Ahaz was the father of Hezekiah.
10 Hezekiah was the father of Manasseh.
Manasseh was the father of Amon.*
Amon was the father of Josiah.

1:1 Greek *Jesus the Messiah, son of David.* **1:3** Greek *Aram,* a variant spelling of Ram; also in 1:4. See 1 Chr 2:9-10. **1:7** Greek *Asaph,* a variant spelling of Asa; also in 1:8. See 1 Chr 3:10. **1:8a** Greek *Joram,* a variant spelling of Jehoram; also in 1:8b. See 1 Kgs 22:50 and note at 1 Chr 3:11. **1:8b** Or *ancestor;* also in 1:11. **1:10** Greek *Amos,* a variant spelling of Amon; also in 1:10b. See 1 Chr 3:14.

• **1:1** Presenting this record of ancestors (called a genealogy) was one of the most interesting ways that Matthew could begin a book for a Jewish audience. Because a person's family line proved his or her standing as one of God's chosen people, Matthew began by showing that Jesus was a descendant of Abraham, the father of all Jews, and a direct descendant of David, fulfilling Old Testament prophecies about the Messiah's line. The facts of this ancestry were carefully preserved. This is the first of many proofs recorded by Matthew to show that Jesus is the true Messiah.

1:1ff More than 400 years had passed since the last Old Testament prophecies, and faithful Jews all over the world were still waiting for the Messiah (Luke 3:15). Matthew wrote this book to Jews to present Jesus as King and Messiah, the promised descendant of David who would reign forever (Isaiah 11:1-5). The Gospel of Matthew links the Old and New Testaments and contains many references that show how Jesus fulfilled Old Testament prophecy.

1:1ff Jesus entered human history when the land of Palestine was controlled by Rome and considered an insignificant outpost of the vast and mighty Roman Empire. The presence of Roman soldiers in Israel gave the Jews military peace, but at the price of oppression, slavery, injustice, and immorality. Into this kind of world came the promised Messiah.

• **1:1-17** In the first 17 verses we meet 46 people whose lifetimes span 2,000 years. All were ancestors of Jesus, but they varied considerably in personality, spirituality, and experience. Some were heroes of faith—like Abraham, Isaac, Ruth, and David. Some had shady reputations—like Rahab and Tamar. Many were very ordinary—like Hezron, Ram, Nahshon, and Akim. And others were evil—like Manasseh and Abijah. God's work in history is not limited by human failures or sins, and he works through ordinary people. Just as God used all kinds of people to bring his Son into the world, he uses all kinds today to accomplish his will. And God wants to use you.

1:3-6 Matthew's inclusion of four particular women (Tamar, Rahab, Ruth, and Bathsheba) reveals his concern to do more than relay historical data. These women raise both ethnic and ethical questions. At least two of them were not Israelites by birth and all four of them had reputations that could have made them unmentionable in an ancestral tree. Yet this was the line into which God's Son was born. Jesus' genealogy makes it clear, not that there were a few disreputable people in his family, but that all of them were sinners. God sent his Son as Savior of *all* people—Jews, Gentiles, men, and women. No matter what the sins of the people, God's plan was never thwarted. It continues to unfold. That plan includes you.

¹¹ Josiah was the father of Jehoiachin* and his brothers (born at the time of the exile to Babylon).
¹² After the Babylonian exile:
Jehoiachin was the father of Shealtiel.
Shealtiel was the father of Zerubbabel.
¹³ Zerubbabel was the father of Abiud.
Abiud was the father of Eliakim.
Eliakim was the father of Azor.
¹⁴ Azor was the father of Zadok.
Zadok was the father of Akim.
Akim was the father of Eliud.
¹⁵ Eliud was the father of Eleazar.
Eleazar was the father of Matthan.
Matthan was the father of Jacob.
¹⁶ Jacob was the father of Joseph, the husband of Mary.
Mary gave birth to Jesus, who is called the Messiah.

¹⁷All those listed above include fourteen generations from Abraham to David, fourteen from David to the Babylonian exile, and fourteen from the Babylonian exile to the Messiah.

An Angel Appears to Joseph (8)

¹⁸This is how Jesus the Messiah was born. His mother, Mary, was engaged to be married to Joseph. But before the marriage took place, while she was still a virgin, she became pregnant through the power of the Holy Spirit. ¹⁹Joseph, her fiancé, was a good man and did not want to disgrace her publicly, so he decided to break the engagement* quietly.

²⁰As he considered this, an angel of the Lord appeared to him in a dream. "Joseph, son of David," the angel said, "do not be afraid to take Mary as your wife. For the child within her was conceived by the Holy Spirit. ²¹And she will have a son, and you are to name him Jesus,* for he will save his people from their sins."

²²All of this occurred to fulfill the Lord's message through his prophet:

1:11 Greek *Jeconiah,* a variant spelling of Jehoiachin; also in 1:12. See 2 Kgs 24:6 and note at 1 Chr 3:16.
1:19 Greek *to divorce her.*   **1:21** *Jesus* means "The LORD saves."

1:11 references: 2 Kgs 24:14-16; 1 Chr 3:15-16; Jer 27:20; Dan 1:1-2. 1:12: 1 Chr 3:17, 19; Ezra 3:2. 1:16: Matt 27:17, 22; Luke 2:11. 1:18: Luke 1:27, 35; Gal 4:4. 1:19: Deut 24:1. 1:20: Luke 1:35. 1:21: Luke 1:31; 2:11, 21; Acts 5:31; 13:23; Heb 7:25.

1:11 The exile to Babylon occurred in 586 B.C. when Nebuchadnezzar, king of Babylon, conquered Judah, destroyed Jerusalem, and took thousands of people captive.

• **1:16** Because Mary was a virgin when she became pregnant, Matthew lists Joseph only as the husband of Mary, not the father of Jesus. Matthew's genealogy gives Jesus' legal (or royal) lineage through Joseph. Mary's ancestral line is recorded in Luke 3:23-38. Both Mary and Joseph were direct descendants of David. Matthew traced the genealogy back to Abraham, while Luke traced it back to Adam. Matthew wrote to the Jews, so Jesus was shown as a descendant of their father, Abraham. Luke wrote to the Gentiles, so he emphasized Jesus as the Savior of all people.

1:17 Matthew breaks Israel's history into three sets of 14 generations, but there were probably more generations than those listed here. Genealogies often compressed history, meaning that not every generation of ancestors was specifically listed. Thus, the phrase *the father of* can also be translated "the ancestor of."

• **1:18** Jewish marriage involved three basic steps. First, the two families agreed to the union. Second, a public announcement was made. At this point, the couple was "engaged." This was similar to engagement today except that their relationship could be broken only through death or divorce (even though sexual relations were not yet permitted). Third, the couple was married and began living together. Because Mary and Joseph were engaged, Mary's apparent unfaithfulness carried a severe social stigma. According to Jewish civil law, Joseph had a right to divorce her, and the Jewish authorities could have had her stoned to death (Deuteronomy 22:23, 24).

1:18 Why is the Virgin Birth important to the Christian faith? Jesus Christ, God's Son, had to be free from the sinful nature passed on to all other human beings by Adam. Because Jesus

was born of a woman, he was a human being; but as the Son of God, Jesus was born without any trace of human sin. Jesus is both fully human and fully divine.

Because Jesus lived as a man, we know that he fully understands our experiences and struggles (Hebrews 4:15, 16). Because he is God, he has the power and authority to deliver us from sin (Colossians 2:13-15). We can tell Jesus all our thoughts, feelings, and needs. He has been where we are now, and he has the ability to help.

• **1:19** Joseph was faced with a difficult choice after discovering that Mary was pregnant. Perhaps Joseph thought he had only two options: divorce Mary quietly or have her stoned. But God gave a third option—marry her (1:20-23). In view of the circumstances, this had not occurred to Joseph. But God often shows us that there are more options available than we think. Although Joseph seemed to be doing the right thing by breaking the engagement, only God's guidance helped him make the best decision. But that did not make it an easy decision. Consenting to marry Mary surely cast doubt on his own innocence regarding the pregnancy, as well as leaving them both with a social stigma they would carry for the rest of their lives. Yet Joseph chose to obey the angel's command (1:24). When our decisions affect the lives of others, we must always seek God's wisdom and then be willing to follow through no matter how difficult it may be.

1:20 The conception and birth of Jesus Christ are supernatural events beyond human logic or reasoning. Because of this, God sent angels to help certain people understand the significance of what was happening (see 2:13, 19; Luke 1:11, 26; 2:9).

Angels are spiritual beings created by God who help carry out his work on earth. They bring God's messages to people (Luke 1:26), protect God's people (Daniel 6:22), offer encouragement (Genesis 16:7ff), give guidance (Exodus 14:19), carry out punish-

1:23
†Isa 7:14; 8:8, 10
John 1:14
1 Tim 3:16

²³ "Look! The virgin will conceive a child!
        She will give birth to a son,
    and they will call him Immanuel,*
        which means 'God is with us.'"

1:23 Isa 7:14; 8:8, 10 (Greek version).

JOSEPH

The strength of what we believe is measured by how much we are willing to suffer for those beliefs. Joseph was a man with strong beliefs. He was prepared to do what was right, despite the pain he knew it would cause. But Joseph had another trait: He not only tried to do what was right, he also tried to do it in the right way.

When Mary told Joseph about her pregnancy, Joseph knew the child was not his. His respect for Mary's character and the explanation she gave him, as well as her attitude toward the expected child, must have made it hard to think his bride had done something wrong. Still, someone else was the child's father—and it was mind-boggling to accept that the "someone else" was God.

Joseph decided he had to break the engagement, but he was determined to do it in a way that would not cause public shame to Mary. He intended to act with justice and love.

At this point, God sent a messenger to Joseph to confirm Mary's story and open another way of obedience for Joseph—to take Mary as his wife. Joseph obeyed God, married Mary, and honored her virginity until the baby was born.

We do not know how long Joseph lived his role as Jesus' earthly father—he is last mentioned when Jesus was 12 years old. But Joseph trained his son in the trade of carpentry, made sure he had good spiritual training in Nazareth, and took the whole family on the yearly trip to Jerusalem for the Passover, which Jesus continued to observe during his adult years.

Joseph knew Jesus was someone special from the moment he heard the angel's words. His strong belief in that fact and his willingness to follow God's leading empowered him to be Jesus' chosen earthly father.

Strengths and accomplishments	• A man of integrity • A descendant of King David • Jesus' legal and earthly father • A person sensitive to God's guidance and willing to do God's will no matter what the consequence
Lessons from his life	• God honors integrity • Social position is of little importance when God chooses to use us • Being obedient to the guidance we have from God leads to more guidance from him • Feelings are not accurate measures of the rightness or wrongness of an action
Vital statistics	• Where: Nazareth, Bethlehem • Occupation: Carpenter • Relatives: Wife: Mary. Children: Jesus, James, Joses, Judas, Simon, and daughters. • Contemporaries: Herod the Great, John the Baptist, Simeon, Anna
Key verses	"Joseph, her fiancé, was a good man and did not want to disgrace her publicly, so he decided to break the engagement quietly. As he considered this, an angel of the Lord appeared to him in a dream. 'Joseph, son of David,' the angel said, 'do not be afraid to take Mary as your wife. For the child within her was conceived by the Holy Spirit'" (Matthew 1:19-20).

Joseph's story is told in Matthew 1:16–2:23; Luke 1:26–2:52.

ment (2 Samuel 24:16), patrol the earth (Zechariah 1:9-14), and fight the forces of evil (2 Kings 6:16-18; Revelation 20:1, 2). There are both good and bad angels (Revelation 12:7), but because bad angels are allied with the devil, or Satan, they have considerably less power and authority than good angels. Eventually the main role of angels will be to offer continuous praise to God (Revelation 7:11, 12).

1:20-23 The angel declared to Joseph that Mary's child was conceived by the Holy Spirit and would be a son. This reveals an important truth about Jesus—he is both God and human. The infinite, unlimited God took on the limitations of humanity so he could live and die for the salvation of all who would believe in him.

Jesus means "the Lord saves." Jesus came to earth to save us because we can't save ourselves from sin and its consequences. No matter how good we are, we can't eliminate the sinful nature present in all of us. Only Jesus can do that. Jesus didn't come to help people save themselves; he came to be their Savior from the power and penalty of sin. Thank Christ for his death on the cross for your sin, and then ask him to take control of your life. Your new life begins at that moment.

Jesus would fulfill the prophecy of Isaiah, for he would be *Immanuel* ("God is with us," see Isaiah 7:14). Jesus was God in the flesh; thus, God was literally among us, "with us." Through the Holy Spirit, Christ is present today in the life of every believer. Perhaps not even Isaiah understood how far-reaching the meaning of *Immanuel* would be.

²⁴When Joseph woke up, he did as the angel of the Lord commanded and took Mary as his wife. ²⁵But he did not have sexual relations with her until her son was born. And Joseph named him Jesus.

1:25
Luke 1:31

Visitors Arrive from Eastern Lands (12)

2 Jesus was born in Bethlehem in Judea, during the reign of King Herod. About that time some wise men* from eastern lands arrived in Jerusalem, asking, ²"Where is the new-born king of the Jews? We saw his star as it rose,* and we have come to worship him."

³King Herod was deeply disturbed when he heard this, as was everyone in Jerusalem. ⁴He called a meeting of the leading priests and teachers of religious law and asked, "Where is the Messiah supposed to be born?"

⁵"In Bethlehem in Judea," they said, "for this is what the prophet wrote:

2:1
Luke 1:5; 2:4-7
2:2
Num 24:17
Jer 23:5
Matt 2:9
Rev 22:16

2:5
John 7:42

2:1 Or *royal astrologers;* Greek reads *magi;* also in 2:7, 16.   **2:2** Or *star in the east.*

• **1:24** Joseph changed his plans quickly after learning that Mary had not been unfaithful to him (1:19). He obeyed God and proceeded with the marriage plans. Although others may have disapproved of his decision, Joseph went ahead with what he knew was right. Sometimes we avoid doing what is right because of what others might think. Like Joseph, we must choose to obey God rather than seek the approval of others.

2:1 Bethlehem is a small town five miles south of Jerusalem. It sits on a high ridge over 2,000 feet above sea level. It is mentioned in more detail in the Gospel of Luke. Luke also explains why Joseph and Mary were in Bethlehem when Jesus was born, rather than in Nazareth, their hometown.

2:1 The land of Israel was divided into four political districts and several lesser territories. Judea was to the south, Samaria in the middle, Galilee to the north, and Idumea to the southwest. Bethlehem of Judea (also called Judah, 2:6) had been prophesied as the Messiah's birthplace (Micah 5:2). Jerusalem was also in Judea and was the seat of government for Herod the Great, king over all four political districts. After Herod's death, the districts were divided among three separate rulers (see the note on 2:19-22). Although he was a ruthless, evil man who murdered many in his own family, Herod the Great supervised the renovation of the Temple, making it much larger and more beautiful. This made him popular with many Jews. Jesus would visit Jerusalem many times because the great Jewish festivals were held there.

2:1, 2 Not much is known about these "wise men." We don't know where they came from or how many there were. Tradition says they were men of high position from Parthia, near the site of ancient Babylon. How did they know that the star represented the Messiah? (1) They could have been Jews who remained in

Babylon after the Exile and knew the Old Testament predictions of the Messiah's coming. (2) They may have been eastern astrologers who studied ancient manuscripts from around the world. Because of the Jewish exile centuries earlier, they would have had copies of the Old Testament in their land. (3) They may have had a special message from God directing them to the Messiah. Some scholars say these wise men were each from a different land, representing the entire world bowing before Jesus. These men from faraway lands recognized Jesus as the Messiah when most of God's chosen people in Israel did not. Matthew pictures Jesus as the King over the whole world, not just Judea.

2:1, 2 The wise men traveled thousands of miles to see the king of the Jews. When they finally found him, they responded with joy, worship, and gifts. This is so different from the approach people often take today. We expect God to come looking for us, to explain himself, prove who he is, and give *us* gifts. But those who are wise still seek and worship Jesus today, not for what they can get, but for who he is.

2:2 The wise men said they saw Jesus' star. Balaam referred to a coming "star . . . from Jacob" (Numbers 24:17). Some say this star may have been a conjunction of Jupiter, Saturn, and Mars in 6 B.C., and others offer other explanations. But couldn't God, who created the heavens, have created a special star to signal the arrival of his Son? Whatever the nature of the star, these wise men traveled thousands of miles searching for a king, and they found him.

• **2:3** Herod the Great was quite disturbed when the wise men asked about a newborn king of the Jews because (1) Herod was not the rightful heir to the throne of David; therefore, many Jews hated him as a usurper. If Jesus really was an heir, trouble would arise. (2) Herod was ruthless, and because of his many enemies, he was suspicious that someone would try to overthrow him. (3) Herod didn't want the Jews, a religious people, to unite around a religious figure. (4) If these wise men were of Jewish descent and from Parthia (the most powerful region next to Rome), they would have welcomed a Jewish king who could swing the balance of power away from Rome. The land of Israel, far from Rome, would have been easy prey for a nation trying to gain more control.

The text tells us that not only was Herod disturbed, but so was everyone in Jerusalem. When Jesus was born to the world, people immediately began to react. His presence did not soothe and comfort most people; instead, it startled and disturbed them. In some he awakened spiritual longings; in others, fear and insecurity. Things have not changed that much. Jesus still disturbs people. If it is true that God entered our world when Jesus was born, we dare not sit idly by ignoring and rationalizing our inaction. We must acknowledge Jesus as the rightful King of our lives.

• **2:4-6** The leading priests and teachers of religious law were aware of Micah 5:2 and other prophecies about the Messiah. Matthew repeatedly highlighted their knowledge and unbelief. The wise men's news troubled Herod because he knew that the Jewish people expected the Messiah to come soon (Luke 3:15). Most Jews expected the Messiah to be a great military and

THE FLIGHT TO EGYPT
Herod planned to kill the baby Jesus, whom he perceived to be a future threat to his position. Warned of this treachery in a dream, Joseph took his family to Egypt until Herod's death, which occurred a year or two later. They then planned to return to Judea, but God led them instead to Nazareth in Galilee.

2:6
†Mic 5:2

6 'And you, O Bethlehem in the land of Judah,
>   are not least among the ruling cities* of Judah,
> for a ruler will come from you
>   who will be the shepherd for my people Israel.'*"

7 Then Herod called for a private meeting with the wise men, and he learned from them the time when the star first appeared. 8 Then he told them, "Go to Bethlehem and search carefully for the child. And when you find him, come back and tell me so that I can go and worship him, too!"

2:9
Matt 2:2

9 After this interview the wise men went their way. And the star they had seen in the east guided them to Bethlehem. It went ahead of them and stopped over the place where the child was. 10 When they saw the star, they were filled with joy! 11 They entered the house and saw the child with his mother, Mary, and they bowed down and worshiped him. Then they opened their treasure chests and gave him gifts of gold, frankincense, and myrrh.

2:11
Ps 72:10
Isa 60:6

2:12
Matt 2:22

12 When it was time to leave, they returned to their own country by another route, for God had warned them in a dream not to return to Herod.

The Escape to Egypt (13)

2:13
Matt 1:20; 2:19

13 After the wise men were gone, an angel of the Lord appeared to Joseph in a dream. "Get up! Flee to Egypt with the child and his mother," the angel said. "Stay there until I tell you to return, because Herod is going to search for the child to kill him."

2:6a Greek the rulers.   **2:6b** Mic 5:2; 2 Sam 5:2.

GOSPEL ACCOUNTS FOUND ONLY IN MATTHEW	Passage	Subject
	1:20-24	Joseph's dream*
	2:1-12	The visit of the wise men
	2:13-15	Escape to Egypt*
	2:16-18	Slaughter of the male children*
	27:3-10	The death of Judas*
	27:19	The dream of Pilate's wife
	27:52	The other resurrections
	28:11-15	The bribery of the guards
	28:19, 20	The baptism emphasis in the great commission*

Matthew records nine special events that are not mentioned in any of the other Gospels. In each case, the most apparent reason for Matthew's choice has to do with his purpose in communicating the gospel to Jewish people. Five cases are fulfillments of Old Testament prophecies (marked with asterisks above). The other four would have been of particular interest to the Jews of Matthew's day.

political deliverer, like Alexander the Great. Herod's counselors would have told Herod this. No wonder this ruthless man took no chances and ordered all the baby boys in Bethlehem killed (2:16)!

2:6 Most religious leaders believed in a literal fulfillment of all Old Testament prophecy; therefore, they believed the Messiah would be born in Bethlehem as foreseen by the prophet Micah seven centuries earlier (Micah 5:2). Ironically, when Jesus was born, these same religious leaders became his greatest enemies. When the Messiah for whom they had been waiting finally came, they didn't recognize him.

• **2:8** Herod did not want to worship Christ—he was lying. This was a trick to get the wise men to return to him and reveal the whereabouts of the newborn king. Herod's plan was to kill Jesus.

2:11 Jesus was probably one or two years old when the wise men found him. By this time, Mary and Joseph were married, living in a house, and intending to stay in Bethlehem for a while. For more on Joseph and Mary's stay there, see the note on Luke 2:39.

2:11 The wise men gave these expensive gifts as worthy acknowledgement for a future king. Bible students have seen in the gifts symbols of Christ's identity and what he would accomplish. Gold was a gift for royalty; frankincense was a gift for deity; and myrrh

was a spice used to anoint a body for burial. These gifts may have provided the financial resources for the trip to Egypt and back.

2:11 The wise men brought gifts and worshiped Jesus for who he was. This is the essence of true worship—honoring Christ for who he is and being willing to give him what is valuable to you. Worship God because he is the perfect, just, and almighty Creator of the universe, worthy of the best you have to give.

2:12 After finding Jesus and worshiping him, the wise men were warned by God not to return through Jerusalem as they had intended. Finding Jesus may mean that your life must take a different direction, one that is responsive and obedient to God's Word. In what ways has Jesus affected the direction of your life?

• **2:13** This was the second dream or vision that Joseph received from God. Joseph's first dream revealed that Mary's child would be the Messiah (1:20, 21). His second dream told him how to protect the child's life. Although Joseph was not Jesus' natural father, he was Jesus' legal father and was responsible for his safety and well-being. Divine guidance comes only to prepared hearts. Joseph remained receptive to God's guidance.

¹⁴That night Joseph left for Egypt with the child and Mary, his mother, ¹⁵and they stayed there until Herod's death. This fulfilled what the Lord had spoken through the prophet: "I called my Son out of Egypt."*

¹⁶Herod was furious when he realized that the wise men had outwitted him. He sent soldiers to kill all the boys in and around Bethlehem who were two years old and under, based on the wise men's report of the star's first appearance. ¹⁷Herod's brutal action fulfilled what God had spoken through the prophet Jeremiah:

¹⁸ "A cry was heard in Ramah—
   weeping and great mourning.
Rachel weeps for her children,
   refusing to be comforted,
   for they are dead."*

The Return to Nazareth (14)

¹⁹When Herod died, an angel of the Lord appeared in a dream to Joseph in Egypt. ²⁰"Get up!" the angel said. "Take the child and his mother back to the land of Israel, because those who were trying to kill the child are dead."

²¹So Joseph got up and returned to the land of Israel with Jesus and his mother. ²²But when he learned that the new ruler of Judea was Herod's son Archelaus, he was afraid to go there. Then, after being warned in a dream, he left for the region of Galilee. ²³So the family went and lived in a town called Nazareth. This fulfilled what the prophets had said: "He will be called a Nazarene."

John the Baptist Prepares the Way for Jesus (16/Mark 1:1-8; Luke 3:1-17)

3 In those days John the Baptist came to the Judean wilderness and began preaching. His message was, ²"Repent of your sins and turn to God, for the Kingdom of Heaven is near.*" ³The prophet Isaiah was speaking about John when he said,

2:15 Hos 11:1.   **2:18** Jer 31:15.   **3:2** Or *has come*, or *is coming soon.*

Marginal references:

2:15 †Hos 11:1

2:18 †Jer 31:15

2:19 Matt 1:20; 2:12

2:20 Exod 4:19

2:22 Matt 2:12

2:23 Luke 2:39; John 1:45-46; Acts 4:10; 24:5

3:2 Matt 4:17; 10:7; Mark 1:15

3:3 †Isa 40:3; Mal 3:1; Luke 1:76

2:14, 15 Going to Egypt was not unusual because there were colonies of Jews in several major Egyptian cities. These colonies had developed during the time of the great captivity (see Jeremiah 43–44). There is an interesting parallel between this flight to Egypt and Israel's history. As an infant nation, Israel went to Egypt, just as Jesus did as a child. God led Israel out (Hosea 11:1); God brought Jesus back. Both events show God working to save his people.

• **2:16** Herod, the king of the Jews, killed all the boys under two years of age in an obsessive attempt to kill Jesus, the newborn king. He stained his hands with blood, but he did not harm Jesus. Herod was king by a human appointment; Jesus was King by a divine appointment. No one can thwart God's plans.

• **2:16** Herod was afraid that this newborn king would one day take his throne. He completely misunderstood the reason for Christ's coming. Jesus didn't want Herod's throne; he wanted to be king of Herod's life. Jesus wanted to give Herod eternal life, not take away his present life. Today people are often afraid that Christ wants to take things away when, in reality, he wants to give them real freedom, peace, and joy. Don't fear Christ—give him the throne of your life.

2:17, 18 Rachel had been the favored wife of Jacob, one of the great men of God in the Old Testament. As such, she was considered the mother of a nation. From Jacob's 12 sons had come the 12 tribes of Israel. Rachel was buried near Bethlehem (Genesis 35:19). For more about the significance of this verse, see the note on Jeremiah 31:15, from which this verse was quoted.

2:19-22 Herod the Great died in 4 B.C. of an incurable disease. Rome trusted him but didn't trust his sons. Herod knew that Rome wouldn't give his successor as much power, so he divided his kingdom into three parts, one for each son. Archelaus received Judea, Samaria, and Idumea; Herod Antipas received Galilee and Perea; Herod Philip II received Traconitis. Archelaus, a violent man, began his reign by slaughtering 3,000 influential people. Nine years later, he was banished. God didn't want Joseph's family to go into the region of this evil ruler.

2:23 Nazareth sat in the hilly area of southern Galilee near the crossroads of great caravan trade routes. The town itself was rather small. The Roman garrison in charge of Galilee was housed there. The people of Nazareth had constant contact with people from all over the world, so world news reached them quickly. The people of Nazareth had an attitude of independence that many of the Jews despised. This may have been why Nathanael commented "Nazareth! . . . Can anything good come from Nazareth?" (John 1:46).

2:23 The Old Testament does not record this specific statement, "He will be called a Nazarene." Many scholars believe, however, that Matthew is referring to Isaiah 11:1, where the Hebrew word for "branch" is similar to the word for "Nazarene." Or he may be referring to a prophecy unrecorded in the Bible. In any case, Matthew paints the picture of Jesus as the true Messiah announced by God through the prophets; and he makes the point that Jesus, the Messiah, had unexpectedly humble beginnings, just as the Old Testament had predicted (see Micah 5:2).

3:1, 2 Almost 30 years had passed since the events of chapter 2. Here John the Baptist burst onto the scene. His theme was "Repent of your sins." The people needed to repent—make a 180-degree turn—from the kind of self-centeredness that leads to wrong actions, such as lying, cheating, stealing, gossiping, taking revenge, abusing, and indulging in sexual immorality. A person who turns from sin stops rebelling and begins following God's way of living prescribed in his Word. The first step in turning to God is to admit your sin, as John urged. Then God will receive you and help you live the way he wants. Remember that only God can get rid of sin. He doesn't expect us to clean up our life *before* we come to him.

3:1, 2 John the Baptist's Profile is found in John 1, p. 1749.

3:2 The Kingdom of Heaven began when God himself entered human history as a man. Today Jesus Christ reigns in the hearts of believers, but the Kingdom of Heaven will not be fully realized until all evil in the world is judged and removed. Christ came to earth first as a suffering servant; he will come again as king and judge to rule victoriously over all the earth.

3:3 The prophecy quoted is Isaiah 40:3. Isaiah was one of the

"He is a voice shouting in the wilderness,
  'Prepare the way for the LORD's coming!
    Clear the road for him!'"*

3:4
Lev 11:22
2 Kgs 1:8

⁴John's clothes were woven from coarse camel hair, and he wore a leather belt around his waist. For food he ate locusts and wild honey. ⁵People from Jerusalem and from all of Judea

3:3 Isa 40:3 (Greek version).

The Bible records history. It has proven itself an accurate and reliable record of people, events, and places. Independent historical accounts verify the Bible's descriptions and details of many famous lives. One of these was the father of the Herodian family, Herod the Great.

Herod is remembered as a builder of cities and the lavish rebuilder of the Temple in Jerusalem. But he also destroyed people. He showed little greatness in either his personal actions or his character. He was ruthless in ruling his territory. His suspicions and jealousy led to the murder of several of his children and the death of his wife Mariamne.

Herod's title, king of the Jews, was granted by Rome but never accepted by the Jewish people. He was not part of the Davidic family line, and he was only partly Jewish. Although Israel benefited from Herod's lavish efforts to repair the Temple in Jerusalem, he won little admiration because he also rebuilt various pagan temples. Herod's costly attempt to gain the loyalty of the people failed because it was superficial. His only loyalty was to himself.

Because his royal title was not genuine, Herod was constantly worried about losing his position. His actions when hearing from the wise men about their search for the new king are consistent with all that we know about Herod. He planned to locate and kill the child before he could become a threat. The murder of innocent children that followed is a tragic lesson in what can happen when actions are motivated by selfishness. Herod's suspicions did not spare even his own family. His life was self-destructive.

Strengths and accomplishments	• Was given the title king of the Jews by the Romans • Held on to his power for more than 30 years • Was an effective, though ruthless, ruler • Sponsored a great variety of large building projects
Weaknesses and mistakes	• Tended to treat those around him with fear, suspicion, and jealousy • Had several of his own children and at least one wife killed • Ordered the killing of the baby boys in Bethlehem • Although claiming to be a God-worshiper, he was still involved in many forms of pagan religion
Lessons from his life	• Great power brings neither peace nor security • No one can prevent God's plans from being carried out • Superficial loyalty does not impress people or God
Vital statistics	• Occupation: King of Judea from 37 to 4 B.C. • Relatives: Father: Antipater. Sons: Archelaus, Antipater, Antipas, Philip, and others. Wives: Doris, Mariamne, and others. • Contemporaries: Zechariah, Elizabeth, Mary, Joseph, Mark Antony, Augustus
Key verse	"Herod was furious when he realized that the wise men had outwitted him. He sent soldiers to kill all the boys in and around Bethlehem who were two years old and under" (Matthew 2:16).

Herod the Great is mentioned in Matthew 2:1-22 and Luke 1:5.

greatest prophets of the Old Testament and one of the most quoted in the New. Like Isaiah, John was a prophet who urged the people to confess their sins and live for God. Both prophets taught that the message of repentance is good news to those who listen and seek the healing forgiveness of God's love, but terrible news to those who refuse to listen and thus cut off their only hope.

3:3 John the Baptist *prepared* the way for Jesus by preparing others to welcome him. People who do not know Jesus need to get ready to meet him. We can prepare them by explaining their need for forgiveness, demonstrating Christ's teachings by our conduct, and telling them how Christ can give their lives meaning. We can "clear the road for him" by correcting misconceptions that might be hindering people from coming to Christ. Someone you know may be open to a relationship with Christ. How are you helping those around you to welcome Jesus?

3:4 John was markedly different from other religious leaders of his day. While many were greedy, selfish, and preoccupied with

winning the praise of the people, John was concerned only with the praise of God. Having separated himself from the evil and hypocrisy of his day, John lived differently from other people to show that his message was new. John not only preached God's law, he *lived* it. Do you practice what you preach? Could people discover what you believe by observing the way you live?

3:4-6 John must have presented a strange image! Many people came to hear this preacher, who wore odd clothes and ate unusual food. Some probably came simply out of curiosity and ended up turning from their sins as they listened to his powerful message. People may be curious about your Christian life-style and values. You can use their simple curiosity as an opener to share how Christ makes a difference in you.

3:5 Why did John attract so many people? He was the first true prophet in 400 years. He publicly blasted both Herod and the religious leaders, daring words that fascinated the common people. But John also had a strong message for his audience: They, too,

and all over the Jordan Valley went out to see and hear John. ⁶And when they confessed their sins, he baptized them in the Jordan River.

⁷But when he saw many Pharisees and Sadducees coming to watch him baptize,* he denounced them. "You brood of snakes!" he exclaimed. "Who warned you to flee God's coming wrath? ⁸Prove by the way you live that you have repented of your sins and turned to God. ⁹Don't just say to each other, 'We're safe, for we are descendants of Abraham.' That means nothing, for I tell you, God can create children of Abraham from these very stones. ¹⁰Even now the ax of God's judgment is poised, ready to sever the roots of the trees. Yes, every tree that does not produce good fruit will be chopped down and thrown into the fire.

¹¹"I baptize with* water those who repent of their sins and turn to God. But someone is coming soon who is greater than I am—so much greater that I'm not worthy even to be his slave and carry his sandals. He will baptize you with the Holy Spirit and with fire.* ¹²He is ready to separate the chaff from the wheat with his winnowing fork. Then he will clean up the threshing area, gathering the wheat into his barn but burning the chaff with never-ending fire."

3:7
Matt 12:34; 23:33
Luke 3:7
John 8:44
Rom 5:9
Eph 5:6
Col 3:6

3:9
John 8:33, 37, 39
Rom 4:12

3:10
Matt 7:19
Luke 13:7
John 15:6

3:11
John 1:26-27, 31, 33
Acts 1:5; 2:3-4; 13:24; 19:4

3:12
Matt 13:30

3:7 Or *coming to be baptized.*   **3:11a** Or *in.*   **3:11b** Or *in the Holy Spirit and in fire.*

were sinners and needed to turn from their sins. His words were powerful and true. The people were expecting a prophet like Elijah (Malachi 4:5; Luke 1:17), and John seemed to be the one!

3:6 When you wash dirty hands, the results are immediately visible. But turning from sins (repentance) happens inside with a cleansing that isn't seen right away. So John used a symbolic action that people could see: baptism. The Jews used baptism to initiate converts, so John's audience was familiar with the rite. Here, baptism was used as a sign of repentance and forgiveness. Turning from sins implies a change in behavior, turning from sin toward God. Have you turned from sin in your life? Can others see the difference it makes in you? A changed life with new and different behavior makes your repentance real and visible.

3:6 The Jordan River is about 70 miles long, its main section stretching between the Sea of Galilee and the Dead Sea. Jerusalem lies about 20 miles west of the Jordan. This river was Israel's eastern border, and many significant events in the nation's history took place there. It was by the Jordan River that the Israelites renewed their covenant with God before entering the Promised Land (Joshua 1–2). Here John the Baptist calls them to renew their covenant with God again, this time through baptism.

3:7 The Jewish religious leaders were divided into several groups. Two of the most prominent groups were the Pharisees and the Sadducees. The Pharisees separated themselves from

anything non-Jewish and carefully followed both the Old Testament laws and the oral traditions handed down through the centuries. The Sadducees believed the Pentateuch alone (Genesis—Deuteronomy) to be God's Word. They were descended mainly from priestly nobility, while the Pharisees came from all classes of people. The two groups disliked each other greatly, and both opposed Jesus. John the Baptist criticized the Pharisees for being legalistic and hypocritical, following the letter of the law while ignoring its true intent. He criticized the Sadducees for using religion to advance their political position. For more information on these two groups, see the chart in Mark 2, p. 1617.

3:8 John the Baptist called people to more than words or ritual; he told them to change their behavior. "Prove by the way you live that you have repented of your sins" means that God looks beyond our words and religious activities to see if our conduct backs up what we say, and he judges our words by the actions that accompany them. Do your actions match your words?

3:9, 10 Just as a fruit tree is expected to bear fruit, God's people should produce a crop of good deeds. God has no use for people who call themselves Christians but who live otherwise. Like many people in John's day who were God's people in name only, we are of no value if we are Christians in name only. If others can't see our faith in the way we treat them, we may not be God's people at all.

3:10 God's message hasn't changed since the Old Testament: People will be judged for their unproductive lives. God calls us to be *active* in our obedience. John compared people who claim they believe God but don't live for God to unproductive trees that will be cut down. To be productive for God, we must obey his teachings, resist temptation, actively serve and help others, and share our faith. How productive are you for God?

3:11 John baptized people as a sign that they had asked God to forgive their sins and had decided to live as he wanted them to live. Baptism was an *outward* sign of commitment. To be effective, it had to be accompanied by an *inward* change of attitude leading to a changed life—the work of the Holy Spirit. John said that Jesus would baptize with the Holy Spirit and fire. This looked ahead to Pentecost (Acts 2), when the Holy Spirit would be sent by Jesus in the form of tongues of fire, empowering his followers to preach the Good News. John's statement also symbolizes the work of the Holy Spirit in bringing God's judgment on those who refuse to turn from their sins. Everyone will one day be baptized—either now by God's Holy Spirit or later by the fire of his judgment.

3:12 A winnowing fork is a pitchfork used to toss wheat in the air to separate grain from chaff. The grain is the part of the plant that is useful; chaff is the worthless outer shell. Because it is useless, chaff is burned; grain, however, is gathered.

JESUS BEGINS HIS MINISTRY

From his childhood home, Nazareth, Jesus set out to begin his earthly ministry. He was baptized by John the Baptist in the Jordan River, tempted by Satan in the wilderness, and then returned to Galilee. Between the temptation and his move to Capernaum (4:12, 13), he ministered in Judea, Samaria, and Galilee (see John 1–4).

3:13-17
Mark 1:9-11
Luke 3:21-22
John 1:31-34
3:16
Isa 11:2
3:17
Gen 22:2
Ps 2:7
Isa 42:1
Matt 12:18; 17:5
Mark 9:7
Luke 9:35

The Baptism of Jesus (**17**/Mark 1:9-11; Luke 3:21-22)

¹³ Then Jesus went from Galilee to the Jordan River to be baptized by John. ¹⁴ But John tried to talk him out of it. "I am the one who needs to be baptized by you," he said, "so why are you coming to me?"

¹⁵ But Jesus said, "It should be done, for we must carry out all that God requires.*" So John agreed to baptize him.

¹⁶ After his baptism, as Jesus came up out of the water, the heavens were opened* and he saw the Spirit of God descending like a dove and settling on him. ¹⁷ And a voice from heaven said, "This is my dearly loved Son, who brings me great joy."

3:15 Or *for we must fulfill all righteousness.*   **3:16** Some manuscripts read *opened to him.*

THE PHARISEES AND SADDUCEES

The Pharisees and Sadducees were the two major religious groups in Israel at the time of Christ. The Pharisees were more religiously minded, while the Sadducees were more politically minded. Although the groups disliked and distrusted each other, they became allies in their common hatred for Jesus.

Name	Positive Characteristics	Negative Characteristics
PHARISEES	• Were committed to obeying all of God's commands • Were admired by the common people for their apparent piety • Believed in a bodily resurrection and eternal life • Believed in angels and demons	• Behaved as though their own religious rules were just as important as God's rules for living • Their piety was often hypocritical, and their efforts often forced others to try to live up to standards they themselves could not live up to • Believed that salvation came from perfect obedience to the law and was not based on forgiveness of sins • Became so obsessed with obeying their legal interpretations in every detail that they completely ignored God's message of mercy and grace • Were more concerned with appearing to be good than obeying God
SADDUCEES	• Believed strongly in the law of Moses and in Levitical purity • Were more practically minded than the Pharisees	• Relied on logic while placing little importance on faith • Did not believe all the Old Testament was God's Word • Did not believe in a bodily resurrection or eternal life • Did not believe in angels or demons • Were often willing to compromise their values with the Romans and others in order to maintain their status and influential positions

---

"Winnowing" is often used as a picture of God's judgment. Unrepentant people will be judged and discarded because they are worthless in doing God's work; those who repent and believe will be saved and used by God.

3:13-15 John had been explaining that Jesus' baptism would be much greater than his, when suddenly Jesus came to him and asked to be baptized! John felt unqualified. He wanted Jesus to baptize *him.* Why did Jesus ask to be baptized? It was not for repentance for sin because Jesus never sinned. "We must carry out all that God requires" refers to accomplishing God's mission. Jesus saw his baptism as advancing God's work. Jesus was baptized because (1) he was confessing sin on behalf of the nation, as Nehemiah, Ezra, Moses, and Daniel had done; (2) he was showing support for what John was doing; (3) he was inaugurating his public ministry; (4) he was identifying with the penitent people of God, not with the critical Pharisees who were only watching. Jesus, the perfect man, didn't need baptism for sin, but he accepted baptism in obedient service to the Father, and God showed his approval.

3:15 Put yourself in John's shoes. Your work is going well, people are taking notice, everything is growing. But you know that the purpose of your work is to prepare the people for Jesus (John 1:35-37). Then Jesus arrives, and his coming tests your integrity. Will you be able to turn your followers over to him? John passed the test by publicly baptizing Jesus. Soon

he would say, "He must become greater and greater, and I must become less and less" (John 3:30). Can we, like John, put our egos and profitable work aside in order to point others to Jesus? Are we willing to lose some of our status so that everyone will benefit?

3:16, 17 The doctrine of the Trinity, which appeared later in church history, teaches that God is three persons and yet one in essence. In this passage, all three persons of the Trinity are present and active. God the Father speaks; God the Son is baptized; God the Holy Spirit descends on Jesus. God is one, yet in three persons at the same time. This is one of God's incomprehensible mysteries. Other Bible references that speak of the Father, Son, and Holy Spirit are Matthew 28:19; John 15:26; 1 Corinthians 12:4-13; 2 Corinthians 13:14; Ephesians 2:18; 1 Thessalonians 1:2-5; and 1 Peter 1:2.

Satan Tempts Jesus in the Wilderness (18/Mark 1:12-13; Luke 4:1-13)

4 Then Jesus was led by the Spirit into the wilderness to be tempted there by the devil. ²For forty days and forty nights he fasted and became very hungry.

³During that time the devil* came and said to him, "If you are the Son of God, tell these stones to become loaves of bread."

⁴But Jesus told him, "No! The Scriptures say,

'People do not live by bread alone,
    but by every word that comes from the mouth of God.'*"

⁵Then the devil took him to the holy city, Jerusalem, to the highest point of the Temple, ⁶and said, "If you are the Son of God, jump off! For the Scriptures say,

'He will order his angels to protect you.
And they will hold you up with their hands
    so you won't even hurt your foot on a stone.'*"

⁷Jesus responded, "The Scriptures also say, 'You must not test the Lord your God.'*"

4:1
Gen 3:1-7
1 Thes 3:5

4:2
Exod 34:28
1 Kgs 19:8

4:4
†Deut 8:3

4:6
†Ps 91:11-12

4:7
†Deut 6:16

4:3 Greek *the tempter.*   **4:4** Deut 8:3.   **4:6** Ps 91:11-12.   **4:7** Deut 6:16.

• **4:1** This time of testing showed that Jesus really was the Son of God, able to overcome the devil and his temptations. A person has not shown true obedience if he or she has never had an opportunity to disobey. We read in Deuteronomy 8:2 that God led Israel into the wilderness to humble and test them. God wanted to see whether or not his people would really obey him. We, too, will be tested. Because we know that testing will come, we should be alert and ready for it. Remember, your convictions are only strong if they hold up under pressure!

• **4:1** The devil, also called Satan, tempted Eve in the Garden of Eden, and here he tempted Jesus in the wilderness. Satan is a fallen angel. He is *real*, not symbolic, and is constantly fighting against those who follow and obey God. Satan's temptations are real, and he is always trying to get us to live his way or our way rather than God's way. Jesus will one day reign over all creation, but Satan tried to force his hand and get him to declare his kingship prematurely. If Jesus had given in, his mission on earth—to die for our sins and give us the opportunity to have eternal life—would have been lost. When temptations seem especially strong, or when you think you can rationalize giving in, consider whether Satan may be trying to block God's purposes for your life or for someone else's life.

• **4:1ff** This temptation by the devil shows us that Jesus was human, and it gave Jesus the opportunity to reaffirm God's plan for his ministry. It also gives us an example to follow when we are tempted. Jesus' temptation was an important demonstration of his sinlessness. He would face temptation and not give in.

Although we may feel dirty after being tempted, we should remember that temptation itself is not sin. We sin when we give in and disobey God. Remembering this will help us turn away from the temptation.

4:1ff Jesus wasn't tempted inside the Temple or at his baptism but in the wilderness, where he was tired, alone, and hungry, and thus most vulnerable. The devil often tempts us when we are vulnerable—when we are under physical or emotional stress (for example, lonely, tired, weighing big decisions, or faced with uncertainty). But he also likes to tempt us through our strengths, where we are most susceptible to pride (see the note on Luke 4:3ff). We must guard at all times against his attacks.

• **4:1-10** The devil's temptations focused on three crucial areas: (1) physical needs and desires, (2) possessions and power, and (3) pride (see 1 John 2:15, 16 for a similar list). But Jesus did not give in. Hebrews 4:15 says that Jesus "faced all of the same testings we do, yet he did not sin." He knows firsthand what we are experiencing, and he is willing and able to help us in our struggles. When you are tempted, turn to him for strength.

• **4:3, 4** Jesus was hungry and weak after fasting for 40 days, but he chose not to use his divine power to satisfy his natural desire for food. Food, hunger, and eating are good, but the timing was wrong. Jesus was in the wilderness to fast, not to eat. And because Jesus had given up the unlimited, independent use of his divine power in order to experience humanity fully, he wouldn't use his power to change the stones to bread. We also may be tempted to satisfy a perfectly normal desire in a wrong way or at the wrong time. If we indulge in sex before marriage or if we steal to get food, we are trying to satisfy God-given desires in wrong ways. Remember, many of your desires are normal and good, but God wants you to satisfy them in the right way and at the right time.

• **4:3, 4** Jesus was able to resist all of the devil's temptations because he not only knew Scripture, but he also obeyed it. Ephesians 6:17 says that God's Word is a sword to use in spiritual combat. Knowing Bible verses is an important step in helping us resist the devil's attacks, but we must also obey the Bible. Note that Satan had memorized Scripture, but he failed to obey it. Knowing and obeying the Bible helps us follow God's desires rather than the devil's.

4:5 The Temple was the religious center of the Jewish nation and the place where the people expected the Messiah to arrive (Malachi 3:1). Herod the Great had renovated the Temple in hopes of gaining the Jews' confidence. The Temple was the tallest building in the area, and this "highest point" was probably the corner wall that jutted out of the hillside, overlooking the valley below. From this spot, Jesus could see all of Jerusalem behind him and the country for miles in front of him.

4:5-7 God is not our magician in the sky ready to perform on request. In response to Satan's temptations, Jesus said not to put God to a test (Deuteronomy 6:16). You may want to ask God to do something to prove his existence or his love for you. Jesus once taught through a parable that people who don't believe what is written in the Bible won't believe even if someone were to come back from the dead to warn them (Luke 16:31)! God wants us to live by faith, not by magic. Don't try to manipulate God by asking for signs.

• **4:6** The devil used Scripture to try to convince Jesus to sin! Sometimes friends or associates will present attractive and convincing reasons why you should try something you know is wrong. They may even find Bible verses that *seem* to support their viewpoint. Study the Bible carefully, especially the broader contexts of specific verses, so that you understand God's principles for living and what he wants for your life. Only if you really understand what the *whole* Bible says will you be able to recognize errors of interpretation when people take verses out of context and twist them to say what they want them to say.

⁸Next the devil took him to the peak of a very high mountain and showed him all the kingdoms of the world and their glory. ⁹"I will give it all to you," he said, "if you will kneel down and worship me."

4:10
†Deut 6:13

¹⁰ "Get out of here, Satan," Jesus told him. "For the Scriptures say,

'You must worship the LORD your God
    and serve only him.'*"

4:11
Luke 22:43
Heb 1:14
Jas 4:7

¹¹ Then the devil went away, and angels came and took care of Jesus.

B. MESSAGE AND MINISTRY OF JESUS, THE KING (4:12—25:46)
Matthew features Jesus' sermons. The record of Jesus' actions is interspersed with great passages of his teaching. This section of Matthew is topical rather than chronological. Matthew records for us the Sermon on the Mount, the parables of the Kingdom, Jesus' teachings on forgiveness, and parables about the end of the age.

1. Jesus begins his ministry
Jesus Preaches in Galilee (**30**/Mark 1:14-15; Luke 4:14-15; John 4:43-45)
¹²When Jesus heard that John had been arrested, he left Judea and returned to Galilee. ¹³He went first to Nazareth, then left there and moved to Capernaum, beside the Sea of

4:10 Deut 6:13.

THE TEMPTATIONS	Temptation	Real needs used as basis for temptation	Possible doubts that made the temptations real	Potential weaknesses Satan sought to exploit	Jesus' answer
	Make bread	Physical need: Hunger	Would God provide food?	Hunger, impatience, need to "prove his sonship"	Deuteronomy 8:3 "Depend on God" Focus: God's purpose
	Dare God to rescue you (based on misapplied Scripture, Psalm 91:11, 12)	Emotional need: Security	Would God protect?	Pride, insecurity, need to test God	Deuteronomy 6:16 "Don't test God" Focus: God's plan
	Worship me! (Satan)	Psychological need: significance, power, achievement	Would God rule?	Desire for quick power, easy solutions, need to prove equality with God	Deuteronomy 6:13 "No compromise with evil" Focus: God's person

As if going through a final test of preparation, Jesus was tempted by Satan in the wilderness. Three specific parts of the Temptation are listed by Matthew. They are familiar because we face the same kinds of temptations. As the chart shows, temptation is often the combination of a real need and a possible doubt that creates an inappropriate desire. Jesus demonstrates both the importance and effectiveness of knowing and applying Scripture to combat temptation.

4:8, 9 Did the devil have the power to give Jesus the nations of the world? Didn't God, the Creator of the world, have control over these nations? The devil may have been lying about his implied power, or he may have based his offer on his temporary control and free rein over the earth because of humanity's sinfulness. The temptation before Jesus was to take the world as a political ruler right then, without carrying out his plan to save the world from sin. Satan was trying to distort Jesus' perspective by making him focus on worldly power and not on God's plans.

• **4:8-10** The devil offered the whole world to Jesus if Jesus would only kneel down and worship him. Today the devil offers us the world by trying to entice us with materialism and power. We can resist temptations the same way Jesus did. If you find yourself craving something that the world offers, quote Jesus' words to the devil: "You must worship the LORD your God and serve only him."

4:11 Angels, like these who waited on Jesus, have a significant role as God's messengers. These spiritual beings were involved in Jesus' life on earth by (1) announcing Jesus' birth to Mary,

(2) reassuring Joseph, (3) naming Jesus, (4) announcing Jesus' birth to the shepherds, (5) protecting Jesus by sending his family to Egypt, and (6) ministering to Jesus in Gethsemane. For more on angels, see the note on 1:20.

4:12, 13 Jesus moved from Nazareth, his hometown, to Capernaum, about 20 miles farther north. Capernaum became Jesus' home base during his ministry in Galilee. Jesus probably moved (1) to get away from intense opposition in Nazareth, (2) to have an impact on the greatest number of people (Capernaum was a busy city, and Jesus' message could reach more people and spread more quickly), and (3) to utilize extra resources and support for his ministry.

Jesus' move fulfilled the prophecy of Isaiah 9:1, 2, which states that the Messiah would be a light to the land of Zebulun and Naphtali, the region of Galilee where Capernaum was located. Zebulun and Naphtali were two of the original 12 tribes of Israel.

Galilee, in the region of Zebulun and Naphtali. ¹⁴This fulfilled what God said through the prophet Isaiah:

¹⁵ "In the land of Zebulun and of Naphtali,
    beside the sea, beyond the Jordan River,
    in Galilee where so many Gentiles live,
¹⁶ the people who sat in darkness
    have seen a great light.
And for those who lived in the land where death casts its shadow,
    a light has shined."*

4:15-16
†Isa 9:1-2; 42:6-7
Luke 2:32

¹⁷From then on Jesus began to preach, "Repent of your sins and turn to God, for the Kingdom of Heaven is near.*"

4:17
Matt 3:2; 10:7

Four Fishermen Follow Jesus (33/Mark 1:16-20)
¹⁸One day as Jesus was walking along the shore of the Sea of Galilee, he saw two brothers— Simon, also called Peter, and Andrew—throwing a net into the water, for they fished for a living. ¹⁹Jesus called out to them, "Come, follow me, and I will show you how to fish for people!" ²⁰And they left their nets at once and followed him.

4:19
Matt 16:17-18
John 1:42

²¹A little farther up the shore he saw two other brothers, James and John, sitting in a boat with their father, Zebedee, repairing their nets. And he called them to come, too. ²²They immediately followed him, leaving the boat and their father behind.

4:20
Mark 10:28
Luke 18:28

Jesus Preaches throughout Galilee (36/Mark 1:35-39; Luke 4:42-44)
²³Jesus traveled throughout the region of Galilee, teaching in the synagogues and announcing the Good News about the Kingdom. And he healed every kind of disease and illness. ²⁴News about him spread as far as Syria, and people soon began bringing to him all who were sick. And whatever their sickness or disease, or if they were demon possessed or epileptic or paralyzed—he healed them all. ²⁵Large crowds followed him wherever he went— people from Galilee, the Ten Towns,* Jerusalem, from all over Judea, and from east of the Jordan River.

4:23
Matt 9:35
Mark 1:39
Luke 4:15

4:15-16 Isa 9:1-2 (Greek version).   **4:17** Or *has come,* or *is coming soon.*   **4:25** Greek *Decapolis.*

4:14-16 By quoting from the book of Isaiah, Matthew continues to tie Jesus' ministry to the Old Testament. This was helpful for his Jewish readers, who were familiar with these Scriptures. In addition, it shows the unity of God's purposes as he works with his people throughout all ages.

4:17 The "Kingdom of Heaven" has the same meaning as the "Kingdom of God" in Mark and Luke. Matthew uses this phrase because the Jews, out of their intense reverence and respect, did not pronounce God's name. The Kingdom of Heaven is still near because it has arrived in our heart. See the note on 3:2 for more on the Kingdom of Heaven.

4:17 Jesus started his ministry with the same message people had heard John the Baptist say: "Repent of your sins." The message is the same today as when Jesus and John gave it. Becoming a follower of Christ means turning away from our self-centeredness and "self" control and turning our life over to Christ's direction and control.

4:18 The Sea of Galilee is really a large lake. About 30 fishing towns surrounded it during Jesus' day, and Capernaum was the largest.

4:18-20 These men already knew Jesus. He had talked to Peter and Andrew previously (John 1:35-42) and had been preaching in the area. When Jesus called them, they knew what kind of man he was and were willing to follow him. Jesus told Peter and Andrew to leave their fishing business and begin fishing "for people," helping others find God. Jesus was calling them away from their productive trade to be productive spiritually. We all need to fish for souls. If we practice Christ's teachings and share the Good News with others, we will be able to draw those around us to Christ like a fisherman who pulls fish into his boat with nets.

4:21, 22 James and his brother, John, along with Peter and Andrew, were the first disciples that Jesus called to work with him. Jesus' call motivated these men to get up and leave their jobs—immediately. They didn't make excuses about why it wasn't a good time. They left at once and followed. Jesus calls each of us to follow him. When Jesus asks us to serve him, we must be like the disciples and do it at once.

4:23 Jesus was teaching, preaching, and healing. These were the three main aspects of his ministry. *Teaching* shows Jesus' concern for understanding; *preaching* shows his concern for commitment; and *healing* shows his concern for wholeness. His miracles of healing authenticated his teaching and preaching, proving that he truly was from God.

4:23 Jesus soon developed a powerful preaching ministry and often spoke in the synagogues. Most towns that had 10 or more Jewish families had a synagogue. The building served as a religious gathering place on the Sabbath and as a school during the week. The leader of the synagogue was not a preacher as much as an administrator. His job was to find and invite rabbis to teach and preach. It was customary to invite visiting rabbis like Jesus to speak.

4:23, 24 Jesus preached the gospel—the Good News—to everyone who wanted to hear it. The Good News is that the Kingdom of Heaven has come, that God is with us, and that he cares for us. Christ can heal us, not just of physical sickness, but of spiritual sickness as well. There's no sin or problem too great or too small for him to handle. Jesus' words were good news because they offered freedom, hope, peace of heart, and eternal life with God.

4:25 The "Ten Towns" was a league of 10 Gentile cities east of the Sea of Galilee, joined together for better trade and mutual defense. The word about Jesus was out, and Jews and Gentiles were coming long distances to hear him.

2. Jesus gives the Sermon on the Mount

Jesus Gives the Beatitudes (**49**/Luke 6:17-26)

5:1
Luke 6:12
John 6:3
5:3-12
Luke 6:20-23
5:3
Isa 57:15
Matt 25:34

5 One day as he saw the crowds gathering, Jesus went up on the mountainside and sat down. His disciples gathered around him, ²and he began to teach them.

3 "God blesses those who are poor and realize their need for him,*
for the Kingdom of Heaven is theirs.

5:3 Greek *poor in spirit.*

	Beatitude	Old Testament anticipation	Clashing worldly values	God's reward	How to develop this attitude
KEY LESSONS FROM THE SERMON ON THE MOUNT	Realize need for God (5:3)	Isaiah 57:15	Pride and personal independence	Kingdom of Heaven	James 4:7-10
	Mourn (5:4)	Isaiah 61:1, 2	Happiness at any cost	Comfort (2 Corinthians 1:4)	Psalm 51 James 4:7-10
	Humble (5:5)	Psalm 37:5-11	Power	Inherit the earth	Matthew 11:27-30
	Hunger and thirst for justice (5:6)	Isaiah 11:4, 5; 42:1-4	Pursuing personal needs	Satisfied	John 16:5-11 Philippians 3:7-11
	Merciful (5:7)	Psalm 41:1	Strength without feeling	Be shown mercy	Ephesians 5:1, 2
	Pure hearts (5:8)	Psalms 24:3, 4; 51:10	Deception is acceptable	See God	1 John 3:1-3
	Work for peace (5:9)	Isaiah 57:18, 19; 60:17	Personal peace is pursued without concern for the world's chaos	Be called children of God	Romans 12:9-21 Hebrews 12:10, 11
	Persecuted (5:10)	Isaiah 52:13; 53:12	Weak commitments	Kingdom of Heaven	2 Timothy 3:12

In his longest recorded sermon, Jesus began by describing the traits he was looking for in his followers. He said that God blesses those who live out those traits. Each beatitude is an almost direct contradiction of society's typical way of life. In the last beatitude, Jesus even points out that a serious effort to develop these traits is bound to create opposition. The best example of each trait is found in Jesus himself. If our goal is to become like him, applying the Beatitudes will challenge the way we live each day.

• **5:1ff** Matthew 5–7 is called the Sermon on the Mount because Jesus gave it on a hillside near Capernaum. This "sermon" probably covered several days of preaching. In it, Jesus proclaimed his attitude toward the law. Position, authority, and money are not important in his Kingdom—what matters is faithful obedience from the heart. The Sermon on the Mount challenged the proud and legalistic religious leaders of the day. It called them back to the messages of the Old Testament prophets, who, like Jesus, taught that heartfelt obedience is more important than legalistic observance.

• **5:1, 2** Enormous crowds were following Jesus—he was the talk of the town, and everyone wanted to see him. The disciples, who were the closest associates of this popular man, were certainly tempted to feel important, proud, and possessive. Being with Jesus gave them not only prestige but also opportunity for receiving money and power.

The crowds were gathering once again. But before speaking to them, Jesus pulled his disciples aside and warned them about the temptations they would face as his associates. Don't expect fame and fortune, Jesus was saying, but mourning, hunger, and persecution. Nevertheless, Jesus assured his disciples that they would be rewarded—but perhaps not in this life. There may be times when following Jesus will bring us great popularity. If we don't live by Jesus' words in this sermon, we will find

ourselves using God's message only to promote our personal interests.

• **5:3-5** Jesus began his sermon with words that seem to contradict each other. But God's way of living usually contradicts the world's. If you want to live for God, you must be ready to say and do what seems strange to the world. You must be willing to give when others take, to love when others hate, to help when others abuse. By giving up your own rights in order to serve others, you will one day receive everything God has in store for you.

• **5:3-12** The Beatitudes can be understood in at least four ways: (1) They are a code of ethics for the disciples and a standard of conduct for all believers. (2) They contrast Kingdom values (what is eternal) with worldly values (what is temporary). (3) They contrast the superficial "faith" of the Pharisees with the real faith that Christ demands. (4) They show how the Old Testament expectations will be fulfilled in the new Kingdom. These Beatitudes are not multiple choice—pick what you like and leave the rest. They must be taken as a whole. They describe what we should be like as Christ's followers.

• **5:3-12** Each beatitude tells how to be *blessed* by God. *Blessed* means more than happiness. It implies the fortunate or enviable state of those who are in God's Kingdom. The Beatitudes don't promise laughter, pleasure, or earthly prosperity. Being "blessed"

⁴ God blesses those who mourn,
    for they will be comforted.

5:4
Isa 61:2-3

⁵ God blesses those who are humble,
    for they will inherit the whole earth.

5:5
Ps 37:11

⁶ God blesses those who hunger and thirst for justice,*
    for they will be satisfied.

5:6
Isa 55:1-2

⁷ God blesses those who are merciful,
    for they will be shown mercy.

5:7
Matt 18:33
Jas 2:13

⁸ God blesses those whose hearts are pure,
    for they will see God.

5:8
Ps 24:3-4

⁹ God blesses those who work for peace,
    for they will be called the children of God.

5:9
Heb 12:14
Jas 3:18

¹⁰ God blesses those who are persecuted for doing right,
    for the Kingdom of Heaven is theirs.

5:10
2 Tim 2:12
1 Pet 3:14

¹¹"God blesses you when people mock you and persecute you and lie about you* and say all sorts of evil things against you because you are my followers. ¹²Be happy about it! Be very glad! For a great reward awaits you in heaven. And remember, the ancient prophets were persecuted in the same way.

5:11
Matt 10:22
1 Pet 4:14
5:12
Acts 7:52
Heb 11:32-38
Jas 5:10

Jesus Teaches about Salt and Light (50)

¹³ "You are the salt of the earth. But what good is salt if it has lost its flavor? Can you make it salty again? It will be thrown out and trampled underfoot as worthless.

5:13
Mark 9:50
Luke 14:34-35

¹⁴"You are the light of the world—like a city on a hilltop that cannot be hidden. ¹⁵No one lights a lamp and then puts it under a basket. Instead, a lamp is placed on a stand, where it gives light to everyone in the house. ¹⁶In the same way, let your good deeds shine out for all to see, so that everyone will praise your heavenly Father.

5:15
Mark 4:21
Luke 8:16; 11:33
5:16
Eph 5:8-9
1 Pet 2:12

Jesus Teaches about the Law (51)

¹⁷ "Don't misunderstand why I have come. I did not come to abolish the law of Moses or the writings of the prophets. No, I came to accomplish their purpose. ¹⁸ I tell you the truth, until

5:17
Rom 3:31
5:18
Luke 16:17; 21:33

5:6 Or *for righteousness.*   **5:11** Some manuscripts do not include *and lie about you.*

---

by God means the experience of hope and joy, independent of outward circumstances. To find hope and joy, the deepest form of happiness, follow Jesus no matter what the cost.

• **5:3-12** With Jesus' announcement that the Kingdom was near (4:17), people were naturally asking, "How do I qualify to be in God's Kingdom?" Jesus said that God's Kingdom is organized differently from worldly kingdoms. In the Kingdom of Heaven, wealth and power and authority are unimportant. Kingdom people seek different blessings and benefits, and they have different attitudes. Are your attitudes a carbon copy of the world's selfishness, pride, and lust for power, or do they reflect the humility and self-sacrifice of Jesus, your king?

• **5:11, 12** Jesus said to be happy when we're persecuted for our faith. Persecution can be good because (1) it takes our eyes off earthly rewards, (2) it strips away superficial belief, (3) it strengthens the faith of those who endure, and (4) our attitude through it serves as an example to others who follow. We can be comforted knowing that God's greatest prophets were persecuted (Elijah, Jeremiah, Daniel). The fact that we are being persecuted proves that we have been faithful; faithless people would be unnoticed. In the future God will reward the faithful by receiving them into his eternal Kingdom, where there is no more persecution.

5:13 If a seasoning has no flavor, it has no value. If Christians make no effort to affect the world around them, they are of little value to God. If we are too much like the world, we are worthless. Christians should not blend in with everyone else. Instead, we should affect others positively, just as seasoning brings out the best flavor in food.

5:14-16 Can you hide a city that is sitting on top of a mountain? Its light at night can be seen for miles. If we live for Christ, we will glow like lights, showing others what Christ is like. We hide

our light by (1) being quiet when we should speak, (2) going along with the crowd, (3) denying the light, (4) letting sin dim our light, (5) not explaining our light to others, or (6) ignoring the needs of others. Be a beacon of truth—don't shut your light off from the rest of the world.

5:17 God's moral and ceremonial laws were given to help people love God with all their hearts and minds. Throughout Israel's history, however, these laws had often been misquoted and misapplied. By Jesus' time, religious leaders had turned the laws into a confusing mass of rules. When Jesus talked about a new way to understand God's law, he was actually trying to bring people back to its *original* purpose. Jesus did not speak against the law itself but against the abuses and excesses to which it had been subjected (see John 1:17).

5:17-20 If Jesus did not come to abolish the law, does that mean all the Old Testament laws still apply to us today? In the Old Testament, there were three categories of law: ceremonial, civil, and moral.

(1) The *ceremonial law* related specifically to Israel's worship (see Leviticus 1:2, 3, for example). Its primary purpose was to point forward to Jesus Christ; these laws, therefore, were no longer necessary after Jesus' death and resurrection. While we are no longer bound by ceremonial law, the principles behind them—to worship and love a holy God—still apply. Jesus was often accused by the Pharisees of violating ceremonial law.

(2) The *civil law* applied to daily living in Israel (see Deuteronomy 24:10, 11, for example). Because modern society and culture are so radically different from that time and setting, all of these guidelines cannot be followed specifically. But the principles behind the commands are timeless and should guide our conduct. Jesus demonstrated these principles by example.

(3) The *moral law* (such as the Ten Commandments) is the direct command of God, and it requires strict obedience (see

5:19
Jas 2:10

heaven and earth disappear, not even the smallest detail of God's law will disappear until its purpose is achieved. [19]So if you ignore the least commandment and teach others to do the same, you will be called the least in the Kingdom of Heaven. But anyone who obeys God's laws and teaches them will be called great in the Kingdom of Heaven.

[20]"But I warn you—unless your righteousness is better than the righteousness of the teachers of religious law and the Pharisees, you will never enter the Kingdom of Heaven!

Jesus Teaches about Anger (52)

5:21
†Exod 20:13
†Deut 5:17
Matt 19:18
Mark 10:19
Luke 18:20
Rom 13:9
Jas 2:11

5:22
Eph 4:26
Jas 1:19-20
1 Jn 3:15

[21]"You have heard that our ancestors were told, ' You must not murder. If you commit murder, you are subject to judgment.'* [22]But I say, if you are even angry with someone,* you are subject to judgment! If you call someone an idiot,* you are in danger of being brought before the court. And if you curse someone,* you are in danger of the fires of hell.*

[23]"So if you are presenting a sacrifice* at the altar in the Temple and you suddenly remember that someone has something against you, [24]leave your sacrifice there at the altar. Go and be reconciled to that person. Then come and offer your sacrifice to God.

5:21 Exod 20:13; Deut 5:17. **5:22a** Some manuscripts add *without cause.* **5:22b** Greek uses an Aramaic term of contempt: *If you say to your brother, 'Raca.'* **5:22c** Greek *if you say, 'You fool.'* **5:22d** Greek *Gehenna;* also in 5:29, 30. **5:23** Greek *gift;* also in 5:24.

SIX WAYS TO THINK LIKE CHRIST

Reference	Example	It's not enough to	We must also
5:21, 22	Murder	Avoid killing	Avoid anger and hatred
5:23-26	Sacrifices	Offer regular gifts	Have right relationships with God and others
5:27-30	Adultery	Avoid adultery	Keep our hearts from lusting and be faithful
5:31, 32	Divorce	Be legally married	Live out marriage commitments
5:33-37	Vows	Keep a vow	Avoid casual and irresponsible commitments to God
5:38-47	Revenge	Seek justice for ourselves	Show mercy and love to others

We, more often than not, avoid the extreme sins but regularly commit the types of sins with which Jesus was most concerned. In these six examples, our real struggle with sin is exposed. Jesus pointed out what kind of lives would be required of his followers. Are you living as Jesus taught?

Exodus 20:13, for example). The moral law reveals the nature and will of God, and it still applies today. Jesus obeyed the moral law completely.

5:19 Some of those in the crowd were experts at telling others what to do, but they missed the central point of God's laws themselves. Jesus made it clear, however, that obeying God's laws is more important than explaining them. It's much easier to study God's laws and tell others to obey them than to put them into practice. How are you doing at obeying God *yourself?*

5:20 The Pharisees were exacting and scrupulous in their attempts to follow their laws. So how could Jesus reasonably call us to greater righteousness than theirs? The Pharisees' weakness was that they were content to obey the laws outwardly without allowing God to change their hearts (or attitudes). They looked pious, but they were far from the Kingdom of Heaven. God judges our hearts as well as our deeds, for it is in the heart that our real allegiance lies.

Jesus was saying that his listeners needed a different kind of righteousness altogether (out of love for God), not just a more intense version of the Pharisees' obedience (which was mere legal compliance). Our righteousness must (1) come from what God does in us, not what we can do by ourselves, (2) be God-centered, not self-centered, (3) be based on reverence for God, not approval from people, and (4) go beyond keeping the law to living by the principles behind the law. We should be just as concerned about our attitudes that people don't see as about our actions that are seen by all.

5:21, 22 When Jesus said, "But I say," he was not doing away with the law or adding his own beliefs. Rather, he was

giving a fuller understanding of why God made that law in the first place. For example, Moses said, "You must not murder" (Exodus 20:13); Jesus taught that we should not even become angry enough to murder, for then we have already committed murder in our heart. The Pharisees read this law and, not having literally murdered anyone, felt that they had obeyed it. Yet they were angry enough with Jesus that they would soon plot his death, though they would not do the dirty work themselves. We miss the intent of God's Word when we read his rules for living without trying to understand why he made them. When do you keep God's rules but close your eyes to his intent?

5:21, 22 Killing is a terrible sin, but *anger* is a great sin, too, because it also violates God's command to love. Anger in this case refers to a seething, brooding bitterness against someone. It is a dangerous emotion that always threatens to leap out of control, leading to violence, emotional hurt, increased mental stress, and spiritual damage. Anger keeps us from developing a spirit pleasing to God. Have you ever been proud that you didn't strike out and say what was really on your mind? Self-control is good, but Christ wants us to practice thought-control as well. Jesus said that we will be held accountable even for our attitudes.

5:23, 24 Broken relationships can hinder our relationship with God. If we have a problem or grievance with a friend, we should resolve the problem as soon as possible. We are hypocrites if we claim to love God while we hate others. Our attitudes toward others reflect our relationship with God (1 John 4:20).

25"When you are on the way to court with your adversary, settle your differences quickly. Otherwise, your accuser may hand you over to the judge, who will hand you over to an officer, and you will be thrown into prison. 26And if that happens, you surely won't be free again until you have paid the last penny.*

Jesus Teaches about Lust (53)

27 "You have heard the commandment that says, 'You must not commit adultery.'* 28But I say, anyone who even looks at a woman with lust has already committed adultery with her in his heart. 29 So if your eye—even your good eye*—causes you to lust, gouge it out and throw it away. It is better for you to lose one part of your body than for your whole body to be thrown into hell. 30And if your hand—even your stronger hand*—causes you to sin, cut it off and throw it away. It is better for you to lose one part of your body than for your whole body to be thrown into hell.

Jesus Teaches about Divorce (54)

31 "You have heard the law that says, 'A man can divorce his wife by merely giving her a written notice of divorce.'* 32But I say that a man who divorces his wife, unless she has been unfaithful, causes her to commit adultery. And anyone who marries a divorced woman also commits adultery.

Jesus Teaches about Vows (55)

33 "You have also heard that our ancestors were told, 'You must not break your vows; you must carry out the vows you make to the LORD.'* 34But I say, do not make any vows! Do not say, 'By heaven!' because heaven is God's throne. 35And do not say, 'By the earth!' because the earth is his footstool. And do not say, 'By Jerusalem!' for Jerusalem is the city of the great King. 36Do not even say, 'By my head!' for you can't turn one hair white or black. 37Just say a simple, 'Yes, I will,' or 'No, I won't.' Anything beyond this is from the evil one.

5:25-26
Matt 18:34-35
Luke 12:58-59

5:27
†Exod 20:14
†Deut 5:18
Matt 19:18
Mark 10:19
Luke 18:20
Rom 13:9
Jas 2:11

5:29-30
Matt 18:8-9
Mark 9:43-47

5:31
†Deut 24:1
Matt 19:7
Mark 10:4

5:32
1 Cor 7:10-11

5:33
Lev 19:12
Num 30:2
Deut 23:21

5:34
Isa 66:1
Jas 5:12

5:35
Isa 66:1

5:37
Jas 5:12

5:26 Greek *the last kodrantes* [i.e., quadrans]. **5:27** Exod 20:14; Deut 5:18. **5:29** Greek *your right eye*. **5:30** Greek *your right hand*. **5:31** Deut 24:1. **5:33** Num 30:2.

5:25, 26 In Jesus' day, someone who couldn't pay a debt was thrown into prison until the debt was paid. Unless someone came to pay the debt for the prisoner, he or she would probably die there. It is practical advice to resolve our differences with our enemies before their anger causes more trouble (Proverbs 25:8-10). You may not get into a disagreement that takes you to court, but even small conflicts mend more easily if you try to make peace right away. In a broader sense, these verses advise us to get things right with our brothers and sisters before we have to stand before God.

5:27, 28 The Old Testament law said that it is wrong for a person to have sex with someone other than his or her spouse (Exodus 20:14). But Jesus said that the *desire* to have sex with someone other than your spouse is mental adultery and thus sin. Jesus emphasized that if the *act* is wrong, then so is the *intention*. To be faithful to your spouse with your body but not your mind is to break the trust so vital to a strong marriage. Jesus is condemning not natural interest in the opposite sex or even healthy sexual desire but the deliberate and repeated filling of one's mind with fantasies that would be evil if acted out.

5:27, 28 Some think that if lustful thoughts are sin, why shouldn't a person go ahead and do the lustful actions, too? Acting out sinful desires is harmful in several ways: (1) It causes people to excuse sin rather than to stop sinning; (2) it destroys marriages; (3) it is deliberate rebellion against God's Word; (4) it always hurts someone else in addition to the sinner. Sinful actions are more dangerous than sinful desires, and that is why desires should not be acted out. Nevertheless, sinful desires are just as damaging to obedience. Left unchecked, wrong desires will result in wrong actions and turn people away from God.

5:29, 30 When Jesus said to get rid of your hand or your eye, he was speaking figuratively. He didn't mean literally to gouge out your eye, because even a blind person can lust. But if that were the only choice, it would be better to go into heaven with one eye or hand than to go to hell with two. We sometimes tolerate sins in our life that, left unchecked, could eventually destroy us. It is better to experience the pain of removal (getting rid of a bad habit or some-

thing we treasure, for instance) than to allow the sin to bring judgment and condemnation. Examine your life for anything that causes you to sin, and take every necessary action to remove it.

5:31, 32 Divorce is as hurtful and destructive today as in Jesus' day. God intends marriage to be a lifetime commitment (Genesis 2:24). When entering into marriage, people should never consider divorce an option for solving problems or a way out of a relationship that seems dead. In these verses, Jesus is also attacking those who purposefully abuse the marriage contract, using divorce to satisfy their lustful desire to marry someone else. Are your actions today helping your marriage grow stronger, or are you tearing it apart?

5:32 Jesus said that divorce is not permissible except for unfaithfulness. This does not mean that divorce should automatically occur when a spouse commits adultery. The word translated "unfaithful" implies a sexually immoral lifestyle, not a confessed and repented act of adultery. Those who discover that their partner has been unfaithful should first make every effort to forgive, reconcile, and restore their relationship. We are always to look for reasons to restore the marriage relationship rather than for excuses to leave it.

5:33ff Here, Jesus was emphasizing the importance of telling the truth. People were breaking vows and using sacred language casually and carelessly. Keeping vows and promises is important; it builds trust and makes committed human relationships possible. The Bible condemns making vows or taking oaths casually, giving your word while knowing that you won't keep it, or swearing falsely in God's name (Exodus 20:7; Leviticus 19:12; Numbers 30:1, 2; Deuteronomy 19:16-20). Vows are needed in certain situations only because we live in a sinful society that breeds distrust.

5:33-37 Vows were common, but Jesus told his followers not to use them—their word alone should be enough (see James 5:12). Are you known as a person of your word? Truthfulness seems so rare that we feel we must end our statements with "I promise." If we tell the truth all the time, we will have less pressure to back up our words with an oath or promise.

5:38
†Exod 21:24
†Lev 24:20
†Deut 19:21

5:39
1 Cor 6:7
1 Pet 3:9

5:40
1 Cor 6:7

5:42
Deut 15:8

5:43
†Lev 19:18
Luke 10:27
Rom 13:9

5:44
Exod 23:4-5
Luke 23:34

5:48
Luke 6:36
1 Pet 1:16

Jesus Teaches about Revenge (56)

38"You have heard the law that says the punishment must match the injury: 'An eye for an eye, and a tooth for a tooth.'* 39But I say, do not resist an evil person! If someone slaps you on the right cheek, offer the other cheek also. 40If you are sued in court and your shirt is taken from you, give your coat, too. 41If a soldier demands that you carry his gear for a mile,* carry it two miles. 42Give to those who ask, and don't turn away from those who want to borrow.

Jesus Teaches about Loving Enemies (57/Luke 6:27-36)

43"You have heard the law that says, 'Love your neighbor'* and hate your enemy. 44But I say, love your enemies!* Pray for those who persecute you! 45In that way, you will be acting as true children of your Father in heaven. For he gives his sunlight to both the evil and the good, and he sends rain on the just and the unjust alike. 46If you love only those who love you, what reward is there for that? Even corrupt tax collectors do that much. 47If you are kind only to your friends,* how are you different from anyone else? Even pagans do that. 48But you are to be perfect, even as your Father in heaven is perfect.

5:38 Greek *the law that says: 'An eye for an eye and a tooth for a tooth.'* Exod 21:24; Lev 24:20; Deut 19:21.
5:41 Greek *milion* [4,854 feet or 1,478 meters]. **5:43** Lev 19:18. **5:44** Some manuscripts add *Bless those who curse you. Do good to those who hate you.* Compare Luke 6:27-28. **5:47** Greek *your brothers.*

JESUS AND THE OLD TESTAMENT LAW

Reference	Examples of Old Testament mercy in justice:
Leviticus 19:18	"Do not seek revenge or bear a grudge against a fellow Israelite, but love your neighbor as yourself. I am the LORD."
Proverbs 24:28, 29	"Don't testify against your neighbors without cause; don't lie about them. And don't say, 'Now I can pay them back for what they've done to me! I'll get even with them!'"
Proverbs 25:21, 22	"If your enemies are hungry, give them food to eat. If they are thirsty, give them water to drink. You will heap burning coals of shame on their heads, and the LORD will reward you."
Lamentations 3:30, 31	"Let them turn the other cheek to those who strike them and accept the insults of their enemies. For no one is abandoned by the Lord forever."

What seems to be a case of Jesus contradicting the laws of the Old Testament deserves a careful look. It is too easy to overlook how much mercy was written into the Old Testament laws. Above are several examples. What God designed as a system of justice with mercy had been distorted over the years into a license for revenge. It was this misapplication of the law that Jesus attacked.

5:38 God's purpose behind this law was an expression of mercy. The law was given to judges and said, in effect, "Make the punishment fit the crime." It was not a guide for personal revenge (Exodus 21:23-25; Leviticus 24:19, 20; Deuteronomy 19:21). These laws were given to *limit* vengeance and help the court administer punishment that was neither too strict nor too lenient. Some people, however, were using this phrase to justify their vendettas against others. People still try to excuse their acts of revenge by saying, "I was just doing to him what he did to me."

5:38-42 When we are wronged, often our first reaction is to get even. Instead, Jesus said we should do *good* to those who wrong us! Our desire should not be to keep score but to love and forgive. This is not natural—it is supernatural. Only God can give us the strength to love as he does. Instead of planning vengeance, pray for those who hurt you.

5:39-44 To many Jews of Jesus' day, these statements were offensive. Any Messiah who would turn the other cheek was not the military leader they wanted to lead a revolt against Rome. Since they were under Roman oppression, they wanted retaliation against their enemies, whom they hated. But Jesus suggested a new, radical response to injustice: Instead of demanding rights, give them up freely! According to Jesus, it is more important to *give* justice and mercy than to receive it.

5:43, 44 By telling us not to retaliate, Jesus keeps us from taking the law into our own hands. By loving and praying for our enemies, we can overcome evil with good.
    The Pharisees interpreted Leviticus 19:18 as teaching that they

should love only those who love in return, and Psalms 139:19-22 and 140:9-11 as meaning that they should hate their enemies. But Jesus says we are to love our enemies. If you love your enemies and treat them well, you will truly show that Jesus is Lord of your life. This is possible only for those who give themselves fully to God, because only he can deliver people from natural selfishness. We must trust the Holy Spirit to help us *show* love to those for whom we may not *feel* love.

5:48 How can we be perfect? (1) *In character:* In this life we cannot be flawless, but we can aspire to be as much like Christ as possible. (2) *In holiness:* Like the Pharisees, we are to separate ourselves from the world's sinful values. But unlike the Pharisees, we are to be devoted to God's desires rather than our own and carry his love and mercy into the world. (3) *In maturity:* We can't achieve Christlike character and holy living all at once, but we must grow toward maturity and wholeness. Just as we expect different behavior from a baby, a child, a teenager, and an adult, so God expects different behavior from us, depending on our stage of spiritual development. (4) *In love:* We can seek to love others as completely as God loves us.
    We can be perfect if our behavior is appropriate for our maturity level—perfect, yet with much room to grow. Our tendency to sin must never deter us from striving to be more like Christ. Christ calls all of his disciples to excel, to rise above mediocrity, and to mature in every area, becoming like him. Those who strive to become perfect will one day be perfect, even as Christ is perfect (1 John 3:2, 3).

Jesus Teaches about Giving to the Needy (58)

6 "Watch out! Don't do your good deeds publicly, to be admired by others, for you will lose the reward from your Father in heaven. ² When you give to someone in need, don't do as the hypocrites do—blowing trumpets in the synagogues and streets to call attention to their acts of charity! I tell you the truth, they have received all the reward they will ever get. ³ But when you give to someone in need, don't let your left hand know what your right hand is doing. ⁴Give your gifts in private, and your Father, who sees everything, will reward you.

6:1-2
Matt 23:5

6:4
Matt 6:6, 18

Jesus Teaches about Prayer (59)

⁵ "When you pray, don't be like the hypocrites who love to pray publicly on street corners and in the synagogues where everyone can see them. I tell you the truth, that is all the reward they will ever get. ⁶But when you pray, go away by yourself, shut the door behind you, and pray to your Father in private. Then your Father, who sees everything, will reward you.

⁷ "When you pray, don't babble on and on as people of other religions do. They think their prayers are answered merely by repeating their words again and again. ⁸ Don't be like them, for your Father knows exactly what you need even before you ask him! ⁹ Pray like this:

6:5
Matt 6:16; 23:5
Luke 18:10-14
6:6
2 Kgs 4:33
Isa 26:20
6:7
Eccl 5:1-2
6:8
Matt 6:32
Luke 12:30
6:9-13
Luke 11:2-4
6:9
1 Pet 1:17
6:10
Matt 26:39, 42
Luke 22:42
6:11
Prov 30:8
John 6:32

> Our Father in heaven,
>   may your name be kept holy.
> ¹⁰ May your Kingdom come soon.
> May your will be done on earth,
>   as it is in heaven.
> ¹¹ Give us today the food we need,*
> ¹² and forgive us our sins,
>   as we have forgiven those who sin against us.

6:11 Or *Give us today our food for the day;* or *Give us today our food for tomorrow.*

• **6:2** The term *hypocrites,* as used here, describes people who do good acts for appearances only—not out of compassion or other good motives. Their actions may be good, but their motives are hollow. These empty acts are their only reward, but God will reward those who are sincere in their faith.

• **6:3** When Jesus says not to tell your left hand what your right hand is doing, he is teaching that our motives for giving to God and to others must be pure. It is easy to give with mixed motives, to do something for someone if it will benefit us in return. But believers should avoid all scheming and give for the pleasure of giving and as a response to God's love. Why do *you* give?

• **6:3, 4** It's easier to do what's right when we gain recognition and praise. To be sure our motives are not selfish, we should do our good deeds quietly or in secret, with no thought of reward. Jesus says we should check our motives in three areas: generosity (6:4), prayer (6:6), and fasting (6:18). Those acts should not be self-centered but God-centered, done not to make us look good but to make God look good. The reward God promises is not material, and it is never given to those who seek it. Doing something only for ourselves is not a loving sacrifice. With your next good deed, ask, Would I still do this if no one would ever know I did it?

• **6:5, 6** Some people, especially the religious leaders, wanted to be seen as "holy," and public prayer was one way to get attention. Jesus saw through their self-righteous acts, however, and taught that the essence of prayer is not public style but private communication with God. There is a place for public prayer, but to pray only where others will notice you indicates that your real audience is not God.

6:6 Some have concluded that Jesus' directions about private prayer call into question all public prayer. Jesus' own practice indicates this wasn't his intention. The Gospels record Jesus at prayer both privately (14:23) and publicly (14:18, 19). Again, Jesus was drawing attention to the motives behind actions. The point really wasn't a choice between public and private prayer but between heartfelt and hypocritical prayer. When asked to pray in public, focus on addressing God, not on how you're coming across to others.

6:7, 8 Repeating the same words over and over like a magic incantation is no way to ensure that God will hear your prayer. It's not wrong to come to God many times with the same requests—Jesus encourages *persistent* prayer. But he condemns the shallow repetition of words that are not offered with a sincere heart. We can never pray too much if our prayers are honest and sincere. Before you start to pray, make sure you mean what you say.

6:9 This is often called the Lord's Prayer because Jesus gave it to the disciples as a model for them (and us) to keep in mind as we pray. Jesus provided a pattern to be imitated as well as duplicated. We should praise God, pray for his work in the world, pray for our daily needs, and pray for help in our daily struggles. To what extent do you use the items in the Lord's Prayer to guide your own prayer times?

6:9 The phrase "Our Father in heaven" indicates that God is not only majestic and holy but also personal and loving. The first line of this model prayer is a statement of praise and a commitment to hallow, or honor, God's holy name. We can honor God's name by being careful to use it respectfully. If we use God's name lightly, we aren't remembering God's holiness.

6:10 The phrase "May your Kingdom come soon" is a reference to God's spiritual reign, not Israel's freedom from Rome. God's Kingdom was announced in the covenant with Abraham (8:11; Luke 13:28), is present in Christ's reign in believers' hearts (Luke 17:21), and will be complete when all evil is destroyed and God establishes the new heaven and earth (Revelation 21:1).

6:10 When we pray "May your will be done," we are not resigning ourselves to fate but praying that God's perfect purpose will be accomplished in this world as well as in the next. And how does God accomplish his will on earth? He does it largely through people willing to obey him. This part of the prayer allows us to offer ourselves as doers of God's will, asking him to guide, lead, and give us the means to accomplish his purposes.

6:11 When we pray "Give us today the food we need," we are acknowledging that God is our sustainer and provider. It is a misconception to think that we provide for our needs ourselves. We must trust God *daily* to provide what he knows we need.

6:13
Luke 22:40, 46
John 17:15

¹³ And don't let us yield to temptation,*
    but rescue us from the evil one.*

6:14
Mark 11:25
Eph 4:32
Col 3:13

¹⁴ "If you forgive those who sin against you, your heavenly Father will forgive you. ¹⁵ But if you refuse to forgive others, your Father will not forgive your sins.

6:15
Matt 18:35

Jesus Teaches about Fasting (60)

6:16
Isa 58:5
Matt 6:5; 23:5

¹⁶ "And when you fast, don't make it obvious, as the hypocrites do, for they try to look misera-ble and disheveled so people will admire them for their fasting. I tell you the truth, that is the only reward they will ever get. ¹⁷ But when you fast, comb your hair and wash your face.

6:18
Matt 6:4, 6

¹⁸Then no one will notice that you are fasting, except your Father, who knows what you do in private. And your Father, who sees everything, will reward you.

Jesus Teaches about Money (61)

6:19
Prov 23:4
Jas 5:2-3

¹⁹ "Don't store up treasures here on earth, where moths eat them and rust destroys them, and where thieves break in and steal. ²⁰Store your treasures in heaven, where moths and rust cannot destroy, and thieves do not break in and steal. ²¹Wherever your treasure is, there the desires of your heart will also be.

6:20
Matt 19:21
Mark 10:21
Luke 18:22
1 Tim 6:19

²² "Your eye is a lamp that provides light for your body. When your eye is good, your whole body is filled with light. ²³But when your eye is bad, your whole body is filled with darkness. And if the light you think you have is actually darkness, how deep that darkness is!

6:23
Matt 20:15
Mark 7:22

²⁴ "No one can serve two masters. For you will hate one and love the other; you will be de-voted to one and despise the other. You cannot serve both God and money.

6:13a Or *And keep us from being tested.* **6:13b** Or *from evil.* Some manuscripts add *For yours is the kingdom and the power and the glory forever. Amen.*

SEVEN REASONS NOT TO WORRY

6:25 . . . . The same God who created life in you can be trusted with the details of your life.

6:26 . . . . Worrying about the future hampers your efforts for today.

6:27 . . . . Worrying is more harmful than helpful.

6:28-30 . . . . God does not ignore those who depend on him.

6:31, 32 . . . . Worrying shows a lack of faith in and understanding of God.

6:33 . . . . Worrying keeps us from real challenges God wants us to pursue.

6:34 . . . . Living one day at a time keeps us from being consumed with worry.

6:13 God sometimes allows us to be tested by temptation. As disciples, we should pray to be delivered from these trying times and for deliverance from Satan ("the evil one") and his deceit. All Christians struggle with temptation. Sometimes it is so subtle that we don't even realize what is happening to us. God has promised that he won't allow us to be tempted beyond what we can bear (1 Corinthians 10:13). Ask God to help you recognize temptation and to give you strength to overcome it and choose God's way instead. For more on temptation, see the notes on 4:1.

6:14, 15 Jesus gives a startling warning about forgiveness: If we refuse to forgive others, God will also refuse to forgive us. Why? Because when we don't forgive others, we are denying our common ground as sinners in need of God's forgiveness. God's forgiveness of sin is not the direct result of our forgiving others, but it is based on our realizing what forgiveness means (see Ephesians 4:32). It is easy to ask God for forgiveness but difficult to grant it to others. Whenever we ask God to forgive us for sin, we should ask, Have I forgiven the people who have wronged me?

• **6:16** Fasting—going without food in order to spend time in prayer—is noble *and* difficult. It gives us time to pray, teaches self-discipline, reminds us that we can live with a lot less, and helps us appreciate God's gifts. Jesus was not condemning fast-ing, but hypocrisy—fasting in order to gain public approval. Fasting was mandatory for the Jewish people once a year on the Day of Atonement (Leviticus 23:32). The Pharisees voluntarily fasted twice a week to impress the people with their "holiness." Jesus commended acts of self-sacrifice done quietly and sincerely.

He wanted people to adopt spiritual disciplines for the right reasons, not from a selfish desire for praise.

• **6:20** Storing treasures in heaven is not limited to tithing but is accomplished by all acts of obedience to God. There is a sense in which giving our money to God's work is like investing in heaven. But we should seek to please God not only in our giving but also in fulfilling God's purposes in all we do.

6:21 Jesus made it clear that having the wrong treasures leads to our hearts being in the wrong place. What we treasure the most controls us, whether we admit it or not. If possessions or money become too important to us, we must reestablish control or get rid of items. Jesus calls for a decision that allows us to live contentedly with whatever we have because we have chosen eternal values over temporary, earthly treasures.

• **6:22, 23** Spiritual vision is our capacity to see clearly what God wants us to do and to see the world from his point of view. But this spiritual insight can be easily clouded. Self-serving desires, interests, and goals block that vision. Serving God is the best way to restore it. A "good" eye is one that is fixed on God.

6:24 Jesus says we can have only one master. We live in a mate-rialistic society where many people serve money. They spend all their lives collecting and storing it, only to die and leave it behind. Their desire for money and what it can buy far outweighs their commitment to God and spiritual matters. Whatever you store up, you will spend much of your time and energy thinking about. Don't fall into the materialistic trap, because "the love of money is the root of all kinds of evil" (1 Timothy 6:10). Can you honestly say that God, and not money, is your master? One test is to ask

Jesus Teaches about Worry (62)

25 "That is why I tell you not to worry about everyday life—whether you have enough food and drink, or enough clothes to wear. Isn't life more than food, and your body more than clothing? 26Look at the birds. They don't plant or harvest or store food in barns, for your heavenly Father feeds them. And aren't you far more valuable to him than they are? 27Can all your worries add a single moment to your life?

28 "And why worry about your clothing? Look at the lilies of the field and how they grow. They don't work or make their clothing, 29 yet Solomon in all his glory was not dressed as beautifully as they are. 30And if God cares so wonderfully for wildflowers that are here today and thrown into the fire tomorrow, he will certainly care for you. Why do you have so little faith?

31 "So don't worry about these things, saying, 'What will we eat? What will we drink? What will we wear?' 32These things dominate the thoughts of unbelievers, but your heavenly Father already knows all your needs. 33Seek the Kingdom of God* above all else, and live righteously, and he will give you everything you need.

34 "So don't worry about tomorrow, for tomorrow will bring its own worries. Today's trouble is enough for today.

6:25
Phil 4:6
1 Tim 6:6, 8
1 Pet 5:7
6:26
Job 38:41

6:29
1 Kgs 10:4-7
6:30
Matt 8:26; 14:31;
16:8

6:32
Matt 6:8
Luke 12:30
6:33
Ps 37:4, 25
Mark 10:29-30

6:34
Exod 16:4

Jesus Teaches about Judging Others (63/Luke 6:37-42)

7 "Do not judge others, and you will not be judged. 2For you will be treated as you treat others.* The standard you use in judging is the standard by which you will be judged.*

3"And why worry about a speck in your friend's eye* when you have a log in your own? 4How can you think of saying to your friend,* 'Let me help you get rid of that speck in your eye,' when you can't see past the log in your own eye? 5Hypocrite! First get rid of the log in your own eye; then you will see well enough to deal with the speck in your friend's eye.

6 "Don't waste what is holy on people who are unholy.* Don't throw your pearls to pigs! They will trample the pearls, then turn and attack you.

7:1-2
Luke 6:37-42
Rom 2:1-3; 14:4
1 Cor 4:5; 5:12
Jas 4:11-12
7:3-5
Luke 6:37-38,
41-42

6:33 Some manuscripts do not include *of God.*   **7:2a** Or *For God will judge you as you judge others.*   **7:2b** Or *The measure you give will be the measure you get back.*   **7:3** Greek *your brother's eye;* also in 7:5.   **7:4** Greek *your brother.*   **7:6** Greek *Don't give the sacred to dogs.*

---

yourself which one occupies more of your thoughts, time, and efforts.

6:24 Jesus contrasted heavenly values with earthly values when he explained that our first loyalty should be to those things that do not fade, cannot be stolen or used up, and never wear out. We should not be fascinated with our possessions, lest *they* possess *us.* God alone deserves to be our master. Either we store our treasures with God (6:20, 21), focus our "eyes" on him (6:22, 23), and serve him alone—or else we do not serve him at all. Where does your ultimate allegiance lie?

6:25 Because of the ill effects of worry, Jesus tells us not to worry about those needs that God promises to supply. Worry may (1) damage your health, (2) disrupt your productivity, (3) negatively affect the way you treat others, and (4) reduce your ability to trust in God. How many ill effects of worry are you experiencing? Here is the difference between worry and genuine concern— worry immobilizes, but concern moves you to action.

• **6:33** To "seek the Kingdom of God above all else" means to put God first in your life, to fill your thoughts with his desires, to take his character for your pattern, and to serve and obey him in everything. What is really important to you? People, objects, goals, and other desires all compete for priority. Any of these can quickly become most important to you if you don't actively choose to give God first place in *every* area of your life.

6:34 Planning for tomorrow is time well spent; worrying about tomorrow is time wasted. Sometimes it's difficult to tell the difference. Careful planning is thinking ahead about goals, steps, and schedules, and trusting in God's guidance. When done well, planning can help alleviate worry. Worriers, by contrast, are consumed by fear and find it difficult to trust God. They let their plans interfere with their relationship with God. Don't let worries about tomorrow affect your relationship with God today.

7:1, 2 Jesus tells us to examine our own motives and conduct instead of judging others. The traits that bother us in others are often the habits we have ourselves. Our bad habits and behavior patterns are the very ones that we most want to change in others. Do you find it easy to magnify others' faults while excusing your own? If you are ready to criticize someone, check to see if you deserve the same criticism. Judge yourself first, and then lovingly forgive and help your neighbor.

7:1-5 Jesus' statement, "Do not judge others," is against the kind of hypocritical, judgmental attitude that tears others down in order to build oneself up. It is not a blanket statement to overlook wrong behavior of others but a call to be *discerning* rather than negative. Jesus said to expose false prophets (7:15-23), and Paul taught that we should exercise church discipline (1 Corinthians 5:1, 2) and trust God to be the final Judge (1 Corinthians 4:3-5).

7:6 Pigs were unclean animals according to God's law (Deuteronomy 14:8). Anyone who touched an unclean animal became "ceremonially unclean" and could not go to the Temple to worship until the uncleanness was removed. Jesus says that we should not entrust holy teachings to unholy or unclean people. It is futile to try to teach holy concepts to people who don't want to listen and will only tear apart what we say. We should not stop giving God's Word to unbelievers, but we should be wise and discerning in our witnessing, so that we will not be wasting our time.

7:7, 8 Jesus tells us to persist in pursuing God. People often give up after a few halfhearted efforts and conclude that God cannot be found. But knowing God takes faith, focus, and follow-through, and Jesus assures us that we will be rewarded. Don't give up in your efforts to seek God. Continue to ask him for more knowledge, patience, wisdom, love, and understanding. He will give them to you.

Jesus Teaches about Asking, Looking, Knocking (64)

7:7-11
Luke 11:9-13

7 "Keep on asking, and you will receive what you ask for. Keep on seeking, and you will find. Keep on knocking, and the door will be opened to you. 8For everyone who asks, receives.

7:7
Matt 21:22
Mark 11:24
Luke 11:9-13
John 14:13-14;
15:7; 16:23-24
Jas 1:5-6
1 Jn 3:21-22;
5:14-15

Everyone who seeks, finds. And to everyone who knocks, the door will be opened.

9 "You parents—if your children ask for a loaf of bread, do you give them a stone instead? 10Or if they ask for a fish, do you give them a snake? Of course not! 11So if you sinful people know how to give good gifts to your children, how much more will your heavenly Father give good gifts to those who ask him.

The Golden Rule

7:12
Luke 6:31
Rom 13:8-10
Gal 5:14

12 "Do to others whatever you would like them to do to you. This is the essence of all that is taught in the law and the prophets.

Jesus Teaches about the Way to Heaven (65)

7:14
John 14:6
Acts 14:22

13 "You can enter God's Kingdom only through the narrow gate. The highway to hell* is broad, and its gate is wide for the many who choose that way. 14 But the gateway to life is very narrow and the road is difficult, and only a few ever find it.

Jesus Teaches about Fruit in People's Lives (66/Luke 6:43-45)

7:15
Jer 23:16
Matt 24:11, 24
Luke 6:26
Acts 20:29
Rom 16:17
2 Pet 2:1
1 Jn 4:1

15 "Beware of false prophets who come disguised as harmless sheep but are really vicious wolves. 16 You can identify them by their fruit, that is, by the way they act. Can you pick grapes from thornbushes, or figs from thistles? 17A good tree produces good fruit, and a bad tree produces bad fruit. 18A good tree can't produce bad fruit, and a bad tree can't produce good fruit. 19 So every tree that does not produce good fruit is chopped down and thrown into the fire. 20 Yes, just as you can identify a tree by its fruit, so you can identify people by their actions.

7:16-20
Matt 12:33

Jesus Teaches about Building on a Solid Foundation (67/Luke 6:46-49)

7:21
Luke 6:46
Jas 1:22

21 "Not everyone who calls out to me, 'Lord! Lord!' will enter the Kingdom of Heaven. Only those who actually do the will of my Father in heaven will enter. 22 On judgment day many will say to me, 'Lord! Lord! We prophesied in your name and cast out demons in your name

7:22
Acts 19:13-15

7:13 Greek *The road that leads to destruction.*

7:9, 10 The children in Jesus' example asked their father for bread and fish—good and necessary items. If the children had asked for a poisonous snake, would the wise father have granted the request? Sometimes God knows we are praying for "snakes" and does not give us what we ask for, even though we persist in our prayers. Nor will God give us "stones" or "snakes" instead of what we need. As we learn to know God better as a loving Father, we learn to ask for what is good for us, and then he grants it.

7:11 Christ is showing us the heart of God the Father. God is not selfish, begrudging, or stingy, and we don't have to beg or grovel as we come with our requests. He is a loving Father, who understands, cares, and comforts. If humans can be kind, imagine how kind God, the Creator of kindness, can be.

7:11 Jesus used the expression "you sinful people" to contrast sinful and fallible human beings with the holy and perfect God.

7:12 This is commonly known as the Golden Rule. In many religions it is stated negatively: "Don't do to others what you don't want done to you." By stating it positively, Jesus made it more significant. It is not very hard to refrain from harming others; it is much more difficult to take the initiative in doing something good for them. The Golden Rule, as Jesus formulated it, is the foundation of active goodness and mercy—the kind of love God shows to us every day. Think of a good and merciful action you can do today.

7:13, 14 The gate that leads to eternal life (John 10:7-9) is called "narrow." This does not mean that it is difficult to become a Christian but that there is only *one* way to eternal life with God and that only a few decide to walk that road. Believing in Jesus is the only way to heaven, because he alone died for our sins and made us right before God. Living his way may not be popular, but it is true and right. Thank God there is one way!

7:15 False prophets were common in Old Testament times. They prophesied only what the king and the people wanted to hear, claiming it was God's message. Jesus indicates that false prophets were just as prevalent in his time. False teachers are just as common today. Jesus says to beware of those whose words sound religious but who are motivated by money, fame, or power. You can tell who they are because in their teaching they minimize Christ and glorify themselves.

7:20 We should evaluate teachers' words by examining their lives. Just as trees are consistent in the kind of fruit they produce, good teachers consistently exhibit good behavior and high moral character as they seek to live out the truths of Scripture. This does not mean we should have witch-hunts, throwing out Sunday school teachers, pastors, and others who are less than perfect. Every one of us is subject to sin, and we must show the same mercy to others that we expect for ourselves. When Jesus talks about worthless trees, he means teachers who deliberately teach false doctrine. We must examine the teachers' motives, the direction they are taking, and the results they are seeking.

• **7:21** Some self-professed athletes can "talk" a great game, but that tells you nothing about their athletic skills. And not everyone who talks about heaven belongs to God's Kingdom. Jesus is more concerned about our *walk* than our *talk*. He wants us to *do* right, not just *say* the right words. What you do cannot be separated from what you believe.

• **7:21-23** Jesus exposed those people who sounded religious but had no personal relationship with him. On "judgment day" only our relationship with Christ—our acceptance of him as Savior and our obedience to him—will matter. Many people think that if they are "good" people and say religious things, they will be rewarded with eternal life. In reality, faith in Christ is what will count at the judgment.

• **7:22** "Judgment day" is the final day of reckoning when God will settle all accounts, judging sin and rewarding faith.

and performed many miracles in your name.' ²³But I will reply, 'I never knew you. Get away from me, you who break God's laws.'

²⁴"Anyone who listens to my teaching and follows it is wise, like a person who builds a house on solid rock. ²⁵ Though the rain comes in torrents and the floodwaters rise and the winds beat against that house, it won't collapse because it is built on bedrock. ²⁶But anyone who hears my teaching and doesn't obey it is foolish, like a person who builds a house on sand. ²⁷ When the rains and floods come and the winds beat against that house, it will collapse with a mighty crash."

²⁸ When Jesus had finished saying these things, the crowds were amazed at his teaching, ²⁹for he taught with real authority—quite unlike their teachers of religious law.

7:23
Matt 25:12, 41
Luke 13:25-27

7:24
2 Tim 2:19
Jas 1:22

7:26
Jas 1:23

7:27
Ezek 13:10-12

7:28
Matt 13:54
Mark 1:22; 6:2
Luke 4:32
John 7:46

3. Jesus performs many miracles

Jesus Heals a Man with Leprosy (**38**/Mark 1:40-45; Luke 5:12-16)

8 Large crowds followed Jesus as he came down the mountainside. ²Suddenly, a man with leprosy approached him and knelt before him. "Lord," the man said, "if you are willing, you can heal me and make me clean."

³Jesus reached out and touched him. "I am willing," he said. "Be healed!" And instantly the leprosy disappeared. ⁴ Then Jesus said to him, "Don't tell anyone about this. Instead, go to the priest and let him examine you. Take along the offering required in the law of Moses for those who have been healed of leprosy.* This will be a public testimony that you have been cleansed."

8:4
Lev 14:1-32

A Roman Officer Demonstrates Faith (**68**/Luke 7:1-10)

⁵When Jesus returned to Capernaum, a Roman officer* came and pleaded with him, ⁶"Lord, my young servant* lies in bed, paralyzed and in terrible pain."

⁷Jesus said, "I will come and heal him."

8:5-7
John 4:43-54

8:4 See Lev 14:2-32.　**8:5** Greek *a centurion*; similarly in 8:8, 13.　**8:6** Or *child*; also in 8:13.

• **7:24** To build "on solid rock" means to be a hearing, responding disciple, not a phony, superficial one. Practicing obedience becomes the solid foundation to weather the storms of life. See James 1:22-27 for more on putting into practice what we hear.

7:24-27 The two lives Jesus compares at the end of the Sermon on the Mount have several points in common: they both build, they both hear Jesus' teaching, and they both experience the same set of circumstances in life. The difference between them isn't caused by ignorance but by one ignoring what Jesus said. Externally, their lives may look similar; but the lasting, structural differences will be revealed by the storms of life. The immediate differences in your life when you follow Jesus may not be obvious, but eventually they will turn out to affect even

**JESUS'
MIRACULOUS
POWER
DISPLAYED**
Jesus finished the sermon he had given on a hillside near Galilee and returned to Capernaum. As he and his disciples crossed the Sea of Galilee, Jesus calmed a fierce storm. Then, in the Gentile Gadarene region, Jesus commanded demons to come out of two men.

your eternal destiny. To what degree does your life reflect the directions Jesus gave in this sermon?

• **7:26, 27** Like a house of cards, the fool's life crumbles. Most people do not deliberately seek to build on a false or inferior foundation; instead, they just don't think about their life's purpose. Many people are headed for destruction, not out of stubbornness but out of thoughtlessness. Part of our responsibility as believers is to help others stop and think about where their lives are headed and to point out the consequences of ignoring Christ's message.

• **7:29** The teachers of religious law (religious scholars) often cited traditions and quoted authorities to support their arguments and interpretations. But Jesus spoke with a new authority—his own. He didn't need to quote anyone because he was the original Word (John 1:1).

8:2, 3 Leprosy, like AIDS today, was a terrifying disease because there was no known cure. In Jesus' day, the Greek word for "leprosy" was used for a variety of similar diseases, and some forms were contagious. If a person contracted the contagious type, a priest declared him a leper and banished him from his home and city. The leper was sent to live in a community with other lepers until he either got better or died. Yet when the leper begged Jesus to heal him, Jesus reached out and touched him, even though his skin was covered with the dread disease.

Sin is also an incurable disease—and we all have it. Only Christ's healing touch can miraculously take away our sins and restore us to real living. But first, just like the leper, we must realize our inability to cure ourselves and ask for Christ's saving help.

8:4 The law required a healed leper to be examined by the priest (Leviticus 14). Jesus wanted this man to give his story firsthand to the priest to prove that his leprosy was completely gone so that he could be restored to his community.

8:5, 6 The Roman officer could have let many obstacles stand between him and Jesus—pride, doubt, money, language, distance, time, self-sufficiency, power, race. But he didn't. If he did

8:8
Ps 107:20

8But the officer said, "Lord, I am not worthy to have you come into my home. Just say the word from where you are, and my servant will be healed. 9I know this because I am under the authority of my superior officers, and I have authority over my soldiers. I only need to say, 'Go,' and they go, or 'Come,' and they come. And if I say to my slaves, 'Do this,' they do it."

8:10-12
Ps 107:3
Matt 13:41-42;
21:43
Acts 10:45; 11:18;
14:27
Eph 3:6

10When Jesus heard this, he was amazed. Turning to those who were following him, he said, "I tell you the truth, I haven't seen faith like this in all Israel! 11And I tell you this, that many Gentiles will come from all over the world—from east and west—and sit down with Abraham, Isaac, and Jacob at the feast in the Kingdom of Heaven. 12But many Israelites— those for whom the Kingdom was prepared—will be thrown into outer darkness, where there will be weeping and gnashing of teeth."

8:13
Matt 9:29; 15:28
John 4:50-51

13Then Jesus said to the Roman officer, "Go back home. Because you believed, it has happened." And the young servant was healed that same hour.

Jesus Heals Peter's Mother-in-Law and Many Others
(**35**/Mark 1:29-34; Luke 4:38-41)
14When Jesus arrived at Peter's house, Peter's mother-in-law was sick in bed with a high fever. 15But when Jesus touched her hand, the fever left her. Then she got up and prepared a meal for him.

16That evening many demon-possessed people were brought to Jesus. He cast out the evil spirits with a simple command, and he healed all the sick. 17This fulfilled the word of the Lord through the prophet Isaiah, who said,

8:17
†Isa 53:4

"He took our sicknesses
    and removed our diseases."*

Jesus Teaches about the Cost of Following Him (**122**/Luke 9:51-62)
18When Jesus saw the crowd around him, he instructed his disciples to cross to the other side of the lake.

19Then one of the teachers of religious law said to him, "Teacher, I will follow you wherever you go."

20But Jesus replied, "Foxes have dens to live in, and birds have nests, but the Son of Man* has no place even to lay his head."

8:17 Isa 53:4.   **8:20** "Son of Man" is a title Jesus used for himself.

---

not let these barriers block his approach to Jesus, we don't need to either. What keeps you from Christ?

8:8-12 This Roman officer (also called a centurion) was a career military officer in the Roman army with control over 100 soldiers. Roman soldiers, of all people, were hated by the Jews for their oppression, control, and ridicule. Yet this man's genuine faith amazed Jesus! This hated Gentile's faith put to shame the pompous piety of many of the Jewish religious leaders.

8:10-12 Jesus told the crowd that many religious Jews who should be in the Kingdom would be excluded because of their lack of faith. Entrenched in their religious traditions, they could not accept Christ and his new message. We must be careful not to become so set in our religious habits that we expect God to work only in specified ways. Don't limit God by your mind-set and lack of faith.

8:11, 12 Faithful people of God from "all over the world" will be gathered to feast with the Messiah (Isaiah 25:6; 55). The Jews should have known that when the Messiah came, his blessings would be for Gentiles too (see Isaiah 66:12, 19). But this message came as a shock because they were too wrapped up in their own affairs and destiny. In claiming God's promises, we must not apply them so personally or culturally that we forget to see what God wants to do to reach *all* the people he loves.

8:11, 12 Matthew emphasizes this universal theme—Jesus' message is for everyone. The Old Testament prophets knew this (see Isaiah 56:3, 6-8; 66:12, 19; Malachi 1:11), but many New Testament Jewish leaders chose to ignore it. Each individual has to choose to accept or reject the Good News, and no one can become part of God's Kingdom on the basis of heritage or connections. Having Christian parents is a wonderful blessing,

but it won't guarantee you eternal life. *You* must believe in and follow Christ.

8:14, 15 Peter's mother-in-law gives us a beautiful example to follow. Her response to Jesus' touch was to wait on Jesus and his disciples—immediately. Has God ever helped you through a dangerous or difficult situation? If so, you should ask, How can I express my gratitude to him? Because God has promised us all the rewards of his Kingdom, we should look for ways to serve him and his followers now.

8:16, 17 Matthew continues to show Jesus' kingly nature. Through a single touch, Jesus healed (8:3, 15); when he spoke a single word, evil spirits fled his presence (8:16). Jesus has authority over all evil powers and all earthly disease. He also has power and authority to conquer sin. Sickness and evil are consequences of living in a fallen world. But in the future, when God removes all sin, there will be no more sickness and death. Jesus' healing miracles were a taste of what the whole world will one day experience in God's Kingdom.

• **8:19, 20** Following Jesus is not always easy or comfortable. Often it means great cost and sacrifice, with no earthly rewards or security. Jesus didn't have a place to call home. You may find that following Christ costs you popularity, friendships, leisure time, or treasured habits. But while the cost of following Christ is high, the value of being Christ's disciple is even higher. Discipleship is an investment that lasts for eternity and yields incredible rewards.

21Another of his disciples said, "Lord, first let me return home and bury my father."

22But Jesus told him, "Follow me now. Let the spiritually dead bury their own dead.*"

8:22
Matt 9:9
Mark 2:14
Luke 9:59
John 1:43; 21:19

Jesus Calms the Storm (87/Mark 4:35-41; Luke 8:22-25)

23Then Jesus got into the boat and started across the lake with his disciples. 24Suddenly, a fierce storm struck the lake, with waves breaking into the boat. But Jesus was sleeping. 25The disciples went and woke him up, shouting, "Lord, save us! We're going to drown!"

26Jesus responded, "Why are you afraid? You have so little faith!" Then he got up and rebuked the wind and waves, and suddenly there was a great calm.

8:26
Pss 89:10;
107:25-32
Matt 6:30

27The disciples were amazed. "Who is this man?" they asked. "Even the winds and waves obey him!"

Jesus Sends Demons into a Herd of Pigs (88/Mark 5:1-20; Luke 8:26-29)

28When Jesus arrived on the other side of the lake, in the region of the Gadarenes,* two men who were possessed by demons met him. They lived in a cemetery and were so violent that no one could go through that area.

29They began screaming at him, "Why are you interfering with us, Son of God? Have you come here to torture us before God's appointed time?"

8:29
Mark 1:24
Luke 4:34
2 Pet 2:4

30There happened to be a large herd of pigs feeding in the distance. 31So the demons begged, "If you cast us out, send us into that herd of pigs."

32 "All right, go!" Jesus commanded them. So the demons came out of the men and entered the pigs, and the whole herd plunged down the steep hillside into the lake and drowned in the water.

8:22 Greek *Let the dead bury their own dead.*   **8:28** Other manuscripts read *Gerasenes;* still others read *Gergesenes.* Compare Mark 5:1; Luke 8:26.

• **8:21, 22** It is possible that this disciple was not asking permission to go to his father's funeral but rather to put off following Jesus until his elderly father died. Perhaps he was the firstborn son and wanted to be sure to claim his inheritance. Perhaps he didn't want to face his father's wrath if he left the family business to follow an itinerant preacher. Whether his concern was financial security, family approval, or something else, he did not want to commit himself to Jesus just yet. Jesus, however, would not accept his excuse.

Jesus was always direct with those who wanted to follow him. He made sure they counted the cost and set aside any conditions they might have for following him. As God's Son, Jesus did not hesitate to demand complete loyalty. Even family loyalty was not to take priority over the demands of obedience. His direct challenge forces us to ask ourselves about our own priorities in following him. The decision to follow Jesus should not be put off, even though other loyalties compete for our attention. Nothing should be placed above a total commitment to living for him.

8:23 The boat used here was probably the kind familiar to many of Jesus' disciples who were fishermen. Josephus, an ancient historian, wrote that there were usually more than 300 fishing boats on the Sea of Galilee at one time. This boat was large enough to hold Jesus and his 12 disciples and was powered both by oars and sails. During a storm, however, the sails were taken down to keep them from ripping and to make the boat easier to control.

8:24 The Sea of Galilee is an unusual body of water. It is relatively small (13 miles long, 7 miles wide), but it is 150 feet deep, and the shoreline is 680 feet below sea level. Sudden storms can appear over the surrounding mountains with little warning, stirring the water into violent 20-foot waves. The disciples had not foolishly set out in a storm. They had been caught without warning, and their danger was great.

8:25 Although the disciples had witnessed many miracles, they panicked in this storm. As experienced sailors, they knew its danger; what they did not know was that Christ could control the forces of nature. We often encounter storms in our life, where we feel God can't or won't work. When we truly understand who God is, however, we will realize that he controls both the storms of nature and the storms of the troubled heart. Jesus' power that calmed this storm can also help us deal with the problems we face. Jesus is willing to help if we only ask him. We should never discount his power even in terrible trials.

8:28 The region of the Gadarenes is located southeast of the Sea of Galilee, near the town of Gadara, one of the most important cities of the region (see map). Gadara was a member of the Ten Towns (see the note on Mark 5:20), towns with independent governments that were largely inhabited by Gentiles. This explains the herd of pigs (8:30), for the Jews did not raise pigs because pigs were considered unclean and thus unfit to eat.

8:28 Demon-possessed people are under the control of one or more demons. Demons are fallen angels who joined Satan in his rebellion against God and are now evil spirits under Satan's control. They help Satan tempt people to sin and have great destructive powers. But whenever they are confronted by Jesus, they lose their power. These demons recognized Jesus as God's Son (8:29), but they didn't think they had to obey him. Just believing is not enough (see James 2:19 for a discussion of belief and demons). Faith is more than belief. By faith, you accept what Jesus has done for you, receive him as the only one who can save you from sin, and live out your faith by obeying his commands.

8:28 Matthew says there were two demon-possessed men, while Mark and Luke refer only to one. Apparently Mark and Luke mention only the man who did the talking.

8:28 According to Jewish ceremonial laws, the men Jesus encountered were unclean in three ways: They were Gentiles (non-Jews), they were demon possessed, and they lived in a cemetery. Jesus helped them anyway. We should not turn our backs on people who are "unclean" or repulsive to us or who violate our moral standards and religious beliefs. Instead, we must realize that every human individual is a unique creation of God, needing to be touched by his love.

8:29 The Bible tells us that at the end of the world the devil and his angels will be thrown into the lake of fire that burns with sulfur (Revelation 20:10). When the demons asked if Jesus had come to torture them "before God's appointed time," they showed they knew their ultimate fate.

8:32 When the demons entered the pigs, they drove the animals into the sea. The demons' action proves their destructive intent—if they could not destroy the men, they would destroy the pigs. Jesus' action, by contrast, shows the value he places on each human life.

8:34
Acts 16:39

33 The herdsmen fled to the nearby town, telling everyone what happened to the demon-possessed men. 34 Then the entire town came out to meet Jesus, but they begged him to go away and leave them alone.

Jesus Heals a Paralyzed Man (**39**/Mark 2:1-12; Luke 5:17-26)

9 Jesus climbed into a boat and went back across the lake to his own town. 2 Some people brought to him a paralyzed man on a mat. Seeing their faith, Jesus said to the paralyzed man, "Be encouraged, my child! Your sins are forgiven."

MATTHEW

More than any other disciple, Matthew had a clear idea of how much it would cost to follow Jesus, yet he did not hesitate a moment. When he left his tax-collecting booth, he guaranteed himself unemployment. For several of the other disciples, there was always fishing to return to, but for Matthew, there was no turning back.

Two changes happened to Matthew when he decided to follow Jesus. First, Jesus gave him a new life. He not only belonged to a new group; he belonged to the Son of God. He was not just accepting a different way of life; he was now an accepted person. For a despised tax collector, that change must have been wonderful! Second, Jesus gave Matthew a new purpose for his skills. When he followed Jesus, the only tool from his past job that he carried with him was his pen. From the beginning, God had made him a record keeper. Jesus' call eventually allowed him to put his skills to their finest work. Matthew was a keen observer, and he undoubtedly recorded what he saw going on around him. The Gospel that bears his name came as a result.

Matthew's experience points out that each of us, from the beginning, is one of God's works in progress. Much of what God has for us he gives long before we are able to consciously respond to him. He trusts us with skills and abilities ahead of schedule. He has made each of us capable of being his servant. When we trust him with what he has given us, we begin a life of real adventure. Matthew couldn't have known that God would use the very skills he had sharpened as a tax collector to record the greatest story ever lived. And God has no less meaningful a purpose for each one of us. Have you recognized Jesus saying to you, "Follow me"? What has been your response?

Strengths and accomplishments	• Was one of Jesus' 12 disciples • Responded immediately to Jesus' call • Invited many friends to his home to meet Jesus • Compiled the Gospel of Matthew • Clarified for his Jewish audience Jesus' fulfillment of Old Testament prophecies
Lessons from his life	• Jesus consistently accepted people from every level of society • Matthew was given a new life, and his God-given skills of record keeping and attention to detail were given a new purpose • Having been accepted by Jesus, Matthew immediately tried to bring others into contact with Jesus
Vital statistics	• Where: Capernaum • Occupations: Tax collector, disciple of Jesus • Relative: Father: Alphaeus • Contemporaries: Jesus, Pilate, Herod, other disciples
Key verse	"As Jesus was walking along, he saw a man named Matthew sitting at his tax collector's booth. 'Follow me and be my disciple,' Jesus said to him. So Matthew got up and followed him" (Matthew 9:9).

Matthew's story is told in the Gospels. He is also mentioned in Acts 1:13.

8:34 Why did the people ask Jesus to leave? Unlike their own pagan gods, Jesus could not be contained, controlled, or appeased. They feared Jesus' supernatural power, a power that they had never before witnessed. And they were upset about losing a herd of pigs more than they were glad about the deliverance of the demon-possessed men. Are you more concerned about property and programs than people? Human beings are created in God's image and have eternal value. How foolish and yet how easy it is to value possessions, investments, and even animals above human life. Would you rather have Jesus leave you than finish his work in you?

9:1 "His own town" was Capernaum, a good choice for Jesus' base of operations. It was a wealthy city due to fishing and trade. Situated on the Sea of Galilee in a densely populated area, Capernaum housed the Roman garrison that kept peace in the region.

The city was a cultural melting pot, greatly influenced by Greek and Roman manners, dress, architecture, and politics.

9:2 Among the first words Jesus said to the paralyzed man were "Your sins are forgiven." Then he healed the man. We must be careful not to concentrate more on God's power to heal physical sickness than on his power to forgive spiritual sickness in the form of sin. Jesus saw that even more than physical health, this man needed spiritual health. Spiritual health comes only from Jesus' healing touch.

9:2 Both the man's body and his spirit were paralyzed—he could not walk, and he did not know Jesus. But the man's spiritual state was Jesus' first concern. If God does not heal us or someone we love, we need to remember that physical healing is not Christ's only concern. We will all be completely healed in Christ's coming Kingdom; but first we have to come to know Jesus.

³But some of the teachers of religious law said to themselves, "That's blasphemy! Does he think he's God?"

9:3
Matt 26:65
John 10:33

⁴Jesus knew* what they were thinking, so he asked them, "Why do you have such evil thoughts in your hearts? ⁵Is it easier to say 'Your sins are forgiven,' or 'Stand up and walk'? ⁶So I will prove to you that the Son of Man* has the authority on earth to forgive sins." Then Jesus turned to the paralyzed man and said, "Stand up, pick up your mat, and go home!"

9:4
Matt 12:25
Luke 6:8; 9:47;
11:17

⁷And the man jumped up and went home! ⁸Fear swept through the crowd as they saw this happen. And they praised God for sending a man with such great authority.*

9:6-8
Matt 15:31
Luke 7:16
Acts 9:33-35

Jesus Eats with Sinners at Matthew's House (40/Mark 2:13-17; Luke 5:27-32)

⁹As Jesus was walking along, he saw a man named Matthew sitting at his tax collector's booth. "Follow me and be my disciple," Jesus said to him. So Matthew got up and followed him.

¹⁰Later, Matthew invited Jesus and his disciples to his home as dinner guests, along with many tax collectors and other disreputable sinners. ¹¹But when the Pharisees saw this, they asked his disciples, "Why does your teacher eat with such scum?*"

9:11
Matt 11:19
Luke 5:30; 15:1-2;
19:7

¹²When Jesus heard this, he said, "Healthy people don't need a doctor—sick people do." ¹³Then he added, "Now go and learn the meaning of this Scripture: 'I want you to show mercy, not offer sacrifices.'* For I have come to call not those who think they are righteous, but those who know they are sinners."

9:13
†Hos 6:6
Mic 6:6-8
Matt 12:7
Luke 19:10
1 Tim 1:15

Religious Leaders Ask Jesus about Fasting (41/Mark 2:18-22; Luke 5:33-39)

¹⁴One day the disciples of John the Baptist came to Jesus and asked him, "Why don't your disciples fast* like we do and the Pharisees do?"

¹⁵Jesus replied, "Do wedding guests mourn while celebrating with the groom? Of course not. But someday the groom will be taken away from them, and then they will fast.

9:15
John 3:29

¹⁶ "Besides, who would patch old clothing with new cloth? For the new patch would shrink and rip away from the old cloth, leaving an even bigger tear than before.

9:4 Some manuscripts read *saw.*   9:6 "Son of Man" is a title Jesus used for himself.   9:8 Greek *for giving such authority to human beings.*   9:11 Greek *with tax collectors and sinners?*   9:13 Hos 6:6 (Greek version).
9:14 Some manuscripts read *fast often.*

9:3 Blaspheming is claiming to be God and applying his characteristics to yourself. The religious leaders rightly saw that Jesus was claiming to be God. What they did not understand was that he *is* God and thus has the authority to heal and to forgive sins.

9:5, 6 It's easy to tell someone his sins are forgiven; it's a lot more difficult to reverse a case of paralysis! Jesus backed up his words by healing the man's legs. Jesus' action showed that his words were true; he had the power to forgive as well as to heal. Talk is cheap, but our words lack meaning if our actions do not back them up. We can say we love God or others, but if we are not taking practical steps to demonstrate that love, our words are empty and meaningless. How well do your actions back up what you say?

9:9 Matthew was a Jew who was appointed by the Romans to be the area's tax collector. He collected taxes from the citizens as well as from merchants passing through town. Tax collectors were expected to take a commission on the taxes they collected, but most of them overcharged and kept the profits. Thus, tax collectors were hated by the Jews because of their reputation for cheating and because of their support of Rome.

9:9 When Jesus called Matthew to be one of his disciples, Matthew got up and followed, leaving a lucrative career. When God calls you to follow or obey him, do you do it with as much abandon as Matthew? Sometimes the decision to follow Christ requires difficult or painful choices. Like Matthew, we must decide to leave behind those things that would keep us from following Christ.

9:10-13 When he visited Matthew, Jesus hurt his own reputation among the religious elites in order to reach out to those who were lost. Matthew's reputation hadn't yet caught up with his new life as a disciple, but he became a bridge for Jesus' message to Matthew's past associates. We should not be afraid to reach out to

people who are living in sin. God's message changes people—and their friends, too!

9:11, 12 The Pharisees constantly tried to trap Jesus, and they thought his association with these "lowlifes" was the perfect opportunity. They were more concerned with their own appearance of holiness than with helping people, with criticism than encouragement, with outward respectability than practical help. But God is concerned for all people, including the sinful and hurting ones. The Christian life is not a popularity contest! Following Jesus' example, we should share the Good News with the poor, immoral, lonely, and outcast, not just the rich, moral, popular, and powerful.

9:13 Those who are sure that they are good enough can't be saved because the first step in following Jesus is acknowledging our need and admitting that we don't have all the answers. For more on "I want you to show mercy, not offer sacrifices," see the chart in Hosea 7, p. 1413.

9:14 John's disciples fasted (went without food) as a sign of mourning for sin and preparation for the Messiah's coming. Jesus' disciples did not need to fast because he is the Messiah and was with them! Jesus did not condemn fasting—he himself fasted (4:2). He emphasized that fasting must be done for the right reasons.

9:14 John the Baptist's message was harsh, and it focused on law. When people look at God's law and compare themselves to it, they realize how far they fall short and how badly they need to repent. Jesus' message focused on life, the result of turning from sin and turning to him. John's disciples had the right start, but they needed to take the next step and trust in Jesus. Where is your focus—on law or on Christ?

9:15 The arrival of the Kingdom of Heaven was like a wedding feast with Jesus as the groom. His disciples, therefore, were filled

¹⁷"And no one puts new wine into old wineskins. For the old skins would burst from the pressure, spilling the wine and ruining the skins. New wine is stored in new wineskins so that both are preserved."

Jesus Heals a Bleeding Woman and Restores a Girl to Life
(89/Mark 5:21-43; Luke 8:40-56)

¹⁸As Jesus was saying this, the leader of a synagogue came and knelt before him. "My daughter has just died," he said, "but you can bring her back to life again if you just come and lay your hand on her."

¹⁹So Jesus and his disciples got up and went with him. ²⁰Just then a woman who had suffered for twelve years with constant bleeding came up behind him. She touched the fringe of his robe, ²¹for she thought, "If I can just touch his robe, I will be healed."

²²Jesus turned around, and when he saw her he said, "Daughter, be encouraged! Your faith has made you well." And the woman was healed at that moment.

²³When Jesus arrived at the official's home, he saw the noisy crowd and heard the funeral music. ²⁴"Get out!" he told them. "The girl isn't dead; she's only asleep." But the crowd laughed at him. ²⁵After the crowd was put outside, however, Jesus went in and took the girl by the hand, and she stood up! ²⁶The report of this miracle swept through the entire countryside.

Jesus Heals the Blind and Mute (90)

²⁷After Jesus left the girl's home, two blind men followed along behind him, shouting, "Son of David, have mercy on us!"

²⁸They went right into the house where he was staying, and Jesus asked them, "Do you believe I can make you see?"

"Yes, Lord," they told him, "we do."

²⁹Then he touched their eyes and said, "Because of your faith, it will happen." ³⁰Then their eyes were opened, and they could see! Jesus sternly warned them, "Don't tell anyone about this." ³¹But instead, they went out and spread his fame all over the region.

9:22
Matt 9:29
Mark 10:52
Luke 7:50; 17:19
Acts 3:16
9:23
2 Chr 35:25
Jer 9:17-18
9:24
John 11:11-13

9:27
Matt 20:29-31
Mark 10:47

9:30
Mark 7:36
9:31
Mark 7:36

---

with joy. It would not be right to mourn or fast when the groom was present.

9:17 In Bible times wine was not kept in glass bottles but in goatskins sewn around the edges to form watertight bags. New wine expanded as it fermented, stretching its wineskin. After the wine had aged, the stretched skin would burst if more new wine was poured into it. New wine, therefore, was always put into new wineskins.

Jesus used this description to explain that he had not come to patch up the old religious system of Judaism with its rules and traditions. His purpose was to bring in something new, though it had been prophesied for centuries. This new message, the Good News, said that Jesus Christ, God's Son, came to earth to offer all people forgiveness of sins and reconciliation with God. The Good News did not fit into the old rigid legalistic system of religion. It needed a fresh start. The message will always remain "new" because it must be accepted and applied in every generation. When we follow Christ, we must be prepared for new ways to live, new ways to look at people, and new ways to serve.

9:18 Mark and Luke say this man's name was Jairus (Mark 5:22; Luke 8:41). As leader of the synagogue, Jairus was responsible for administration—looking after the building, supervising worship, running the school on weekdays, and finding rabbis to teach on the Sabbath. For more information on synagogues, read the first note on Mark 1:21.

9:20-22 This woman had suffered for 12 years with a hemorrhage (perhaps a menstrual disorder). In our times of desperation, we don't have to worry about the correct way to reach out to God. Like this woman, we can simply reach out in faith. He will respond.

9:22 God changed a situation that had been a problem for years. Like the leper and the demon-possessed men (see the note on 8:2, 3 and the second note on 8:28), this woman was considered unclean. For 12 years, she, too, had been one of the "untouchables" and had not been able to lead a normal life. But Jesus changed that and restored her. Sometimes we are tempted to give up on people or situations that have not changed for many years. God can change what seems unchangeable, giving new purpose and hope.

9:23-26 The synagogue leader didn't come to Jesus until his daughter was dead—it was too late for anyone else to help. But Jesus simply went to the girl and raised her! In our lives, Christ can make a difference when it seems too late for anyone else to help. He can bring healing to broken relationships, release from addicting habits, and forgiveness and healing to emotional scars. If your situation looks hopeless, remember that Christ can do the impossible.

9:27 "Son of David" was a popular way of addressing Jesus as the Messiah because it was known that the Messiah would be a descendant of David (Isaiah 9:7). This is the first time the title is used in Matthew. Jesus' ability to give sight to the blind was prophesied in Isaiah 29:18; 35:5; 42:7.

9:27-30 Jesus didn't respond immediately to the blind men's pleas. He waited to see if they had faith. Not everyone who says he wants help really believes God can help him. Jesus may have waited and questioned these men to emphasize and increase their faith. When you think that God is too slow in answering your prayers, consider that he might be testing you as he did the blind men. Do you believe that God can help you? Do you *really* want his help?

9:28 These blind men were persistent. They went right into the house where Jesus was staying. They knew Jesus could heal them, and they would let nothing stop them from finding him. That's real faith in action. If you believe Jesus is the answer to your every need, don't let anything or anyone stop you from reaching out to him.

9:30 Jesus told the people to keep quiet about his healings because he did not want to be known only as a miracle worker. He healed because he had compassion on people, but he also wanted to bring *spiritual* healing to a sin-sick world.

³²When they left, a demon-possessed man who couldn't speak was brought to Jesus. ³³So Jesus cast out the demon, and then the man began to speak. The crowds were amazed. "Nothing like this has ever happened in Israel!" they exclaimed.

³⁴But the Pharisees said, "He can cast out demons because he is empowered by the prince of demons."

Jesus Urges the Disciples to Pray for Workers (92)

³⁵Jesus traveled through all the towns and villages of that area, teaching in the synagogues and announcing the Good News about the Kingdom. And he healed every kind of disease and illness. ³⁶When he saw the crowds, he had compassion on them because they were confused and helpless, like sheep without a shepherd. ³⁷He said to his disciples, "The harvest is great, but the workers are few. ³⁸So pray to the Lord who is in charge of the harvest; ask him to send more workers into his fields."

Jesus Sends Out the Twelve Disciples (93/Mark 6:7-13; Luke 9:1-6)

10 Jesus called his twelve disciples together and gave them authority to cast out evil* spirits and to heal every kind of disease and illness. ²Here are the names of the twelve apostles:

first, Simon (also called Peter),
then Andrew (Peter's brother),
James (son of Zebedee),
John (James's brother),
³ Philip,
Bartholomew,
Thomas,
Matthew (the tax collector),
James (son of Alphaeus),
Thaddaeus,*
⁴ Simon (the zealot*),
Judas Iscariot (who later betrayed him).

9:32-33
Matt 12:22
Mark 7:32, 35;
9:17, 25
Luke 11:14

9:34
Matt 12:24
Mark 3:22
Luke 11:15

9:35
Matt 4:23

9:36
†Num 27:17
†2 Chr 18:16
†Zech 10:2
Mark 6:34

9:37-38
Luke 10:2
John 4:35

10:2-4
John 1:40-49
Acts 1:13

10:4
Matt 26:25; 27:3
Mark 14:44

10:1 Greek *unclean.*   **10:3** Other manuscripts read *Lebbaeus;* still others read *Lebbaeus who is called Thaddaeus.*
10:4 Greek *the Cananean,* an Aramaic term for Jewish nationalists.

9:32 While Jesus was on earth, demonic forces were especially active. Although we cannot always be sure why or how demon possession occurs, it causes both physical and mental problems. In this case, the demon made the man unable to talk. For more on demons and demon possession, read the notes on 8:28 and Mark 1:23.

9:34 In chapter 9, the Pharisees accuse Jesus of four different sins: blasphemy, befriending outcasts, impiety, and serving Satan. Matthew shows how Jesus was maligned by those who should have received him most gladly. Why did the Pharisees do this? (1) Jesus bypassed their religious authority. (2) He weakened their control over the people. (3) He challenged their cherished beliefs. (4) He exposed their insincere motives.

While the Pharisees questioned, probed, and dissected Jesus, people were being healed and lives changed right in front of them. Their skepticism was based not on insufficient evidence but on jealousy of Jesus' popularity.

9:36 Jesus was overwhelmed with compassionate pity for the people. His response echoes the deep inner mercy of God, often described in the Old Testament. Ezekiel also compared Israel to sheep without a shepherd (Ezekiel 34:5, 6). Jesus came to be the Shepherd, the one who could show people how to avoid life's pitfalls (see John 10:14).

9:37, 38 Jesus looked at the crowds following him and referred to them as a field ripe for harvest. Many people are ready to give their lives to Christ if someone would show them how. Jesus commands us to pray that people will respond to this need for workers. Often, when we pray for something, God answers our prayers by using *us.* Be prepared for God to use you to show another person the way to him.

10:1 Jesus *called* his 12 disciples. He didn't draft them, force them, or ask them to volunteer; he chose them to serve him in a special way. Christ calls us today. He doesn't twist our arms and make us do something we don't want to do. We can choose to join him or remain behind. When Christ calls you to follow him, how do you respond?

10:2-4 The list of Jesus' 12 disciples doesn't give us many details—probably because there weren't many impressive details to tell. Jesus called people from all walks of life—fishermen, political activists, tax collectors. He called common people and uncommon leaders; rich and poor; educated and uneducated. Today, many people think only certain people are fit to follow Christ, but this was not the attitude of the Master himself. God can use anyone, no matter how insignificant he or she appears. When you feel small and useless, remember that God uses ordinary people to do his extraordinary work.

10:3 Bartholomew is probably another name for Nathanael, whom we meet in John 1:45-51. Thaddaeus is also known as Judas son of James. The disciples are also listed in Mark 3:16-19; Luke 6:14-16; and Acts 1:13.

10:4 Simon the Zealot may have been a member of the Zealots, a radical political party working for the violent overthrow of Roman rule in Israel.

10:5
2 Kgs 17:24
John 4:9

10:6
Jer 50:6
Matt 15:24

10:7
Matt 3:2; 4:17

10:9-10
1 Cor 9:14
1 Tim 5:18

10:15
Gen 18:20–19:29
Matt 11:23-24
2 Pet 2:6
Jude 1:7

5 Jesus sent out the twelve apostles with these instructions: "Don't go to the Gentiles or the Samaritans, 6but only to the people of Israel—God's lost sheep. 7Go and announce to them that the Kingdom of Heaven is near.* 8 Heal the sick, raise the dead, cure those with leprosy, and cast out demons. Give as freely as you have received!

9 "Don't take any money in your money belts—no gold, silver, or even copper coins. 10 Don't carry a traveler's bag with a change of clothes and sandals or even a walking stick. Don't hesitate to accept hospitality, because those who work deserve to be fed.

11"Whenever you enter a city or village, search for a worthy person and stay in his home until you leave town. 12 When you enter the home, give it your blessing. 13 If it turns out to be a worthy home, let your blessing stand; if it is not, take back the blessing. 14 If any household or town refuses to welcome you or listen to your message, shake its dust from your feet as you leave. 15 I tell you the truth, the wicked cities of Sodom and Gomorrah will be better off than such a town on the judgment day.

10:7 Or *has come,* or *is coming soon.*

COUNTING THE COST OF FOLLOWING CHRIST	Who may oppose us?	Natural response	Possible pressures	Needed truth
	GOVERNMENT 10:18-19		Threats 10:26	→ The truth will be revealed (10:26)
	RELIGIOUS PEOPLE 10:17	Fear and worry	Physical harm 10:28	→ Our soul cannot be harmed (10:28)
			Public ridicule 10:22	→ God himself will acknowledge us if we acknowledge him (10:32)
	FAMILY 10:21		Rejection by loved ones 10:34-37	→ God's love can sustain us (10:31)

Jesus helped his disciples prepare for the rejection many of them would experience by being Christians. Being God's person will usually create reactions from others who are resisting him.

10:5, 6 Why didn't Jesus send the disciples to the Gentiles or the Samaritans? A Gentile is anyone who is not a Jew. The Samaritans were a race that resulted from intermarriage between Jews and Gentiles after the Old Testament captivities (see 2 Kings 17:24). Jesus asked his disciples to go only to the Jews because he came *first* to the Jews (Romans 1:16). God chose them to tell the rest of the world about him. Jewish disciples and apostles preached the Good News of the risen Christ all around the Roman Empire, and soon Gentiles were pouring into the church. The Bible clearly teaches that God's message of salvation is for *all* people, regardless of race, sex, or national origin (Genesis 12:3; Isaiah 25:6; 56:3-7; Malachi 1:11; Acts 10:34, 35; Romans 3:29, 30; Galatians 3:28).

10:7 The Jews were waiting for the Messiah to usher in his Kingdom. They hoped for a political and military kingdom that would free them from Roman rule and bring back the days of glory under David and Solomon. But Jesus was talking about a spiritual Kingdom. The Good News today is that the Kingdom is still *near.* Jesus, the Messiah, has already begun his Kingdom on earth in the hearts of his followers. One day the Kingdom will be fully realized. Then evil will be destroyed and all people will live in peace with one another.

10:8 Jesus gave the disciples a principle to guide their actions as they ministered to others: "Give as freely as you have received." Because God has showered us with his blessings, we should give generously to others of our time, love, and possessions.

10:10 Jesus said that those who minister are to be cared for. The disciples could expect food and shelter in return for the spiritual service they provided. Who ministers to you? Make sure you take care of the pastors, missionaries, and teachers who serve God by serving you (see 1 Corinthians 9:9, 10; 1 Timothy 5:17).

10:10 Mark's account (6:8) says to take a walking stick, and Matthew and Luke (9:3) say not to. Jesus may have meant that they were not to take an *extra* pair of sandals, walking stick, and bag. In any case, the principle was that they were to go out ready for duty and travel, unencumbered by excess material goods.

10:14 Why did Jesus tell his disciples to shake the dust off their feet if a city or home didn't welcome them? When leaving Gentile cities, pious Jews often shook the dust from their feet to show their separation from Gentile practices. If the disciples shook the dust of a *Jewish* town from their feet, it would show their separation from Jews who rejected their Messiah. This gesture was to show the people that they were making a wrong choice—that the opportunity to choose Christ might not present itself again. Are you receptive to teaching from God? If you ignore the Spirit's prompting, you may not get another chance.

10:15 The cities of Sodom and Gomorrah were destroyed by fire from heaven because of their wickedness (Genesis 19:24, 25). Those who reject the Good News when they hear it will be worse off than the wicked people of these destroyed cities, who never heard the Good News at all.

Jesus Prepares the Disciples for Persecution (94)

16 "Look, I am sending you out as sheep among wolves. So be as shrewd as snakes and harmless as doves. 17 But beware! For you will be handed over to the courts and will be flogged with whips in the synagogues. 18 You will stand trial before governors and kings because you are my followers. But this will be your opportunity to tell the rulers and other unbelievers about me.* 19 When you are arrested, don't worry about how to respond or what to say. God will give you the right words at the right time. 20 For it is not you who will be speaking—it will be the Spirit of your Father speaking through you.

21 "A brother will betray his brother to death, a father will betray his own child, and children will rebel against their parents and cause them to be killed. 22 And all nations will hate you because you are my followers.* But everyone who endures to the end will be saved. 23 When you are persecuted in one town, flee to the next. I tell you the truth, the Son of Man* will return before you have reached all the towns of Israel.

24 "Students* are not greater than their teacher, and slaves are not greater than their master. 25 Students are to be like their teacher, and slaves are to be like their master. And since I, the master of the household, have been called the prince of demons,* the members of my household will be called by even worse names!

26 "But don't be afraid of those who threaten you. For the time is coming when everything that is covered will be revealed, and all that is secret will be made known to all. 27 What I tell you now in the darkness, shout abroad when daybreak comes. What I whisper in your ear, shout from the housetops for all to hear!

28 "Don't be afraid of those who want to kill your body; they cannot touch your soul. Fear only God, who can destroy both soul and body in hell.* 29 What is the price of two sparrows—one copper coin*? But not a single sparrow can fall to the ground without your Father knowing it. 30 And the very hairs on your head are all numbered. 31 So don't be afraid; you are more valuable to God than a whole flock of sparrows.

32 "Everyone who acknowledges me publicly here on earth, I will also acknowledge before my Father in heaven. 33 But everyone who denies me here on earth, I will also deny before my Father in heaven.

34 "Don't imagine that I came to bring peace to the earth! I came not to bring peace, but a sword.

10:16
Luke 10:3
Acts 20:29

10:17
Acts 5:40; 22:19;
26:11

10:19-20
Luke 12:11-12
Acts 4:8

10:21
Mic 7:6

10:22
John 15:21

10:24
John 13:16; 15:20

10:26
Mark 4:22

10:28
Isa 8:12-13
Heb 10:31

10:29
Luke 12:6

10:30
1 Sam 14:45
2 Sam 14:11
Luke 21:18
Acts 27:34

10:32
Rom 10:9
Rev 3:5

10:33
Mark 8:38
Luke 9:26
2 Tim 2:12

10:18 Or *But this will be your testimony against the rulers and other unbelievers.* 10:22 Greek *on account of my name.* 10:23 "Son of Man" is a title Jesus used for himself. 10:24 Or *Disciples.* 10:25 Greek *Beelzeboul; other manuscripts read Beezeboul; Latin version reads Beelzebub.* 10:28 Greek *Gehenna.* 10:29 Greek *one assarion* [i.e., one "as," a Roman coin equal to 1/16 of a denarius].

10:16 The opposition of the Pharisees would be like ravaging wolves. The disciples' only hope would be to look to their Shepherd for protection. We may face similar hostility. Like the disciples, we are not to be sheeplike in our attitude but sensible and prudent. We are not to be gullible pawns, but neither are we to be deceitful connivers. We must find a balance between wisdom and vulnerability to accomplish God's work.

• **10:17, 18** Later the disciples experienced these hardships (Acts 5:40; 12:1-3), not only from without (governments, courts), but also from within (friends, family; 10:21). Living for God often brings on persecution, but with it comes the opportunity to tell the Good News of salvation. In times of persecution, we can be confident because Jesus has "overcome the world" (John 16:33). And those who endure to the end will be saved (Matthew 10:22).

• **10:19, 20** Jesus told the disciples that when arrested for preaching the Good News, they should not worry about what to say in their defense—God's Spirit would speak through them. This promise was fulfilled in Acts 4:8-14 and elsewhere. Some mistakenly think this means we don't have to prepare to present the Good News because God will take care of everything. Scripture teaches, however, that we are to make carefully prepared, thoughtful statements (Colossians 4:6). Jesus is telling us not to stop preparing but to stop worrying.

• **10:22** Enduring to the end is not a way to be saved but the evidence that a person is really committed to Jesus. Persistence is not a means to earn salvation; it is the by-product of a truly devoted life.

• **10:25** The prince of demons was Satan, also known as Beelzebub and the lord of flies. The Pharisees accused Jesus of using Satan's power to drive out demons (see 12:24). Good is sometimes labeled evil. If Jesus, who is perfect, was called evil, his followers should expect that similar accusations will be directed at them. But those who endure will be vindicated (10:22).

• **10:29-31** Jesus said that God is aware of everything that happens even to sparrows, and you are far more valuable to him than they are. You are so valuable that God sent his only Son to die for you (John 3:16). Because God places such value on you, you need never fear personal threats or difficult trials. These can't shake God's love or dislodge his Spirit from within you.

This doesn't mean, however, that God will take away all your troubles (see 10:16). The real test of value is how well something holds up under the wear, tear, and stress of everyday life. Those who stand up for Christ in spite of their troubles truly have lasting value and will receive great rewards (see 5:11, 12).

10:32 Anyone who acknowledges Jesus Christ (that is, publicly confesses faith in or declares allegiance to him) will be acknowledged by Christ before his Father in heaven. Jesus' followers would face earthly courts of law where they would have to publicly claim to belong to Jesus Christ, usually at their peril (10:17-25). Genuine discipleship always involves acknowledging Jesus Christ, whether or not we face pressure and persecution.

• **10:34** Jesus did not come to bring the kind of peace that glosses over deep differences just for the sake of superficial harmony. Conflict and disagreement will arise between those who choose to follow Christ and those who don't. Yet we can look forward to

10:35-36
†Mic 7:6

35 'I have come to set a man against his father,
    a daughter against her mother,
and a daughter-in-law against her mother-in-law.

10:37
Luke 14:26

36   Your enemies will be right in your own household!'*

10:38
Mark 8:34
Luke 9:23; 14:27

37 "If you love your father or mother more than you love me, you are not worthy of being

10:39
Matt 16:25
Mark 8:35
Luke 9:24; 17:33
John 12:25

mine; or if you love your son or daughter more than me, you are not worthy of being mine. 38 If you refuse to take up your cross and follow me, you are not worthy of being mine. 39 If you cling to your life, you will lose it; but if you give up your life for me, you will find it.

10:40
John 12:44; 13:20

40 "Anyone who receives you receives me, and anyone who receives me receives the Father who sent me. 41If you receive a prophet as one who speaks for God,* you will be given

10:41
1 Kgs 17:9-24
2 Kgs 4:8-37

the same reward as a prophet. And if you receive righteous people because of their righteousness, you will be given a reward like theirs. 42And if you give even a cup of cold water to one of the least of my followers, you will surely be rewarded."

4. Jesus teaches about the Kingdom

Jesus Eases John's Doubt (**70**/Luke 7:18-35)

11 When Jesus had finished giving these instructions to his twelve disciples, he went out to teach and preach in towns throughout the region.

2John the Baptist, who was in prison, heard about all the things the Messiah was doing. So

11:3
Mal 3:1

he sent his disciples to ask Jesus, 3 "Are you the Messiah we've been expecting,* or should we keep looking for someone else?"

11:5
Isa 35:4-6;
42:7, 18; 61:1
Luke 4:18-19

4Jesus told them, "Go back to John and tell him what you have heard and seen—5the blind see, the lame walk, the lepers are cured, the deaf hear, the dead are raised to life, and the Good News is being preached to the poor. 6And tell him, 'God blesses those who do not turn

11:6
Matt 13:57

away because of me.*' "

11:7
Matt 3:5

7As John's disciples were leaving, Jesus began talking about him to the crowds. " What kind of man did you go into the wilderness to see? Was he a weak reed, swayed by every breath of wind? 8Or were you expecting to see a man dressed in expensive clothes? No, peo-

11:9
Matt 14:5; 21:26
Luke 1:76

ple with expensive clothes live in palaces. 9Were you looking for a prophet? Yes, and he is more than a prophet. 10John is the man to whom the Scriptures refer when they say,

11:10
Exod 23:20
†Mal 3:1
Mark 1:2
Luke 7:27

'Look, I am sending my messenger ahead of you,
    and he will prepare your way before you.'*

10:35-36 Mic 7:6.   **10:41** Greek *receive a prophet in the name of a prophet.*   **11:3** Greek *Are you the one who is coming?*   **11:6** Or *who are not offended by me.*   **11:10** Mal 3:1.

---

the day when all conflict will be resolved. For other verses on Jesus as peacemaker, see Isaiah 9:6; Matthew 5:9; John 14:27.

• **10:34-39** Christian commitment may separate friends and loved ones. In saying this, Jesus was not encouraging disobedience to parents or conflict at home. Rather, he was showing that his presence demands a decision. Because some will follow Christ and some won't, conflict will inevitably arise. As we take up our cross and follow him, our different values, morals, and goals will set us apart from others. Christ calls us to a higher mission than to find comfort and tranquility in this life. Love of family is a law of God, but even this love can be self-serving and used as an excuse not to serve God or do his work. Don't neglect your family, but remember that your commitment to God is even more important. God should be your first priority.

• **10:38** To take up our cross and follow Jesus means to be willing to publicly identify with him, to experience certain opposition, and to be willing to face even suffering and death for his sake.

• **10:39** This verse is a positive and negative statement of the same truth: Clinging to this life may cause us to forfeit the best from Christ in this world *and* in the next. The more we love this life's rewards (leisure, power, popularity, financial security), the more we will discover how empty they really are. The best way to enjoy life, therefore, is to loosen our greedy grasp on earthly rewards so that we can be free to follow Christ. In doing so, we will inherit eternal life and begin at once to experience the benefits of following Christ.

10:42 How much we love God can be measured by how well we treat others. Jesus' example of giving a cup of cold water to a thirsty child is a good model of unselfish service. A child usually can't or won't return a favor. God notices every good deed we do or don't do as if he were the one receiving it. Is there something unselfish you can do for someone else today? Although no one else may see you, God will notice.

11:2, 3 John had been put in prison by Herod. Herod had married his own sister-in-law, and John publicly rebuked Herod's flagrant sin (14:3-5). John's Profile is found in John 1, p. 1749. Herod's Profile is found in Mark 6, p. 1629.

11:4-6 As John sat in prison, he began to have some doubts about whether Jesus really was the Messiah. If John's purpose was to prepare people for the coming Messiah (3:3), and if Jesus really was that Messiah, then why was John in prison when he could have been preaching to the crowds, preparing their hearts?

Jesus answered John's doubts by pointing to the acts of healing the blind, lame, and deaf, curing the lepers, raising the dead, and preaching the Good News to the poor. With so much evidence, Jesus' identity was obvious. If you sometimes doubt your salvation, the forgiveness of your sins, or God's work in your life, look at the evidence in Scripture and the changes in your life. When you doubt, don't turn away from Christ; turn *to* him.

¹¹ "I tell you the truth, of all who have ever lived, none is greater than John the Baptist. Yet even the least person in the Kingdom of Heaven is greater than he is! ¹²And from the time John the Baptist began preaching until now, the Kingdom of Heaven has been forcefully advancing,* and violent people are attacking it. ¹³ For before John came, all the prophets and the law of Moses looked forward to this present time. ¹⁴And if you are willing to accept what I say, he is Elijah, the one the prophets said would come.* ¹⁵Anyone with ears to hear should listen and understand!

11:12-13
Luke 16:16

11:14
Mal 4:5
Matt 17:10-13
Mark 9:11-13
Luke 1:17
John 1:21

¹⁶ "To what can I compare this generation? It is like children playing a game in the public square. They complain to their friends,

11:15
Matt 13:9, 43
Mark 4:9, 23
Luke 8:8; 14:35
Rev 2:7

¹⁷ 'We played wedding songs,
    and you didn't dance,
so we played funeral songs,
    and you didn't mourn.'

¹⁸ For John didn't spend his time eating and drinking, and you say, 'He's possessed by a demon.' ¹⁹ The Son of Man,* on the other hand, feasts and drinks, and you say, 'He's a glutton and a drunkard, and a friend of tax collectors and other sinners!' But wisdom is shown to be right by its results."

11:18
Matt 3:4
Luke 1:15

11:19
Matt 9:11, 14

Jesus Promises Rest for the Soul (71)

²⁰ Then Jesus began to denounce the towns where he had done so many of his miracles, because they hadn't repented of their sins and turned to God. ²¹ "What sorrow awaits you, Korazin and Bethsaida! For if the miracles I did in you had been done in wicked Tyre and Sidon, their people would have repented of their sins long ago, clothing themselves in burlap and throwing ashes on their heads to show their remorse. ²²I tell you, Tyre and Sidon will be better off on judgment day than you.

11:21-22
Isa 23:1-8
Ezek 26–28
Joel 3:4-8
Amos 1:9-10
Zech 9:2-4
Matt 10:15

²³ "And you people of Capernaum, will you be honored in heaven? No, you will go down to the place of the dead.* For if the miracles I did for you had been done in wicked Sodom, it would still be here today. ²⁴I tell you, even Sodom will be better off on judgment day than you."

11:23
†Isa 14:13, 15

²⁵At that time Jesus prayed this prayer: "O Father, Lord of heaven and earth, thank you for hiding these things from those who think themselves wise and clever, and for revealing them to the childlike. ²⁶ Yes, Father, it pleased you to do it this way!

11:25-27
Eph 1:17-18

²⁷ "My Father has entrusted everything to me. No one truly knows the Son except the Father, and no one truly knows the Father except the Son and those to whom the Son chooses to reveal him."

11:27
Matt 28:18
John 3:35; 10:15;
17:2, 25-26

11:12 Or *the Kingdom of Heaven has suffered from violence.*   **11:14** See Mal 4:5.   **11:19** "Son of Man" is a title Jesus used for himself.   **11:23** Greek *to Hades.*

11:11   No person ever fulfilled his God-given purpose better than John. Yet in God's coming Kingdom all members will have a greater spiritual heritage than John because they will have seen and known Christ and his finished work on the cross.

11:12   There are three common views about the meaning of this verse: (1) Jesus may have been referring to a vast movement toward God, the momentum that began with John's preaching. (2) He may have been reflecting the Jewish activists' expectation that God's Kingdom would come through a violent overthrow of Rome. (3) Or he may have meant that entering God's Kingdom takes courage, unwavering faith, determination, and endurance because of the growing opposition leveled at Jesus' followers. In any case, Jesus was pointing out that John's ministry had ushered in the Kingdom of Heaven.

11:14   John was not a resurrected Elijah, but he took on Elijah's prophetic role—boldly confronting sin and pointing people to God (Malachi 3:1). See Elijah's Profile in 1 Kings 17, p. 545.

11:16-19   Jesus condemned the attitude of his generation. No matter what he said or did, they took the opposite view. They were cynical and skeptical because he challenged their comfortable, secure, and self-centered lives. Too often we justify our inconsistencies because listening to God may require us to change the way we live.

11:21-24   Tyre, Sidon, and Sodom were ancient cities with a long-standing reputation for wickedness (Genesis 18–19; Ezekiel 27–28). Each was destroyed by God for its evil. The people of Bethsaida, Korazin, and Capernaum saw Jesus first-hand, and yet they stubbornly refused to repent of their sins and believe in him. Jesus said that if some of the wickedest cities in the world had seen him, they would have repented. Because Bethsaida, Korazin, and Capernaum saw Jesus and didn't believe, they would suffer even greater punishment than would the wicked cities that didn't see Jesus. Similarly, nations and cities with churches on every corner and Bibles in every home will have no excuse on judgment day if they do not repent and believe.

11:25   Jesus mentioned two kinds of people in his prayer: the "wise and clever"—arrogant in their own knowledge—and the "childlike"—humbly open to receive the truth of God's Word. Are you wise in your own eyes, or do you seek the truth in childlike faith, realizing that only God holds all the answers?

11:27   In the Old Testament, *know* means more than knowledge. It implies an intimate relationship. The communion between God the Father and God the Son is the core of their relationship. For anyone else to know God, God must reveal himself to that person, by the Son's choice. How fortunate we are that Jesus

11:29
†Jer 6:16

11:30
1 Jn 5:3

28 Then Jesus said, "Come to me, all of you who are weary and carry heavy burdens, and I will give you rest. 29 Take my yoke upon you. Let me teach you, because I am humble and gentle at heart, and you will find rest for your souls. 30For my yoke is easy to bear, and the burden I give you is light."

12:2
Exod 20:10
Deut 5:14
Luke 13:14; 14:3
John 5:10; 7:23;
9:16

12:3
1 Sam 21:1-6

12:4
Lev 24:5-9

12:5
Num 28:9-10

12:6
Matt 12:41-42
Luke 11:31-32

12:7
Mic 6:6-8

The Disciples Pick Wheat on the Sabbath (**45**/Mark 2:23-28; Luke 6:1-5)

12 At about that time Jesus was walking through some grainfields on the Sabbath. His disciples were hungry, so they began breaking off some heads of grain and eating them. 2But some Pharisees saw them do it and protested, "Look, your disciples are breaking the law by harvesting grain on the Sabbath."

3 Jesus said to them, "Haven't you read in the Scriptures what David did when he and his companions were hungry? 4He went into the house of God, and he and his companions broke the law by eating the sacred loaves of bread that only the priests are allowed to eat. 5And haven't you read in the law of Moses that the priests on duty in the Temple may work on the Sabbath? 6I tell you, there is one here who is even greater than the Temple! 7But you would not have condemned my innocent disciples if you knew the meaning of this Scripture: 'I want you to show mercy, not offer sacrifices.'* 8For the Son of Man* is Lord, even over the Sabbath!"

12:7 Hos 6:6 (Greek version).   **12:8** "Son of Man" is a title Jesus used for himself.

has clearly revealed God to us, as well as his truth and how we can know him.

11:28-30 A yoke is a heavy wooden harness that fits over the shoulders of an ox or oxen. It is attached to a piece of equipment the oxen are to pull. A person may be carrying heavy burdens of (1) sin, (2) excessive demands of religious leaders (23:4; Acts 15:10), (3) oppression and persecution, or (4) weariness in the search for God.

Jesus frees people from all these burdens. The rest that Jesus promises is love, healing, and peace with God, not the end of all labor. A relationship with God changes meaningless, wearisome toil into spiritual productivity and purpose.

11:30 In what sense was Jesus' yoke easy? The yoke emphasizes the challenges, work, and difficulties of partnering with Christ in life. Responsibilities weigh us down, even the effort of staying true to God. But Jesus' yoke remains easy compared to the crushing alternative.

Jesus doesn't offer a life of luxurious ease—the yoke is still an oxen's tool for working hard. But it's a shared yoke, with weight falling on bigger shoulders than yours. Someone with more pulling power is up front helping. Suddenly you are participating in life's responsibilities with a great Partner—and now that frown can turn into a smile, and that gripe into a song.

12:1, 2 The Pharisees had established 39 categories of actions forbidden on the Sabbath, based on interpretations of God's law and on Jewish custom. Harvesting was one of those forbidden actions. By picking wheat and rubbing it in their hands, the disciples were technically harvesting, according to the Pharisees. Jesus and the disciples were picking grain because they were hungry, not because they wanted to harvest the grain for a profit. They were not working on the Sabbath. The Pharisees, however, could not (and did not want to) see beyond their law's technicalities. They had no room for compassion, and they were determined to accuse Jesus of wrongdoing.

12:4 This story is recorded in 1 Samuel 21:1-6. The Bread of the Presence was replaced every week, and the old loaves were eaten by the priests. The loaves given to David were the old loaves that had just been replaced with fresh ones. Although the priests were the only ones allowed to eat this bread, God did not punish David because his need for food was more important.than the priestly regulations. Jesus was saying, "If you condemn me, you must also condemn David," something the religious leaders could never do without causing a great uproar among the people. Jesus was not condoning disobedience to God's laws. Instead, he was emphasizing discernment and compassion in enforcing the laws.

12:5 The Ten Commandments require that the Sabbath be kept holy (Exodus 20:8-11). The Pharisees had interpreted that to require a long list of actions that could not be done on the Sabbath, forcing the people to "rest." That was the *letter* of the law. But because the *purpose* of the Sabbath is to rest and to worship God, the priests were allowed to work by performing sacrifices and conducting worship services. This "Sabbath work" was serving and worshiping God. Jesus always emphasized the intent of the law, the meaning behind the letter. The Pharisees had lost the spirit of the law and were rigidly demanding that the letter (and their interpretation of it) be obeyed.

12:6 The Pharisees were so concerned about religious rituals that they missed the whole purpose of the Temple—to bring people to God. And because Jesus Christ is even greater than the Temple, how much better can he bring people to God. God is far more important than the created instruments of worship. If we become more concerned with the means of worship than with the one we worship, we will miss God even as we think we are worshiping him.

12:7 Jesus repeated to the Pharisees words the Jewish people had heard time and again throughout their history (1 Samuel 15:22, 23; Psalm 40:6-8; Isaiah 1:11-17; Jeremiah 7:21-23; Hosea 6:6). Our heart attitude toward God comes first. Only then can we properly obey and observe religious regulations and rituals.

12:8 When Jesus said he was master of the Sabbath, he claimed to be greater than the law and above the law. To the Pharisees, this was heresy. They did not realize that Jesus, the divine Son of God, had created the Sabbath. The Creator is always greater than his creation; thus, Jesus had the authority to overrule their traditions and regulations.

Jesus Heals a Man's Hand on the Sabbath (46/Mark 3:1-6; Luke 6:6-11)

9 Then Jesus went over to their synagogue, 10 where he noticed a man with a deformed hand. The Pharisees asked Jesus, "Does the law permit a person to work by healing on the Sabbath?" (They were hoping he would say yes, so they could bring charges against him.)

11 And he answered, "If you had a sheep that fell into a well on the Sabbath, wouldn't you work to pull it out? Of course you would. 12 And how much more valuable is a person than a sheep! Yes, the law permits a person to do good on the Sabbath."

13 Then he said to the man, "Hold out your hand." So the man held out his hand, and it was restored, just like the other one! 14 Then the Pharisees called a meeting to plot how to kill Jesus.

Large Crowds Follow Jesus (47/Mark 3:7-12)

15 But Jesus knew what they were planning. So he left that area, and many people followed him. He healed all the sick among them, 16 but he warned them not to reveal who he was. 17 This fulfilled the prophecy of Isaiah concerning him:

18 "Look at my Servant, whom I have chosen.
   He is my Beloved, who pleases me.
I will put my Spirit upon him,
   and he will proclaim justice to the nations.
19 He will not fight or shout
   or raise his voice in public.
20 He will not crush the weakest reed
   or put out a flickering candle.
   Finally he will cause justice to be victorious.
21 And his name will be the hope
   of all the world."*

Religious Leaders Accuse Jesus of Getting His Power from Satan (74/Mark 3:20-30)

22 Then a demon-possessed man, who was blind and couldn't speak, was brought to Jesus. He healed the man so that he could both speak and see. 23 The crowd was amazed and asked, "Could it be that Jesus is the Son of David, the Messiah?"

24 But when the Pharisees heard about the miracle, they said, "No wonder he can cast out demons. He gets his power from Satan,* the prince of demons."

12:10 Luke 13:14; 14:3 John 9:16

12:11 Luke 14:5

12:12 Matt 6:26; 10:31

12:18-21 †Isa 42:1-4

12:22-23 Matt 9:32-33

12:24 Matt 9:34

12:18-21 Isa 42:1-4 (Greek version for 42:4).   **12:24** Greek *Beelzeboul;* also in 12:27. Other manuscripts read *Beezeboul;* Latin version reads *Beelzebub.*

12:10 As they pointed to the man with the deformed hand, the Pharisees tried to trick Jesus by asking him if it was legal to heal on the Sabbath. Their Sabbath rules said that people could be helped on the Sabbath only if their lives were in danger. Jesus healed on the Sabbath several times, and none of those healings were in response to emergencies. If Jesus had waited until another day, he would have been submitting to the Pharisees' authority, showing that their petty rules were equal to God's law. If he healed the man on the Sabbath, the Pharisees could claim that because Jesus broke their rules, his power was not from God. But Jesus made it clear how ridiculous and petty their rules were. God is a God of people, not rules. The best time to reach out to someone is when he or she needs help.

12:10-12 The Pharisees placed their laws above human need. They were so concerned about Jesus breaking one of their rules that they did not care about the man's deformed hand. What is your attitude toward others? If your convictions don't allow you to help certain people, your convictions may not be in tune with God's Word. Don't allow rule keeping to blind you to human need.

12:14 The Pharisees plotted Jesus' death because they were proud, fearful, and outraged. Jesus had overruled their authority

(Luke 6:11) and had exposed their evil attitudes in front of the entire crowd in the synagogue. Jesus had showed that the Pharisees were more loyal to their religious system than to God.

12:15 Up to this point, Jesus had been aggressively confronting the Pharisees' hypocrisy. Here he decided to withdraw from the synagogue before a major confrontation developed because it was not yet time for him to die. Jesus had many lessons still to teach his disciples and the people.

12:16 Jesus did not want those he healed to tell others about his miracles because he didn't want the people coming to him for the wrong reasons. That would hinder his teaching ministry and arouse false hopes about an earthly kingdom. But the news of Jesus' miracles spread, and many came to see for themselves (see Mark 3:7, 8).

12:17-21 The people expected the Messiah to be a king. This quotation from Isaiah's prophecy (Isaiah 42:1-4) showed that the Messiah was indeed a king, but it illustrated what *kind* of king— a gentle ruler who brings justice to the nations. Like the crowd in Jesus' day, we may want Christ to rule as a king and bring great and visible victories in our life. But often Christ's work is quiet, and it happens according to *his* perfect timing, not ours.

12:24 The Pharisees had already accused Jesus of being empowered by the prince of demons (9:34). They were trying to discredit him by using an emotional argument. Refusing to believe that Jesus came from God, they said he was in league with Satan. Jesus easily exposed the foolishness of their argument.

12:25
Matt 9:4

12:27
Matt 9:34
Acts 19:13

12:28
Acts 10:38

12:30
Mark 9:40
Luke 9:50

12:31-32
Mark 3:28-30
Luke 12:10

12:33
Matt 7:16-20
Luke 6:43-45

12:34
Matt 3:7; 23:33

12:38
Matt 16:1
Mark 8:11-12
Luke 11:16
John 2:18; 6:30
1 Cor 1:22

12:38-42
Matt 16:4

12:40
Jon 1:17

12:41
Jon 1:2; 3:5

25Jesus knew their thoughts and replied, "Any kingdom divided by civil war is doomed. A town or family splintered by feuding will fall apart. 26And if Satan is casting out Satan, he is divided and fighting against himself. His own kingdom will not survive. 27And if I am empowered by Satan, what about your own exorcists? They cast out demons, too, so they will condemn you for what you have said. 28But if I am casting out demons by the Spirit of God, then the Kingdom of God has arrived among you. 29For who is powerful enough to enter the house of a strong man like Satan and plunder his goods? Only someone even stronger—someone who could tie him up and then plunder his house.

30"Anyone who isn't with me opposes me, and anyone who isn't working with me is actually working against me.

31"So I tell you, every sin and blasphemy can be forgiven—except blasphemy against the Holy Spirit, which will never be forgiven. 32Anyone who speaks against the Son of Man can be forgiven, but anyone who speaks against the Holy Spirit will never be forgiven, either in this world or in the world to come.

33"A tree is identified by its fruit. If a tree is good, its fruit will be good. If a tree is bad, its fruit will be bad. 34You brood of snakes! How could evil men like you speak what is good and right? For whatever is in your heart determines what you say. 35A good person produces good things from the treasury of a good heart, and an evil person produces evil things from the treasury of an evil heart. 36And I tell you this, you must give an account on judgment day for every idle word you speak. 37The words you say will either acquit you or condemn you."

Religious Leaders Ask Jesus for a Miraculous Sign (75)
38One day some teachers of religious law and Pharisees came to Jesus and said, "Teacher, we want you to show us a miraculous sign to prove your authority."

39But Jesus replied, "Only an evil, adulterous generation would demand a miraculous sign; but the only sign I will give them is the sign of the prophet Jonah. 40For as Jonah was in the belly of the great fish for three days and three nights, so will the Son of Man be in the heart of the earth for three days and three nights.

41 "The people of Nineveh will stand up against this generation on judgment day and

---

12:25 In the Incarnation, Jesus gave up the complete and unlimited use of his supernatural abilities. But he still had profound insight into human nature. His discernment stopped the religious leaders' attempts to trick him. The resurrected Christ knows all our thoughts. This can be comforting because he knows what we really mean when we speak to him. It can be threatening because we cannot hide from him, and he knows any selfish motives.

12:29 At Jesus' birth, Satan's power and control were disrupted. In the wilderness Jesus overcame Satan's temptations, and at the Resurrection he defeated Satan's ultimate weapon—death. Eventually Satan will be constrained forever (Revelation 20:10), and evil will no longer pervade the earth. Jesus has complete power and authority over Satan and all his forces.

12:30 It is impossible to be neutral about Christ. Anyone who is not actively following him has chosen to reject him. Any person who tries to remain neutral in the struggle against evil is choosing to be separated from God, who alone is good. To refuse to follow Christ is to choose to be on Satan's team.

12:31, 32 The Pharisees had blasphemed against the Spirit by attributing the power by which Christ did miracles to Satan (12:24) instead of the Holy Spirit. The unpardonable sin is the deliberate refusal to acknowledge God's power in Christ. It indicates a deliberate and irreversible hardness of heart. Sometimes believers worry that they have accidentally committed this unforgivable sin. But only those who have turned their backs on God and rejected all faith have any need to worry. Jesus said they can't be forgiven—not because their sin is worse than any other but because they will never ask for forgiveness. Whoever rejects the prompting of the Holy Spirit removes himself or herself from the only force that can lead him or her to repentance and restoration to God.

12:34-36 Jesus reminds us that what we say reveals what is in our heart. What kinds of words come from your mouth? That is an indication of what is in your heart. You can't solve your heart problem, however, just by cleaning up your speech. You must

allow the Holy Spirit to fill you with new attitudes and motives; then your speech will be cleansed at its source.

12:38-40 The Pharisees were asking for another miraculous sign, but they were not sincerely seeking to know Jesus. Jesus knew they had already seen enough miraculous proof to convince them that he was the Messiah if they would just open their hearts. But they had already decided not to believe in him, and more miracles would not change that.

Many people have said, "If I could just see a real miracle, then I could really believe in God." But Jesus' response to the Pharisees applies to us. We have plenty of evidence—Jesus' birth, death, resurrection, and ascension, and centuries of his work in believers around the world. Instead of looking for additional evidence or miracles, accept what God has already given and move forward. He may use your life as evidence to reach another person.

12:39-41 Jonah was a prophet sent to the Assyrian city of Nineveh (see the book of Jonah). Because Assyria was such a cruel and warlike nation, Jonah tried to run from his assignment and ended up spending three days in the belly of a huge fish. When Jonah got out, he grudgingly went to Nineveh, preached God's message, and saw the city repent. By contrast, when Jesus came to his people, they refused to repent. Here Jesus is clearly saying that his resurrection will prove he is the Messiah. Three days after his death, Jesus will come back to life, just as Jonah was given a new chance at life after three days in the fish.

12:41, 42 In Jonah's day, Nineveh was the capital of the Assyrian Empire, and it was as evil as it was powerful (Jonah 1:2). But the entire city repented at Jonah's preaching. The queen of Sheba traveled far to see Solomon, king of Israel, and learn about his great wisdom (1 Kings 10:1-10; also see the note on Luke 11:31, 32 for more on the queen of Sheba). These Gentiles recognized the truth about God when it was presented to them, unlike the religious leaders, who ignored the truth even though it stared them in the face. How have you responded to the evidence and truth that you have?

condemn it, for they repented of their sins at the preaching of Jonah. Now someone greater than Jonah is here—but you refuse to repent. [42] The queen of Sheba* will also stand up against this generation on judgment day and condemn it, for she came from a distant land to hear the wisdom of Solomon. Now someone greater than Solomon is here—but you refuse to listen.

12:42
1 Kgs 10:1-10
2 Chr 9:1-12
Matt 12:6

[43] "When an evil* spirit leaves a person, it goes into the desert, seeking rest but finding none. [44] Then it says, 'I will return to the person I came from.' So it returns and finds its former home empty, swept, and in order. [45]Then the spirit finds seven other spirits more evil than itself, and they all enter the person and live there. And so that person is worse off than before. That will be the experience of this evil generation."

12:45
2 Pet 2:20

Jesus Describes His True Family (76/Mark 3:31-35; Luke 8:19-21)

[46]As Jesus was speaking to the crowd, his mother and brothers stood outside, asking to speak to him. [47] Someone told Jesus, "Your mother and your brothers are outside, and they want to speak to you."*

12:46
Mark 6:3
John 2:12; 7:3-5
Acts 1:14

[48]Jesus asked, "Who is my mother? Who are my brothers?" [49]Then he pointed to his disciples and said, "Look, these are my mother and brothers. [50]Anyone who does the will of my Father in heaven is my brother and sister and mother!"

12:50
John 15:14

Jesus Tells the Parable of the Four Soils (77/Mark 4:1-9; Luke 8:4-8)

13 Later that same day Jesus left the house and sat beside the lake. [2]A large crowd soon gathered around him, so he got into a boat. Then he sat there and taught as the people stood on the shore. [3]He told many stories in the form of parables, such as this one:

"Listen! A farmer went out to plant some seeds. [4]As he scattered them across his field, some seeds fell on a footpath, and the birds came and ate them. [5] Other seeds fell on shallow soil with underlying rock. The seeds sprouted quickly because the soil was shallow. [6] But the plants soon wilted under the hot sun, and since they didn't have deep roots, they died. [7]Other seeds fell among thorns that grew up and choked out the tender plants. [8] Still other seeds fell on fertile soil, and they produced a crop that was thirty, sixty, and even a hundred times as much as had been planted! [9]Anyone with ears to hear should listen and understand."

13:9
Matt 11:15; 13:43

Jesus Explains the Parable of the Four Soils (78/Mark 4:10-25; Luke 8:9-18)

[10]His disciples came and asked him, "Why do you use parables when you talk to the people?"

13:11
Matt 11:25; 16:17
1 Cor 2:10, 14
Col 1:27
1 Jn 2:20, 27

[11]He replied, "You are permitted to understand the secrets* of the Kingdom of Heaven, but others are not. [12] To those who listen to my teaching, more understanding will be given, and they will have an abundance of knowledge. But for those who are not listening, even what little understanding they have will be taken away from them. [13]That is why I use these parables,

13:12
Matt 25:29
Mark 4:25
Luke 19:26

13:13
Jer 5:21

12:42 Greek *The queen of the south.*   **12:43** Greek *unclean.*   **12:47** Some manuscripts do not include verse 47. Compare Mark 3:32 and Luke 8:20.   **13:11** Greek *the mysteries.*

12:43-45 Jesus was describing the attitude of the nation of Israel and the religious leaders in particular. Just cleaning up one's life without filling it with God leaves plenty of room for Satan to enter. The book of Ezra records how the people rid themselves of idolatry but failed to replace it with love for God and obedience to him. Ridding our life of sin is the first step. We must also take the second step: filling our life with God's Word and the Holy Spirit. Unfilled and complacent people are easy targets for Satan.

12:46-50 Jesus was not denying his responsibility to his earthly family. On the contrary, he criticized the religious leaders for not following the Old Testament command to honor their parents (15:1-9). He provided for his mother's security as he hung on the cross (John 19:25-27). His mother and brothers were present in the upper room at Pentecost (Acts 1:14). Instead, Jesus was pointing out that spiritual relationships are as binding as physical ones, and he was paving the way for a new community of believers (the universal church), our spiritual family.

• **13:2, 3** Jesus used many stories, or parables (13:34), when speaking to the crowds. These stories compare something familiar to something unfamiliar, helping us understand spiritual truth by using everyday objects and relationships. Jesus' parables compel listeners to discover truth, while at the same time concealing the truth from those too lazy or too stubborn to see it. To those who are honestly searching, the truth becomes clear. We must be careful not to read too much into parables, forcing them to say what they don't mean. Each parable has a central meaning unless otherwise specified by Jesus.

• **13:8** This parable should encourage spiritual "farmers"—those who teach, preach, and seek to lead others to the Lord. The farmer sowed good seed, but not all the seed sprouted; even the plants that grew had varying yields. Don't be discouraged if you do not always see results as you faithfully teach the Word. Belief cannot be forced to follow a mathematical formula (i.e., a 4:1 ratio of seeds planted to seeds sprouted). Rather, it is a miracle of God's Holy Spirit using your words to produce faith in Christ.

• **13:9, 10** Human ears hear many sounds, but there is a deeper kind of listening that results in spiritual understanding. When speaking in parables, Jesus was not hiding truth from sincere seekers, because those who were receptive to spiritual truth understood the illustrations. To others they were only stories without meaning.

13:12 This phrase means that we are responsible to use well what we have. When people reject Jesus, their hardness of heart drives away or renders useless even the little understanding they had.

> For they look, but they don't really see.
> They hear, but they don't really listen or understand.

13:14-15
†Isa 6:9-10

14 This fulfills the prophecy of Isaiah that says,

> 'When you hear what I say,
> 　you will not understand.
> When you see what I do,
> 　you will not comprehend.
> 15 For the hearts of these people are hardened,
> 　and their ears cannot hear,
> and they have closed their eyes—
> 　so their eyes cannot see,
> and their ears cannot hear,
> 　and their hearts cannot understand,
> and they cannot turn to me
> 　and let me heal them.'*

13:17
John 8:56
Heb 11:13
1 Pet 1:10-12

16 "But blessed are your eyes, because they see; and your ears, because they hear. 17 I tell you the truth, many prophets and righteous people longed to see what you see, but they didn't see it. And they longed to hear what you hear, but they didn't hear it.

18 "Now listen to the explanation of the parable about the farmer planting seeds: 19 The seed that fell on the footpath represents those who hear the message about the Kingdom and don't understand it. Then the evil one comes and snatches away the seed that was planted in their hearts. 20 The seed on the rocky soil represents those who hear the message and immediately receive it with joy. 21But since they don't have deep roots, they don't last long. They fall away as soon as they have problems or are persecuted for believing God's

13:22
Matt 19:23
Luke 12:16-21
1 Tim 6:9-10, 17

word. 22The seed that fell among the thorns represents those who hear God's word, but all too quickly the message is crowded out by the worries of this life and the lure of wealth, so no fruit is produced. 23 The seed that fell on good soil represents those who truly hear and understand God's word and produce a harvest of thirty, sixty, or even a hundred times as much as had been planted!"

Jesus Tells the Parable of the Weeds (**80**)

13:24
Mark 4:26-29

24Here is another story Jesus told: "The Kingdom of Heaven is like a farmer who planted good seed in his field. 25But that night as the workers slept, his enemy came and planted weeds among the wheat, then slipped away. 26 When the crop began to grow and produce grain, the weeds also grew.

27 "The farmer's workers went to him and said, 'Sir, the field where you planted that good seed is full of weeds! Where did they come from?'

28 "'An enemy has done this!' the farmer exclaimed.

"'Should we pull out the weeds?' they asked.

13:30
Matt 3:12

29 "'No,' he replied, 'you'll uproot the wheat if you do. 30Let both grow together until the harvest. Then I will tell the harvesters to sort out the weeds, tie them into bundles, and burn them, and to put the wheat in the barn.'"

13:14-15 Isa 6:9-10 (Greek version).

● **13:22** How easy it is to agree with Christ with no intention of obeying. It is easy to denounce worries of this life and the deceitfulness of wealth and still do nothing to change our ways. In light of eternal life with God, are your present worries justified? If you had everything you could want but forfeited eternal life with God, would those things be so desirable?

● **13:23** The four types of soil represent different responses to God's message. People respond differently because they are in different states of readiness. Some are hardened, others are shallow, others are contaminated by distracting worries, and some are receptive. How has God's Word taken root in your life? What kind of soil are you?

13:24ff Jesus gives the meaning of this parable in verses 36-43. All the parables in this chapter teach us about God and his Kingdom. They explain what the Kingdom is really like as opposed to our expectations of it. The Kingdom of Heaven is not a geographic location but a spiritual realm where God rules and where we share in his eternal life. We join that Kingdom when we trust in Christ as Savior.

13:30 The young weeds and the young blades of wheat look the same and can't be distinguished until they are grown and ready for harvest. Weeds (unbelievers) and wheat (believers) must live side by side in this world. God allows unbelievers to remain for a while, just as a farmer allows weeds to remain in his field so the surrounding wheat isn't uprooted with them. At the harvest, however, the weeds will be uprooted and thrown away. God's harvest (judgment) of all people is coming. We are to make ourselves ready by making sure that our faith is sincere.

Jesus Tells the Parable of the Mustard Seed (81/Mark 4:30-34)

³¹Here is another illustration Jesus used: "The Kingdom of Heaven is like a mustard seed planted in a field. ³² It is the smallest of all seeds, but it becomes the largest of garden plants; it grows into a tree, and birds come and make nests in its branches."

13:32
Ps 104:12
Ezek 17:23; 31:6

Jesus Tells the Parable of the Yeast (82)

³³ Jesus also used this illustration: "The Kingdom of Heaven is like the yeast a woman used in making bread. Even though she put only a little yeast in three measures of flour, it permeated every part of the dough."

13:33
Luke 13:20-21
1 Cor 5:6
Gal 5:9

³⁴ Jesus always used stories and illustrations like these when speaking to the crowds. In fact, he never spoke to them without using such parables. ³⁵This fulfilled what God had spoken through the prophet:

13:34
John 16:25
13:35
†Ps 78:2

"I will speak to you in parables.
I will explain things hidden since the creation of the world.*"

Jesus Explains the Parable of the Weeds (83)

³⁶ Then, leaving the crowds outside, Jesus went into the house. His disciples said, "Please explain to us the story of the weeds in the field."

13:36
Matt 15:15

³⁷ Jesus replied, "The Son of Man* is the farmer who plants the good seed. ³⁸ The field is the world, and the good seed represents the people of the Kingdom. The weeds are the people who belong to the evil one. ³⁹ The enemy who planted the weeds among the wheat is the devil. The harvest is the end of the world,* and the harvesters are the angels.

13:38
John 8:44
1 Jn 3:10
13:39
Joel 3:13
Rev 14:15

⁴⁰ "Just as the weeds are sorted out and burned in the fire, so it will be at the end of the world. ⁴¹ The Son of Man will send his angels, and they will remove from his Kingdom everything that causes sin and all who do evil. ⁴²And the angels will throw them into the fiery furnace, where there will be weeping and gnashing of teeth. ⁴³ Then the righteous will shine like the sun in their Father's Kingdom. Anyone with ears to hear should listen and understand!

13:41
Matt 24:31
Mark 13:27
13:42
Matt 8:12; 13:50;
22:13; 24:51; 25:30
Luke 13:28

Jesus Tells the Parable of the Hidden Treasure (84)

⁴⁴ "The Kingdom of Heaven is like a treasure that a man discovered hidden in a field. In his excitement, he hid it again and sold everything he owned to get enough money to buy the field.

13:44
Phil 3:7-8

13:35 Some manuscripts do not include *of the world.* Ps 78:2.   **13:37** "Son of Man" is a title Jesus used for himself.
13:39 Or *the age;* also in 13:40, 49.

13:31, 32 The mustard seed was the smallest seed a farmer used. Jesus used this parable to show that the Kingdom has small beginnings but will grow and produce great results.

13:33 In other Bible passages, yeast is used as a symbol of evil or uncleanness. Here it is a positive symbol of growth.

NAZARETH REJECTS JESUS

Chronologically, this return to Nazareth occurred after Jesus was in the Gadarene region and healed the demon-possessed men (8:28-34), then recrossed the sea to Capernaum. From there he traveled to Nazareth, where he had grown up, only to discover that the people refused to believe he was the Christ.

Although yeast looks like a minor ingredient, it permeates the whole loaf. Although the Kingdom began small and was nearly invisible, it would soon grow and have a great impact on the world.

13:40-43 At the end of the world, angels will separate the evil from the good. There are true and false believers in churches today, but we should be cautious in our judgments because only Christ is qualified to make the final separation. If you start judging, you may damage some of the good "plants." It's more important to judge our own response to God than to analyze others' responses.

13:42 Jesus often uses these terms to refer to the coming judgment. The weeping indicates sorrow or remorse, and gnashing of teeth shows extreme anxiety or pain. Those who say they don't care what happens to them after they die don't realize what they are saying. They will be punished for living in selfishness and indifference to God.

13:43 Those who will shine like the sun in God's Kingdom stand in contrast to those who receive his judgment. A similar illustration is used in Daniel 12:3.

13:44 The Kingdom of Heaven is more valuable than anything else we can have, and a person must be willing to give up everything to obtain it. The man who discovered the treasure hidden in the field stumbled upon it by accident but knew its value when he found it. Although the transaction cost the man everything, he paid nothing for the priceless treasure itself. It came free, with the field. Nothing is more precious than the Kingdom of Heaven; yet God gives it to us as a gift.

Jesus Tells the Parable of the Pearl Merchant (85)

45 "Again, the Kingdom of Heaven is like a merchant on the lookout for choice pearls. 46 When he discovered a pearl of great value, he sold everything he owned and bought it!

Jesus Tells the Parable of the Fishing Net (86)

47 "Again, the Kingdom of Heaven is like a fishing net that was thrown into the water and caught fish of every kind. 48When the net was full, they dragged it up onto the shore, sat down, and sorted the good fish into crates, but threw the bad ones away. 49 That is the way it will be at the end of the world. The angels will come and separate the wicked people from the righteous, 50 throwing the wicked into the fiery furnace, where there will be weeping and gnashing of teeth. 51Do you understand all these things?"

"Yes," they said, "we do."

52 Then he added, "Every teacher of religious law who becomes a disciple in the Kingdom of Heaven is like a homeowner who brings from his storeroom new gems of truth as well as old."

5. Jesus encounters differing reactions to his ministry

The People of Nazareth Refuse to Believe (91/Mark 6:1-6)

53 When Jesus had finished telling these stories and illustrations, he left that part of the country. 54He returned to Nazareth, his hometown. When he taught there in the synagogue, everyone was amazed and said, "Where does he get this wisdom and the power to do miracles?" 55 Then they scoffed, "He's just the carpenter's son, and we know Mary, his mother, and his brothers—James, Joseph,* Simon, and Judas. 56All his sisters live right here among us. Where did he learn all these things?" 57And they were deeply offended and refused to believe in him.

Then Jesus told them, "A prophet is honored everywhere except in his own hometown and among his own family." 58And so he did only a few miracles there because of their unbelief.

Herod Kills John the Baptist (95/Mark 6:14-29; Luke 9:7-9)

14 When Herod Antipas, the ruler of Galilee,* heard about Jesus, 2 he said to his advisers, "This must be John the Baptist raised from the dead! That is why he can do such miracles."

3 For Herod had arrested and imprisoned John as a favor to his wife Herodias (the former wife of Herod's brother Philip). 4 John had been telling Herod, "It is against God's law for you

13:55 Other manuscripts read *Joses;* still others read *John.*   14:1 Greek *Herod the tetrarch.* Herod Antipas was a son of King Herod and was ruler over Galilee.

Margin references:
13:47 Matt 22:10
13:50 Matt 8:12; 13:42; 22:13; 24:51; 25:30 Luke 13:28
13:53 Matt 7:28
13:54 John 7:15
13:55 Matt 12:46 Luke 3:23 John 6:42
13:57 Luke 4:24 John 4:44
14:3 Luke 3:19-20
14:4 Lev 18:16; 20:21

13:45, 46 In this parable, the Kingdom of Heaven is not the precious pearl, but the merchant. In contrast to the previous picture, Jesus is now displaying another aspect of the Kingdom. The contrast becomes vivid in the transaction—the Kingdom pays the ultimate price to possess the pearl, the price God was willing to pay to redeem us.

13:47-49 The parable of the fishing net has the same meaning as the parable of the wheat and weeds. We are to obey God and tell others about his grace and goodness, but we cannot dictate who is part of the Kingdom of Heaven and who is not. This sorting will be done at the last judgment by those infinitely more qualified than we.

13:52 Anyone who understands God's real purpose in the law as revealed in the Old Testament has a real treasure. The Old Testament points the way to Jesus, the Messiah. Jesus always upheld its authority and relevance. But there is a double benefit for those who understand Jesus' teaching about the Kingdom of Heaven. This was a new treasure that Jesus was revealing. Both the old and new teaching give practical guidelines for faith and for living in the world. The teachers of religious law, however, were trapped in the old and blind to the new. They were looking for a future kingdom *preceded* by judgment. Jesus, however, taught that the Kingdom was *now*, and the judgment was future. The religious leaders were looking for a physical and temporal kingdom (via military rebellion and physical rule), but they were blind to the spiritual significance of the Kingdom that Christ brought.

13:55 The residents of Jesus' hometown had known Jesus since he was a young child and were acquainted with his family; they could not bring themselves to believe in his message. They were too close to the situation. Jesus had come to them as a prophet, one who challenged them to respond to unpopular spiritual truth. They did not listen to the timeless message because they could not see beyond the man.

13:57 Jesus was not the first prophet to be rejected in his own country. Jeremiah experienced rejection in his hometown, even by members of his own family (Jeremiah 12:5, 6).

13:58 Jesus did few miracles in his hometown "because of their unbelief." Unbelief blinds people to the truth and robs them of hope. These people missed the Messiah. How does your faith measure up? If you can't see God's work, perhaps it is because of your unbelief. Believe, ask God for a mighty work in your life, and expect him to act. Look with the eyes of faith.

14:1 Herod Antipas was one of three rulers over the four districts of Palestine. His territory included the regions of Galilee and Perea. He was the son of Herod the Great, who ordered the killing of the babies in Bethlehem (2:16). He heard Jesus' case before Jesus' crucifixion (Luke 23:6-12). His Profile is found in Mark 6, p. 1629.

14:2 For more information on John the Baptist, see his Profile in John 1, p. 1749.

14:3 Philip, Herod's half brother, was another of Palestine's three rulers. His territories were Iturea and Traconitis, northeast of the Sea of Galilee (Luke 3:1). Philip's wife, Herodias, left Philip to live with Herod Antipas. John the Baptist condemned the two for living immorally (see Mark 6:17, 18).

to marry her." 5Herod wanted to kill John, but he was afraid of a riot, because all the people believed John was a prophet.

14:5
Matt 11:9; 21:26

6But at a birthday party for Herod, Herodias's daughter performed a dance that greatly pleased him, 7so he promised with a vow to give her anything she wanted. 8At her mother's urging, the girl said, "I want the head of John the Baptist on a tray!" 9Then the king regretted what he had said; but because of the vow he had made in front of his guests, he issued the necessary orders. 10So John was beheaded in the prison, 11 and his head was brought on a tray and given to the girl, who took it to her mother. 12Later, John's disciples came for his body and buried it. Then they went and told Jesus what had happened.

14:10
Matt 17:12

14:12
Acts 8:2

Jesus Feeds Five Thousand (**96**/Mark 6:30-44; Luke 9:10-17; John 6:1-15)

13As soon as Jesus heard the news, he left in a boat to a remote area to be alone. But the crowds heard where he was headed and followed on foot from many towns. 14 Jesus saw the huge crowd as he stepped from the boat, and he had compassion on them and healed their sick.

14:14
Matt 9:36
Mark 1:41
Heb 2:17-18; 4:15;
5:1-3

15That evening the disciples came to him and said, "This is a remote place, and it's already getting late. Send the crowds away so they can go to the villages and buy food for themselves."

16But Jesus said, "That isn't necessary—you feed them."

17 "But we have only five loaves of bread and two fish!" they answered.

14:16-20
2 Kgs 4:42-44

18 "Bring them here," he said. 19Then he told the people to sit down on the grass. Jesus took the five loaves and two fish, looked up toward heaven, and blessed them. Then, breaking the loaves into pieces, he gave the bread to the disciples, who distributed it to the people. 20They all ate as much as they wanted, and afterward, the disciples picked up twelve baskets of leftovers. 21About 5,000 men were fed that day, in addition to all the women and children!

14:19-22
Matt 15:35-39
Mark 8:6-10

Jesus Walks on Water (**97**/Mark 6:45-52; John 6:16-21)

22Immediately after this, Jesus insisted that his disciples get back into the boat and cross to the other side of the lake, while he sent the people home. 23After sending them home, he went up into the hills by himself to pray. Night fell while he was there alone.

14:23
Luke 9:28

24Meanwhile, the disciples were in trouble far away from land, for a strong wind had risen, and they were fighting heavy waves. 25About three o'clock in the morning* Jesus came toward them, walking on the water. 26When the disciples saw him walking on the water, they were terrified. In their fear, they cried out, "It's a ghost!"

14:26
Luke 24:37

14:25 Greek *In the fourth watch of the night.*

14:9 Herod did not want to kill John the Baptist, but he gave the order so that he wouldn't be embarrassed in front of his guests. How easy it is to give in to the crowd and to let ourselves be pressured into doing wrong. Don't get in a situation where it will be too embarrassing to do what is right. Determine to do what is right, no matter how embarrassing or painful it may be.

14:13, 14 Jesus sought solitude after the news of John's death. Sometimes we may need to deal with our grief alone. Jesus did not dwell on his grief but returned to the ministry he came to do.

JESUS WALKS ON THE SEA
The miraculous feeding of the 5,000 occurred on the shores of the Sea of Galilee near Bethsaida. Jesus then sent his disciples across the lake. Several hours later they encountered a storm, and Jesus came to them—walking on the water. The boat then landed at Gennesaret.

Mediterranean Sea

GALILEE

↑ N

Capernaum • Bethsaida
Gennesaret • Sea of Galilee

DECAPOLIS
(Ten Towns)

Jordan River

SAMARIA

PEREA

Jerusalem •

Dead Sea

JUDEA

IDUMEA

0   20 Mi.
├──┬──┤
0   20 Km.

• **14:14** Jesus performed some miracles as signs of his identity. He used other miracles to teach important truths. But here we read that he healed people because he "had compassion on them." Jesus was, and is, a loving, caring, and feeling person. When you are suffering, remember that Jesus hurts with you. He has compassion on you.

• **14:19-21** Jesus multiplied five loaves and two fish to feed over 5,000 people. What he was originally given seemed insufficient, but in his hands it became more than enough. We often feel that our contribution to Jesus is meager, but he can use and multiply whatever we give him, whether it is talent, time, or treasure. It is when we give them to Jesus that our resources are multiplied.

• **14:21** The text states that there were 5,000 men present, *besides* women and children. Therefore, the total number of people Jesus fed could have been 10,000 to 15,000. The number of men is listed separately because in the Jewish culture of the day, men and women usually ate separately when in public. The children ate with the women.

14:23 Seeking solitude was an important priority for Jesus (see also 14:13). He made room in his busy schedule to be alone with the Father. Spending time with God in prayer nurtures a vital

27 But Jesus spoke to them at once. "Don't be afraid," he said. "Take courage. I am here!*"

28 Then Peter called to him, "Lord, if it's really you, tell me to come to you, walking on the water."

29 "Yes, come," Jesus said.

14:31
Matt 6:30

14:33
Ps 2:7
Matt 16:16; 26:63; 27:54
Mark 1:1
Luke 22:70
John 1:49; 6:69
Rom 1:4

So Peter went over the side of the boat and walked on the water toward Jesus. 30 But when he saw the strong* wind and the waves, he was terrified and began to sink. "Save me, Lord!" he shouted.

31 Jesus immediately reached out and grabbed him. "You have so little faith," Jesus said. "Why did you doubt me?"

32 When they climbed back into the boat, the wind stopped. 33 Then the disciples worshiped him. "You really are the Son of God!" they exclaimed.

Jesus Heals All Who Touch Him (98/Mark 6:53-56)

14:36
Matt 9:20-21

34 After they had crossed the lake, they landed at Gennesaret. 35 When the people recognized Jesus, the news of his arrival spread quickly throughout the whole area, and soon people were bringing all their sick to be healed. 36 They begged him to let the sick touch at least the fringe of his robe, and all who touched him were healed.

Jesus Teaches about Inner Purity (102/Mark 7:1-23)

15:2
Luke 11:38

15 1 Some Pharisees and teachers of religious law now arrived from Jerusalem to see Jesus. They asked him, 2 "Why do your disciples disobey our age-old tradition? For they ignore our tradition of ceremonial hand washing before they eat."

15:4
†Exod 20:12; 21:17
†Lev 20:9
†Deut 5:16
Matt 19:19
Mark 10:19
Luke 18:20
Eph 6:2

3 Jesus replied, "And why do you, by your traditions, violate the direct commandments of God? 4 For instance, God says, 'Honor your father and mother,'* and 'Anyone who speaks disrespectfully of father or mother must be put to death.'* 5 But you say it is all right for people to say to their parents, 'Sorry, I can't help you. For I have vowed to give to God what I would have given to you.' 6 In this way, you say they don't need to honor their parents.* And so you cancel the word of God for the sake of your own tradition. 7 You hypocrites! Isaiah was right when he prophesied about you, for he wrote,

14:27 Or *The 'I Am' is here;* Greek reads *I am.* See Exod 3:14.   **14:30** Some manuscripts do not include *strong.*
15:4a Exod 20:12; Deut 5:16.   **15:4b** Exod 21:17 (Greek version); Lev 20:9 (Greek version).   **15:6** Greek *their father;* other manuscripts read *their father or their mother.*

---

relationship with him and equips us to meet life's challenges and struggles. Develop the discipline of spending time alone with God. It will help you grow spiritually and become more and more like Christ.

• **14:28** Peter was not putting Jesus to the test, something we are told not to do (4:7). Instead, he was the only one in the boat to react in faith. His impulsive request led him to experience a rather unusual demonstration of God's power. Peter started to sink because he took his eyes off Jesus and focused on the high waves around him. His faith wavered when he realized what he was doing. We probably will not walk on water, but we may walk through tough situations. If we focus on the waves of difficult circumstances around us without faith in Jesus to help, we, too, may despair and sink. To maintain your faith when situations are difficult, focus on Jesus' power rather than on your inadequacies.

• **14:30, 31** Although we start out with good intentions, sometimes our faith falters. This doesn't necessarily mean we have failed. When Peter's faith faltered, he reached out to Christ, the only one who could help. He was afraid, but he still looked to Christ. When you are apprehensive about the troubles around you and doubt Christ's presence or ability to help, remember that he is always with you and is the *only* one who can really help.

14:34 Gennesaret was located on the west side of the Sea of Galilee in a fertile, well-watered area.

• **14:35, 36** The people recognized Jesus as a great healer, but how many understood who he truly was? They came to Jesus for physical healing, but did they come for spiritual healing? They came to prolong their lives on earth, not to seek eternal life. People may follow Jesus to learn valuable lessons from his life or in hopes of finding relief from pain. But we miss Jesus' whole message if we seek him only to heal our bodies but not our souls, if we look to him for help only in this life, rather than for his eter-

nal plan for us. Only when we understand the real Jesus Christ can we appreciate how he can truly change our life.

• **14:36** Jewish men wore fringe on the lower edges of their robes according to God's command (Deuteronomy 22:12). By Jesus' day, elaborate versions of this fringe were seen as a sign of holiness (23:5). There is no indication that the fringe on Jesus' robe was anything more than typical. It was natural that people seeking healing should reach out and touch the fringe of his robe. But as one sick woman learned, healing came from faith and not from Jesus' robe (9:19-22).

15:1, 2 The Pharisees and teachers of religious law came from Jerusalem, the center of Jewish authority, to scrutinize Jesus' activities. Over the centuries since the Jews' return from Babylonian captivity, hundreds of religious traditions had been added to God's laws. The Pharisees and teachers of religious law considered them all equally important. Many traditions are not bad in themselves. Certain religious traditions can add richness and meaning to life. But we must not assume that because our traditions have been practiced for years, they should be elevated to a sacred standing. God's principles never change, and his law doesn't need additions. Traditions should help us understand God's laws better, not become laws themselves.

15:5, 6 This was the practice of *Corban* (literally, "offering"; see Mark 7:11). Anyone who made a Corban vow was required to dedicate money to God's Temple that otherwise would have gone to support his parents. Corban had become a religiously acceptable way to neglect parents, circumventing the child's responsibility to them. Although the action—giving money to God—seemed worthy and no doubt conferred prestige on the giver, many people who took the Corban vow were disregarding God's command to care for needy parents. These religious leaders were ignoring God's clear command to honor their parents.

8 'These people honor me with their lips,
 but their hearts are far from me.
9 Their worship is a farce,
 for they teach man-made ideas as commands from God.'* "

15:8-9
†Isa 29:13

15:9
Col 2:20-22

10 Then Jesus called to the crowd to come and hear. "Listen," he said, "and try to understand. 11It's not what goes into your mouth that defiles you; you are defiled by the words that come out of your mouth."

15:11
Matt 12:34
Acts 10:14-15

12 Then the disciples came to him and asked, "Do you realize you offended the Pharisees by what you just said?"

13Jesus replied, "Every plant not planted by my heavenly Father will be uprooted, 14 so ignore them. They are blind guides leading the blind, and if one blind person guides another, they will both fall into a ditch."

15:13
Isa 60:21; 61:3
John 15:2
1 Cor 3:9

15:14
Matt 23:16, 24
Luke 6:39
Rom 2:19

15Then Peter said to Jesus, "Explain to us the parable that says people aren't defiled by what they eat."

16 "Don't you understand yet?" Jesus asked. 17 "Anything you eat passes through the stomach and then goes into the sewer. 18 But the words you speak come from the heart—that's what defiles you. 19For from the heart come evil thoughts, murder, adultery, all sexual immorality, theft, lying, and slander. 20 These are what defile you. Eating with unwashed hands will never defile you."

15:18
Matt 12:34
Jas 3:6

15:19
Rom 1:29-31
1 Cor 5:10-11;
6:9-10
Gal 5:19-21

Jesus Sends a Demon Out of a Girl (103/Mark 7:24-30)

21Then Jesus left Galilee and went north to the region of Tyre and Sidon. 22A Gentile* woman who lived there came to him, pleading, "Have mercy on me, O Lord, Son of David! For my daughter is possessed by a demon that torments her severely."

23But Jesus gave her no reply, not even a word. Then his disciples urged him to send her away. "Tell her to go away," they said. "She is bothering us with all her begging."

24Then Jesus said to the woman, "I was sent only to help God's lost sheep—the people of Israel."

15:24
Matt 10:6
Rom 15:8

15:8-9 Isa 29:13 (Greek version). **15:22** Greek *Canaanite*.

15:8, 9 The prophet Isaiah also criticized hypocrites (Isaiah 29:13), and Jesus applied Isaiah's words to these religious leaders. The Pharisees knew a lot about God, but they didn't know God. When we claim to honor God while our heart is far from him, our worship means nothing. It is not enough to study about religion or even to study the Bible; it is not enough to act religious. Our actions and our attitudes must be sincere. If they are not, Isaiah's words also describe us.

15:11 Jesus was referring to the Jewish regulations concerning food and drink. This verse could be paraphrased: "You aren't made unclean by eating nonkosher food! It is what you *say* and *think*

MINISTRY IN PHOENICIA
After preaching again in Capernaum, Jesus left Galilee for Phoenicia, where he preached in Tyre and Sidon. On his return, he traveled through the region of Decapolis (Ten Towns), fed the 4,000 beside the sea, then crossed to Magadan.

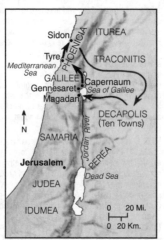

that makes you unclean!" This statement offended the Pharisees, who were very concerned about what people ate and drank.

15:13, 14 Jesus told his disciples to leave the Pharisees alone because the Pharisees were blind to God's truth. Anyone who listened to their teaching would risk spiritual blindness as well. Not all religious leaders clearly see God's truth. Make sure that those you listen to and learn from are those with good spiritual eyesight—they teach and follow the principles of Scripture.

15:15 Later Peter would be faced with the issue of clean and unclean food (see the notes on 15:11 and Acts 10:12). Then he would learn that nothing should be a barrier to proclaiming the Good News to the Gentiles (non-Jews).

15:16-20 We work hard to keep our outward appearance attractive, but what is deep down in our heart (where others can't see) is more important to God. What are you like inside? When people become Christians, God makes them different on the inside. He will continue the process of change inside them if they only ask. God wants us to have healthy thoughts and motives, not just healthy bodies.

• **15:23** Puzzled by Jesus' silence, the disciples asked him to get rid of the woman because she was bothering them with her persistent begging. They showed no compassion for her or sensitivity to her needs. It is possible to become so occupied with spiritual matters that we become oblivious to the needs around us. This may be true especially if we are prejudiced against needy people or if they cause us inconvenience. Instead of being annoyed, be aware of the opportunities that surround you, and make an effort to look for ways to minister to others.

• **15:24** Jesus' words do not contradict the truth that God's message is for all people (Psalm 22:27; Isaiah 56:7; Matthew 28:19; Romans 15:9-12). After all, when Jesus said these words, he was in Gentile territory on a mission to Gentile people. He ministered to Gentiles on many other occasions also. Jesus was simply telling

15:25
Matt 8:2

25 But she came and worshiped him, pleading again, "Lord, help me!"

26 Jesus responded, "It isn't right to take food from the children and throw it to the dogs."

27 She replied, "That's true, Lord, but even dogs are allowed to eat the scraps that fall beneath their masters' table."

15:28
Matt 8:10

28 "Dear woman," Jesus said to her, "your faith is great. Your request is granted." And her daughter was instantly healed.

Jesus Heals Many People (**104**/Mark 7:31-37)

15:30
Isa 35:5-6
Matt 4:23; 11:5
Luke 7:22

29 Jesus returned to the Sea of Galilee and climbed a hill and sat down. 30 A vast crowd brought to him people who were lame, blind, crippled, those who couldn't speak, and many others. They laid them before Jesus, and he healed them all. 31 The crowd was amazed! Those who hadn't been able to speak were talking, the crippled were made well, the lame were walking, and the blind could see again! And they praised the God of Israel.

Jesus Feeds Four Thousand (**105**/Mark 8:1-10)

15:32
Matt 9:36

32 Then Jesus called his disciples and told them, "I feel sorry for these people. They have been here with me for three days, and they have nothing left to eat. I don't want to send them away hungry, or they will faint along the way."

15:33
Mark 6:37
John 6:5

33 The disciples replied, "Where would we get enough food here in the wilderness for such a huge crowd?"

15:34-37
Matt 14:17-20
Mark 6:38-43
Luke 9:13-17
John 6:9-13

34 Jesus asked, "How much bread do you have?"

They replied, "Seven loaves, and a few small fish."

35 So Jesus told all the people to sit down on the ground. 36 Then he took the seven loaves and the fish, thanked God for them, and broke them into pieces. He gave them to the disciples, who distributed the food to the crowd.

15:37
Matt 16:10

37 They all ate as much as they wanted. Afterward, the disciples picked up seven large baskets of leftover food. 38 There were 4,000 men who were fed that day, in addition to all the women and children. 39 Then Jesus sent the people home, and he got into a boat and crossed over to the region of Magadan.

15:38
Matt 14:21
Mark 6:44

Leaders Demand a Miraculous Sign (**106**/Mark 8:11-13)

16:1
Matt 12:38
Luke 11:16
John 6:30

16 One day the Pharisees and Sadducees came to test Jesus, demanding that he show them a miraculous sign from heaven to prove his authority.

16:2-3
Luke 12:54-56

2 He replied, "You know the saying, 'Red sky at night means fair weather tomorrow; 3 red sky in the morning means foul weather all day.' You know how to interpret the weather signs in the sky, but you don't know how to interpret the signs of the times!* 4 Only an evil,

16:4
Matt 12:39
Luke 11:29

16:2-3 Several manuscripts do not include any of the words in 16:2-3 after *He replied.*

---

the woman that Jews were to have the first opportunity to accept him as the Messiah because God wanted them to present the message of salvation to the rest of the world (see Genesis 12:3). Jesus was not rejecting the Gentile woman. He may have wanted to test her faith, or he may have wanted to use the situation as another opportunity to teach that faith is available to all people.

15:26-28 *Dog* was a term the Jews commonly applied to Gentiles because the Jews considered these pagan people no more likely than dogs to receive God's blessing. Jesus was not degrading the woman by using this term; he was reflecting the Jews' attitude so as to contrast it with his own. The woman did not argue. Instead, using Jesus' choice of words, she agreed to be considered a dog as long as she could receive God's blessing for her daughter. Ironically, many Jews would lose God's blessing and salvation because they rejected Jesus, and many Gentiles would find salvation because they recognized and accepted him.

• **15:29-31** A vast crowd was brought to Jesus to be healed, and he healed them all. Jesus is still able to heal people who are suffering physically, emotionally, and spiritually, and we can be the ones who bring suffering people to him. Whom do you know that needs Christ's healing touch? You can bring them to Jesus through prayer or through explaining to them the reason for the hope that you have (1 Peter 3:15). Then let Christ do the healing.

• **15:32ff** This feeding of 4,000 is a separate event from the feeding of the 5,000 (14:13-21), confirmed by Mark 8:19, 20. This was the beginning of Jesus' expanded ministry to the Gentiles.

• **15:33** Jesus had already fed more than 5,000 people with five loaves and two fish. Here, in a similar situation, the disciples were again perplexed. How easily we throw up our hands in despair when faced with difficult situations. Like the disciples, we often forget that if God has cared for us in the past, he will do the same now. When facing a difficult situation, remember that God cares for you and trust him to work faithfully again.

16:1 The Pharisees and Sadducees were Jewish religious leaders of two different parties, and their views were diametrically opposed on many issues. The Pharisees carefully followed their religious rules and traditions, believing that this was the way to God. They also believed in the authority of all Scripture and in the resurrection of the dead. The Sadducees accepted only the books of Moses as Scripture and did not believe in life after death. In Jesus, however, these two groups had a common enemy, and they joined forces to try to kill him. For more information on the Pharisees and Sadducees, see the charts in chapter 3, p. 1541 and Mark 2, p. 1617.

16:1 The Pharisees and Sadducees demanded a sign "from heaven." They tried to explain away Jesus' other miracles as sleight of hand, coincidence, or use of evil power, but they believed that only God could do a sign in the sky. This, they were sure, would be a feat beyond Jesus' power. Although Jesus could have easily impressed them, he refused. He knew that even a miracle in the sky would not convince them he was the Messiah because they had already decided not to believe in him.

adulterous generation would demand a miraculous sign, but the only sign I will give them is the sign of the prophet Jonah.*" Then Jesus left them and went away.

Jesus Warns against Wrong Teaching (**107**/Mark 8:14-21)
5Later, after they crossed to the other side of the lake, the disciples discovered they had forgotten to bring any bread. 6 "Watch out!" Jesus warned them. "Beware of the yeast of the Pharisees and Sadducees."

16:6
Luke 12:1

7At this they began to argue with each other because they hadn't brought any bread. 8Jesus knew what they were saying, so he said, "You have so little faith! Why are you arguing with each other about having no bread? 9 Don't you understand even yet? Don't you remember the 5,000 I fed with five loaves, and the baskets of leftovers you picked up? 10Or the 4,000 I fed with seven loaves, and the large baskets of leftovers you picked up? 11Why can't you understand that I'm not talking about bread? So again I say, 'Beware of the yeast of the Pharisees and Sadducees.' "

16:9
Matt 14:14-21
Mark 6:34-44
Luke 9:11-17
John 6:1-13

16:10
Matt 15:32-38
Mark 8:1-9

12Then at last they understood that he wasn't speaking about the yeast in bread, but about the deceptive teaching of the Pharisees and Sadducees.

16:11
Luke 12:1

Peter Says Jesus Is the Messiah (**109**/Mark 8:27-30; Luke 9:18-20)
13When Jesus came to the region of Caesarea Philippi, he asked his disciples, "Who do people say that the Son of Man is?"*

16:14
Mark 6:14-15

14 "Well," they replied, "some say John the Baptist, some say Elijah, and others say Jeremiah or one of the other prophets."

16:16
Matt 1:16; 14:33
Mark 14:61
John 1:34, 49;
6:69; 11:27; 20:31

15Then he asked them, "But who do you say I am?"

16Simon Peter answered, "You are the Messiah,* the Son of the living God."

17 Jesus replied, "You are blessed, Simon son of John,* because my Father in heaven has revealed this to you. You did not learn this from any human being. 18 Now I say to you that

16:18
John 1:42
1 Cor 3:11
Eph 2:20-22;
4:15-16
1 Pet 2:4-5

16:4 Greek *the sign of Jonah.*   **16:13** "Son of Man" is a title Jesus used for himself.   **16:16** Or *the Christ. Messiah* (a Hebrew term) and *Christ* (a Greek term) both mean "the anointed one."   **16:17** Greek *Simon bar-Jonah;* see John 1:42; 21:15-17.

16:4 By using the sign of Jonah, who was inside a great fish for three days, Jesus was predicting his death and resurrection (see also 12:38-42).

16:4 Many people, like these Jewish leaders, say they want to see a miracle so that they can believe. But Jesus knew that miracles never convince the skeptical. Jesus had been healing, raising people from the dead, and feeding thousands, and still people wanted him to prove himself. Do you doubt Christ because you haven't *seen* a miracle? Do you expect God to prove himself to you personally before you believe? Jesus says, "Blessed are those who believe without seeing me" (John 20:29). We have miracles recorded in the Old and New Testaments, 2,000 years of church history, and the witness of thousands. With all this

evidence, those who won't believe are either too proud or too stubborn. If you simply step forward in faith and believe, then you will begin to see the miracles that God can do in your life!

16:12 Yeast is put into bread to make it rise, and it takes only a little to affect a whole batch of dough. Jesus used yeast as an example of how a small amount of evil can affect a large group of people. The wrong teachings of the Pharisees and Sadducees were leading many people astray. Beware of the tendency to say, "How can this little wrong possibly affect anyone?"

16:13 Caesarea Philippi was located several miles north of the Sea of Galilee, in the territory ruled by Philip. The influence of Greek and Roman culture was everywhere, and pagan temples and idols abounded. When Philip became ruler, he rebuilt and renamed the city after the emperor (Caesar) and himself. The city was originally called Caesarea, the same name as the capital city of Philip's brother Herod's territory.

JOURNEY TO CAESAREA PHILIPPI
Jesus left Magadan, crossed the lake, and landed in Bethsaida. There he healed a man who had been born blind. From there, he and his disciples went to Caesarea Philippi, where Peter confessed Jesus as the Messiah and Son of God.

• **16:13-17** The disciples answered Jesus' question with the common view—that Jesus was one of the great prophets come back to life. This belief may have stemmed from Deuteronomy 18:18, where God said he would raise up a prophet from among the people. (John the Baptist's Profile is in John 1, p. 1749; Elijah's Profile is in 1 Kings 17, p. 545; and Jeremiah's Profile is in Jeremiah 2, p. 1201.) Peter, however, confessed Jesus as divine and as the promised and long-awaited Messiah. If Jesus were to ask you this question, how would you answer? Is he your Lord and Messiah?

• **16:18** The rock on which Jesus would build his church has been identified as (1) Jesus himself (his work of salvation by dying for us on the cross); (2) Peter (the first great leader in the church at Jerusalem); (3) the confession of faith that Peter gave and that all subsequent true believers would give. It seems most likely that the rock refers to Peter as the leader of the church. Just as Peter had revealed the true identity of Christ, so Jesus revealed Peter's identity and role.

Later, Peter reminds Christians that they are the church built

16:19
Isa 22:22
Matt 18:18
John 20:23
Rev 1:18; 3:7

you are Peter (which means 'rock'),* and upon this rock I will build my church, and all the powers of hell* will not conquer it. ¹⁹ And I will give you the keys of the Kingdom of Heaven. Whatever you forbid* on earth will be forbidden in heaven, and whatever you permit* on earth will be permitted in heaven."

²⁰Then he sternly warned the disciples not to tell anyone that he was the Messiah.

Jesus Predicts His Death the First Time (**110**/Mark 8:31–9:1; Luke 9:21-27)

16:21
John 2:19
1 Cor 15:3-4

²¹From then on Jesus* began to tell his disciples plainly that it was necessary for him to go to Jerusalem, and that he would suffer many terrible things at the hands of the elders, the leading priests, and the teachers of religious law. He would be killed, but on the third day he would be raised from the dead.

16:23
Matt 4:10

²² But Peter took him aside and began to reprimand him* for saying such things. "Heaven forbid, Lord," he said. "This will never happen to you!"

16:24
Matt 10:38
Luke 14:27

²³ Jesus turned to Peter and said, "Get away from me, Satan! You are a dangerous trap to me. You are seeing things merely from a human point of view, not from God's."

16:25
Matt 10:39
Luke 17:33
John 12:25

²⁴Then Jesus said to his disciples, "If any of you wants to be my follower, you must turn from your selfish ways, take up your cross, and follow me. ²⁵ If you try to hang on to your life, you will lose it. But if you give up your life for my sake, you will save it. ²⁶And what do you

16:26
Ps 49:7-9
Matt 4:8-9

benefit if you gain the whole world but lose your own soul?* Is anything worth more than

16:18a Greek *that you are Peter.* **16:18b** Greek *and the gates of Hades.* **16:19a** Or *bind,* or *lock.* **16:19b** Or *loose,* or *open.* **16:21** Some manuscripts read *Jesus the Messiah.* **16:22** Or *began to correct him.* **16:26** Or *your self?* also in 16:26b.

---

on the foundation of the apostles and prophets, with Jesus Christ as the cornerstone (1 Peter 2:4-6). All believers are joined into this church by faith in Jesus Christ as Savior, the same faith that Peter expressed here (see also Ephesians 2:20, 21). Jesus praised Peter for his confession of faith. It is faith like Peter's that is the foundation of Christ's Kingdom.

16:19 The meaning of this verse has been a subject of debate for centuries. Some say the "keys" represent the authority to carry out church discipline, legislation, and administration (18:15-18), while others say the keys give the authority to announce the forgiveness of sins (John 20:23). Still others say the keys may be the opportunity to bring people to the Kingdom of Heaven by presenting them with the message of salvation found in God's Word (Acts 15:7-9). The religious leaders thought they held the keys of the Kingdom, and they tried to shut some people out. We cannot decide to open or close the Kingdom of Heaven for others, but God uses us to help others find the way inside. To all who believe in Christ and obey his words, the Kingdom doors are swung wide open.

• **16:20** Jesus warned the disciples not to publicize Peter's confession because they did not yet fully understand the kind of Messiah he had come to be—not a military commander but a suffering servant. They needed to come to a full understanding of Jesus and their mission as disciples before they could proclaim it to others in a way that would not cause a rebellion. They would have a difficult time understanding what Jesus came to do until his earthly mission was complete.

• **16:21** The phrase "From then on" marks a turning point. In 4:17 it signaled Jesus' announcement of the Kingdom of Heaven. Here it points to his new emphasis on his death and resurrection. The disciples still didn't grasp Jesus' true purpose because of their preconceived notions about what the Messiah should be. This is the first of three times that Jesus predicted his death (see 17:22, 23; 20:18 for others).

16:21-28 This passage corresponds to Daniel's prophecies: The Messiah would be cut off (Daniel 9:26); there would be a period of trouble (Daniel 9:27); and the king would come in glory (Daniel 7:13, 14). The disciples would endure the same suffering as their King and, like him, would be rewarded in the end.

• **16:22** Peter, Jesus' friend and devoted follower who had just eloquently proclaimed Jesus' true identity, sought to protect him from the suffering he prophesied. But if Jesus hadn't

suffered and died, Peter would have died in his sins. Great temptations can come from those who love us and seek to protect us. Be cautious of advice from a friend who says, "Surely God doesn't want you to face this." Often our most difficult temptations come from those who are only trying to protect us from discomfort.

16:23 In his wilderness temptations, Jesus heard the message that he could achieve greatness without dying (4:9). Here he heard the same message from Peter. Peter had just recognized Jesus as Messiah; here, however, he forsook God's perspective and evaluated the situation from a human one. Satan is always trying to get us to leave God out of the picture. Jesus rebuked Peter for this attitude.

16:24 When Jesus used this picture of his followers taking up their crosses to follow him, the disciples knew what he meant. Crucifixion was a common Roman method of execution, and condemned criminals had to carry their cross through the streets to the execution site. Following Jesus, therefore, meant a true commitment, the risk of death, and no turning back (see 10:39).

16:25 The possibility of losing their lives was very real for the disciples as well as for Jesus. Real discipleship implies real commitment—pledging our whole existence to his service. If we try to save our physical life from death, pain, or discomfort, we may risk losing eternal life. If we protect ourselves from the pain God calls us to suffer, we begin to die spiritually and emotionally. Our lives turn inward, and we lose our intended purpose. When we give our life in service to Christ, however, we discover the real purpose of living.

• **16:26** When we don't know Christ, we make choices as though there were no afterlife. In reality, this life is just the introduction to eternity. How we live this brief span determines our eternal state. What we accumulate on earth has no value in gaining eternal life. Even the highest social or civic honors cannot earn us entrance into heaven. Evaluate your lifestyle from an eternal perspective, and you will find your values and decisions changing.

your soul? 27 For the Son of Man will come with his angels in the glory of his Father and will judge all people according to their deeds. 28And I tell you the truth, some standing here right now will not die before they see the Son of Man coming in his Kingdom."

16:27
Prov 24:12
Matt 25:31
Rev 22:12

Jesus Is Transfigured on the Mountain (111/Mark 9:2-13; Luke 9:28-36)

17 Six days later Jesus took Peter and the two brothers, James and John, and led them up a high mountain to be alone. 2As the men watched, Jesus' appearance was transformed so that his face shone like the sun, and his clothes became as white as light. 3Suddenly, Moses and Elijah appeared and began talking with Jesus.

17:2
2 Pet 1:16-18

4Peter exclaimed, "Lord, it's wonderful for us to be here! If you want, I'll make three shelters as memorials*—one for you, one for Moses, and one for Elijah."

5But even as he spoke, a bright cloud overshadowed them, and a voice from the cloud said, "This is my dearly loved Son, who brings me great joy. Listen to him." 6The disciples were terrified and fell face down on the ground.

17:5
Ps 2:7
Matt 3:17; 12:18
Mark 1:11
Luke 3:22
2 Pet 1:17

7Then Jesus came over and touched them. "Get up," he said. "Don't be afraid." 8And when they looked up, Moses and Elijah were gone, and they saw only Jesus.

9As they went back down the mountain, Jesus commanded them, "Don't tell anyone what you have seen until the Son of Man* has been raised from the dead."

10Then his disciples asked him, "Why do the teachers of religious law insist that Elijah must return before the Messiah comes?*"

17:10-11
Mal 4;5-6
Luke 1:16-17

11Jesus replied, "Elijah is indeed coming first to get everything ready. 12 But I tell you, Elijah has already come, but he wasn't recognized, and they chose to abuse him. And in the same way they will also make the Son of Man suffer." 13Then the disciples realized he was talking about John the Baptist.

17:12
Matt 11:14

Jesus Heals a Demon-Possessed Boy (112/Mark 9:14-29; Luke 9:37-43)

14At the foot of the mountain, a large crowd was waiting for them. A man came and knelt before Jesus and said, 15 "Lord, have mercy on my son. He has seizures and suffers terribly. He often falls into the fire or into the water. 16 So I brought him to your disciples, but they couldn't heal him."

17:4 Greek *three tabernacles.* **17:9** "Son of Man" is a title Jesus used for himself. **17:10** Greek *that Elijah must come first?*

16:27 Jesus Christ has been given the authority to judge all the earth (Romans 14:9-11; Philippians 2:9-11). Although his judgment is already working in our lives, there is a future, final judgment when Christ returns (25:31-46) and everyone's life will be reviewed and evaluated. This will not be confined to unbelievers; Christians, too, will face a judgment. Their eternal destiny is secure, but Jesus will look at how they handled gifts, opportunities, and responsibilities in order to determine their heavenly rewards. At the time of judgment, God will deliver the righteous and condemn the wicked. We should not judge others' salvation; that is God's work.

16:28 Because all the disciples died *before* Christ's return, many believe that Jesus' words were fulfilled at the Transfiguration when Peter, James, and John saw his glory (17:1-3). Others say this statement refers to the Resurrection (Matthew 28; Mark 16; Luke 24; John 20) and Ascension of Jesus (Acts 1). Still others believe that Pentecost (Acts 2) and the beginning of Christ's church fulfilled Jesus' words. In any case, certain disciples were eyewitnesses to the power and glory of Christ's Kingdom.

17:1ff The Transfiguration was a vision, a brief glimpse of the true glory of the King (16:27, 28). This was a special revelation of Jesus' divinity to three of the disciples, and it was God's divine affirmation of everything Jesus had done and was about to do.

17:3 The Transfiguration was a foretaste of heaven; the participants were doing something worth noting—talking together. In God's world, interactions count highly. People are individuals, with minds, hearts, and opinions. People are also part of a wider whole, connected by relationships built on sharing between whole persons. Friendship is the key. Make time and opportunities to talk with others. Good conversations act as training for eternity.

17:3-5 Moses and Elijah were the two greatest prophets in the Old Testament. Moses represents the law, or the old covenant.

He wrote the Pentateuch, and he predicted the coming of a great prophet (Deuteronomy 18:15-19). Elijah represents the prophets who foretold the coming of the Messiah (Malachi 4:5, 6). Moses' and Elijah's presence with Jesus confirmed Jesus' messianic mission: to fulfill God's law and the words of God's prophets. Just as God's voice in the cloud over Mount Sinai gave authority to his law (Exodus 19:9), God's voice at the Transfiguration gave authority to Jesus' words.

17:4 Peter wanted to build three memorials for these three great men. Peter had the right idea about Christ, but his timing was wrong. Peter wanted to act, but this was a time for worship and adoration. He wanted to memorialize the moment, but he was supposed to learn and move on.

• **17:5** Jesus is more than just a great leader, a good example, a good influence, or a great prophet. He is the Son of God. When you understand this profound truth, the only adequate response is worship. When you have a correct understanding of Christ, you will obey him.

• **17:9** Jesus told Peter, James, and John not to tell anyone what they had seen until after his resurrection because Jesus knew that they didn't fully understand it and could not explain what they didn't understand. Their question (17:10ff) revealed their misunderstandings. They knew that Jesus was the Messiah, but they had much more to learn about the significance of his death and resurrection.

17:10-12 Based on Malachi 4:5, 6, the teachers of the Old Testament law believed that Elijah must appear before the Messiah would appear. Jesus referred to John the Baptist, not to the Old Testament prophet Elijah. John the Baptist took on Elijah's prophetic role, boldly confronting sin and pointing people to God. Malachi had prophesied that a prophet like Elijah would come (Malachi 4:5).

17:17
Deut 32:5, 20
17:18
Matt 8:13; 9:22;
15:28
17:20
Matt 21:21
Mark 11:23
Luke 17:6
1 Cor 13:2

¹⁷ Jesus said, "You faithless and corrupt people! How long must I be with you? How long must I put up with you? Bring the boy here to me." ¹⁸Then Jesus rebuked the demon in the boy, and it left him. From that moment the boy was well.

¹⁹Afterward the disciples asked Jesus privately, "Why couldn't we cast out that demon?"

²⁰ "You don't have enough faith," Jesus told them. "I tell you the truth, if you had faith even as small as a mustard seed, you could say to this mountain, 'Move from here to there,' and it would move. Nothing would be impossible.*"

Jesus Predicts His Death the Second Time (**113**/Mark 9:30-32; Luke 9:44-45)
²²After they gathered again in Galilee, Jesus told them, "The Son of Man is going to be betrayed into the hands of his enemies. ²³He will be killed, but on the third day he will be raised from the dead." And the disciples were filled with grief.

Peter Finds the Coin in the Fish's Mouth (**114**)

17:24
Exod 30:13
17:25
Matt 22:17-22
Rom 13:7

²⁴On their arrival in Capernaum, the collectors of the Temple tax* came to Peter and asked him, "Doesn't your teacher pay the Temple tax?"

²⁵"Yes, he does," Peter replied. Then he went into the house.

But before he had a chance to speak, Jesus asked him, "What do you think, Peter?* Do kings tax their own people or the people they have conquered?*"

²⁶"They tax the people they have conquered," Peter replied.

"Well, then," Jesus said, "the citizens are free! ²⁷However, we don't want to offend them, so go down to the lake and throw in a line. Open the mouth of the first fish you catch, and you will find a large silver coin.* Take it and pay the tax for both of us."

The Disciples Argue about Who Would Be the Greatest
(**115**/Mark 9:33-37; Luke 9:46-48)

18 About that time the disciples came to Jesus and asked, "Who is greatest in the Kingdom of Heaven?"

17:20 Some manuscripts add verse 21, *But this kind of demon won't leave except by prayer and fasting.* Compare Mark 9:29.   **17:24** Greek *the two-drachma [tax];* also in 17:24b. See Exod 30:13-16; Neh 10:32-33.   **17:25a** Greek *Simon?*   **17:25b** Greek *their sons or others?*   **17:27** Greek *a stater* [a Greek coin equivalent to four drachmas].

17:17 The disciples had been given the authority to do the healing, but they had not yet learned how to appropriate the power of God. Jesus' frustration is with the unbelieving and unresponsive generation. His disciples were merely a reflection of that attitude in this instance. Jesus' purpose was not to criticize the disciples but to encourage them to greater faith.

17:17-20 The disciples had been unable to cast out this demon, and they asked Jesus why. He said their faith was too small. It is the power of God, plus our faith, that moves mountains. The mustard seed was the smallest particle imaginable. Jesus said that even faith as small or undeveloped as a mustard seed would have been sufficient. Perhaps the disciples had tried to cast out the demon with their own ability rather than God's. There is great potential in even a little faith when we trust in God's power to act. If we feel weak or powerless as Christians, we should examine our faith, making sure we are trusting God's power, not our own ability to produce results.

17:20 Jesus wasn't condemning the disciples for substandard faith; he was trying to show how important faith would be in their future ministry. If you are facing a problem that seems as big and immovable as a mountain, turn your eyes from the mountain and look to Christ for more faith. Only then will you be able to overcome the obstacles that may stand in your way.

• **17:22, 23** Once again Jesus predicted his death (see also 16:21); but more important, he told of his resurrection. Unfortunately, the disciples heard only the first part of Jesus' words and became discouraged. They couldn't understand why Jesus wanted to go back to Jerusalem, where he would walk right into trouble.

The disciples didn't fully comprehend the purpose of Jesus' death and resurrection until Pentecost (Acts 2). They didn't know that Jesus' death and resurrection would make his Kingdom possible. We shouldn't get upset at ourselves for being unable to understand everything about Jesus. After all, the disciples spent three years with him, saw his miracles, heard his words, and still

had difficulty understanding. Despite their questions and doubts, however, they believed. We should do no less.

17:24 All Jewish males had to pay a Temple tax to support Temple upkeep (Exodus 30:11-16). Tax collectors set up booths to collect these taxes. Only Matthew records this incident—perhaps because he had been a tax collector himself.

17:24-27 Peter answered a question without really knowing the answer, putting Jesus and the disciples in an awkward position. Jesus used this situation, however, to emphasize his kingly role. Just as kings pay no taxes and collect none from their family, Jesus, the King, owed no taxes. But Jesus supplied the tax payment for both himself and Peter rather than offend those who didn't understand his kingship. Although Jesus supplied the tax money, Peter had to go and get it. Ultimately all that we have comes to us from God's supply, but he may want us to be active in the process.

17:24-27 As God's people, we are foreigners on earth because our loyalty is always to our real King—Jesus. Still we have to cooperate with the authorities and be responsible citizens. An ambassador to another country keeps the local laws in order to represent well the one who sent him. We are Christ's ambassadors (2 Corinthians 5:20). Are you being a good foreign ambassador for him to this world?

18:1 From Mark's Gospel we learn that Jesus precipitated this conversation by asking the disciples what they had been discussing among themselves earlier (Mark 9:33, 34).

18:1-4 Jesus used a child to help his self-centered disciples get the point. We are not to be *childish* (like the disciples, arguing over petty issues) but *childlike*, with humble and sincere hearts. In what areas of your life do you tend to struggle with childishness? In what ways are you making progress with childlikeness?

2 Jesus called a little child to him and put the child among them. 3 Then he said, "I tell you the truth, unless you turn from your sins and become like little children, you will never get into the Kingdom of Heaven. 4 So anyone who becomes as humble as this little child is the greatest in the Kingdom of Heaven.

5 "And anyone who welcomes a little child like this on my behalf* is welcoming me. 6 But if you cause one of these little ones who trusts in me to fall into sin, it would be better for you to have a large millstone tied around your neck and be drowned in the depths of the sea.

Jesus Warns against Temptation (117/Mark 9:42-50)

7 "What sorrow awaits the world, because it tempts people to sin. Temptations are inevitable, but what sorrow awaits the person who does the tempting. 8 So if your hand or foot causes you to sin, cut it off and throw it away. It's better to enter eternal life with only one hand or one foot than to be thrown into eternal fire with both of your hands and feet. 9 And if your eye causes you to sin, gouge it out and throw it away. It's better to enter eternal life with only one eye than to have two eyes and be thrown into the fire of hell.*

Jesus Warns against Looking Down on Others (118)

10 "Beware that you don't look down on any of these little ones. For I tell you that in heaven their angels are always in the presence of my heavenly Father.*

12 "If a man has a hundred sheep and one of them wanders away, what will he do? Won't he leave the ninety-nine others on the hills and go out to search for the one that is lost? 13 And if he finds it, I tell you the truth, he will rejoice over it more than over the ninety-nine that didn't wander away! 14 In the same way, it is not my heavenly Father's will that even one of these little ones should perish.

Jesus Teaches How to Treat a Believer Who Sins (119)

15 "If another believer* sins against you,* go privately and point out the offense. If the other person listens and confesses it, you have won that person back. 16 But if you are unsuccessful, take one or two others with you and go back again, so that everything you say may be confirmed by two or three witnesses. 17 If the person still refuses to listen, take your case to the church. Then if he or she won't accept the church's decision, treat that person as a pagan or a corrupt tax collector.

18 "I tell you the truth, whatever you forbid* on earth will be forbidden in heaven, and whatever you permit* on earth will be permitted in heaven.

18:5 Greek *in my name.* **18:9** Greek *the Gehenna of fire.* **18:10** Some manuscripts add verse 11, *And the Son of Man came to save those who are lost.* Compare Luke 19:10. **18:15a** Greek *If your brother.* **18:15b** Some manuscripts do not include *against you.* **18:18a** Or *bind,* or *lock.* **18:18b** Or *loose,* or *open.*

18:3
Matt 19:14
Mark 10:15
Luke 18:17
1 Pet 2:2

18:4
Matt 20:26-27
Mark 10:43-44
Luke 22:26

18:5
Matt 10:40
Luke 10:16
John 13:20

18:6-9
1 Cor 8:12-13

18:8-9
Matt 5:29-30

18:10
Acts 12:15
Heb 1:14

18:15
Lev 19:17
Gal 6:1
Jas 5:19-20

18:16
†Deut 19:15
2 Cor 13:1
1 Tim 5:19

18:17
1 Cor 6:1-6

18:18
Matt 16:19
John 20:23

18:3, 4 The disciples had become so preoccupied with the organization of Jesus' earthly kingdom that they had lost sight of its divine purpose. Instead of seeking a place of service, they sought positions of advantage. It is easy to lose our eternal perspective and compete for promotions or status in the church. It is difficult, but healthy, to identify with "children"—weak and dependent people with no status or influence.

18:6 Children are trusting by nature. Because they trust adults, they are easily led to faith in Christ. God holds parents and other adults accountable for how they influence these little ones. Jesus warned that anyone who turns little children away from faith in him will receive severe punishment.

18:7ff Jesus warned the disciples about two ways to cause others to sin: tempting them (18:7-9) and neglecting or demeaning them (18:10-14). As leaders, we are to help young people or new believers avoid anything or anyone that could cause them to stumble in their faith and lead them to sin. We must never take lightly the spiritual education and protection of those young in age or young in the faith.

18:8, 9 We must remove stumbling blocks that cause us to sin. This does not mean to cut off a part of the body. For the church it means that any person, program, or teaching that threatens the spiritual growth of the body must be removed. For the individual, any relationship, practice, or activity that leads to sin should be stopped. Jesus says it would be better to go to heaven with one hand than to hell with both. Sin, of course, affects more than our hands; it affects our mind and hearts.

18:12-14 Just as a shepherd is concerned enough about one lost sheep to go search the hills for it, so God is concerned about every human being he has created (he "does not want anyone to be destroyed," 2 Peter 3:9). If you come in contact with children in your neighborhood who need Christ, steer them toward him by your example, your words, and your acts of kindness.

18:15-17 These are Jesus' guidelines for dealing with those who sin against us. They were meant for (1) Christians, not unbelievers, (2) sins committed against *you* and not others, and (3) conflict resolution in the context of the church, not the community at large. Jesus' words are not a license for a frontal attack on every person who hurts or slights us. They are not a license to start a destructive gossip campaign or to call for a church trial. They are designed to reconcile those who disagree so that all Christians can live in harmony.

When someone wrongs us, we often do the opposite of what Jesus recommends. We turn away in hatred or resentment, seek revenge, or engage in gossip. By contrast, we should go to that person *first*, as difficult as that may be. Then we should forgive that person as often as he or she needs it (18:21, 22). This will create a much better chance of restoring the relationship.

18:18 This *forbidding* and *permitting* refers to the decisions of the church in conflicts. Among believers, there should need to be no court of appeals beyond the church. Ideally, the church's decisions should be God-guided and based on discernment of his Word. Believers have the responsibility, therefore, to bring their problems to the church, and the church has the responsibility

18:19
Matt 7:7; 21:22
Mark 11:24
John 15:7; 16:23
1 Jn 3:22; 5:14-15

18:20
Matt 28:20
John 14:23

18:21-22
Luke 17:3-4

18:23
Matt 25:19

18:25
Lev 25:39
2 Kgs 4:1
Neh 5:5

18:27
Luke 7:42

18:34
Matt 5:25-26
Luke 12:58-59

18:35
Matt 6:15
Mark 11:25
Eph 4:32
Col 3:13

¹⁹ "I also tell you this: If two of you agree here on earth concerning anything you ask, my Father in heaven will do it for you. ²⁰ For where two or three gather together as my followers,* I am there among them."

Jesus Tells the Parable of the Unforgiving Debtor (120)

²¹ Then Peter came to him and asked, "Lord, how often should I forgive someone* who sins against me? Seven times?"

²² "No, not seven times," Jesus replied, "but seventy times seven!*

²³ "Therefore, the Kingdom of Heaven can be compared to a king who decided to bring his accounts up to date with servants who had borrowed money from him. ²⁴ In the process, one of his debtors was brought in who owed him millions of dollars.* ²⁵ He couldn't pay, so his master ordered that he be sold—along with his wife, his children, and everything he owned—to pay the debt.

²⁶ "But the man fell down before his master and begged him, 'Please, be patient with me, and I will pay it all.' ²⁷ Then his master was filled with pity for him, and he released him and forgave his debt.

²⁸ "But when the man left the king, he went to a fellow servant who owed him a few thousand dollars.* He grabbed him by the throat and demanded instant payment.

²⁹ "His fellow servant fell down before him and begged for a little more time. 'Be patient with me, and I will pay it,' he pleaded. ³⁰But his creditor wouldn't wait. He had the man arrested and put in prison until the debt could be paid in full.

³¹ "When some of the other servants saw this, they were very upset. They went to the king and told him everything that had happened. ³²Then the king called in the man he had forgiven and said, ' You evil servant! I forgave you that tremendous debt because you pleaded with me. ³³Shouldn't you have mercy on your fellow servant, just as I had mercy on you?' ³⁴Then the angry king sent the man to prison to be tortured until he had paid his entire debt.

³⁵ "That's what my heavenly Father will do to you if you refuse to forgive your brothers and sisters* from your heart."

18:20 Greek *gather together in my name.* **18:21** Greek *my brother.* **18:22** Or *seventy-seven times.* **18:24** Greek *10,000 talents* [375 tons or 340 metric tons of silver]. **18:28** Greek *100 denarii.* A denarius was equivalent to a laborer's full day's wage. **18:35** Greek *your brother.*

JESUS AND FORGIVENESS

Jesus forgave . . .	Reference
the paralyzed man lowered on a mat through the roof	Matthew 9:2-8
the woman caught in adultery.	John 8:3-11
the woman who anointed his feet with perfume	Luke 7:44-50
Peter, for denying he knew Jesus	John 18:15-18, 25-27; 21:15-19
the criminal on the cross.	Luke 23:39-43
the people who crucified him	Luke 23:34

Jesus not only taught frequently about forgiveness, he also demonstrated his own willingness to forgive. Here are several examples that should be an encouragement to recognize his willingness to forgive us also.

---

to use God's guidance in seeking to resolve conflicts. Handling problems God's way will have an impact now and for eternity.

18:19, 20 Jesus looked ahead to a new day when he would be present with his followers not in body, but through his Holy Spirit. In the body of believers (the church), the sincere agreement of two people in prayer is more powerful than the superficial agreement of thousands, because Christ's Holy Spirit is with them. Two or more believers, *filled with the Holy Spirit,* will pray according to God's will, not their own; thus, their requests will be granted.

18:22 The rabbis taught that people should forgive those who offend them—but only three times. Peter, trying to be especially generous, asked Jesus if seven (the "perfect" number) was enough times to forgive someone. But Jesus answered, "Seventy times seven," meaning that we shouldn't even keep track of how many times we forgive someone. We

should always forgive those who are truly repentant, no matter how many times they ask.

18:30 In Bible times, serious consequences awaited those who could not pay their debts. A person lending money could seize the borrower who couldn't pay and force him or his family to work until the debt was paid. The debtor could also be thrown into prison, or his family could be sold into slavery to help pay off the debt. It was hoped that the debtor, while in prison, would sell off his landholdings or that relatives would pay the debt. If not, the debtor could remain in prison for life.

18:35 Because God has forgiven all our sins, we should not withhold forgiveness from others. As we realize how completely Christ has forgiven us, it should produce an attitude of forgiveness toward others. When we don't forgive others, we are setting ourselves above Christ's law of love.

6. Jesus faces conflict with the religious leaders

Jesus Teaches about Marriage and Divorce (**173**/Mark 10:1-12)

19 When Jesus had finished saying these things, he left Galilee and went down to the region of Judea east of the Jordan River. ²Large crowds followed him there, and he healed their sick.

19:2
Matt 4:23

³Some Pharisees came and tried to trap him with this question: "Should a man be allowed to divorce his wife for just any reason?"

19:3
Matt 5:31

⁴ "Haven't you read the Scriptures?" Jesus replied. "They record that from the beginning 'God made them male and female.'* ⁵And he said, 'This explains why a man leaves his father and mother and is joined to his wife, and the two are united into one.'* ⁶ Since they are no longer two but one, let no one split apart what God has joined together."

19:4
†Gen 1:27; 5:2
19:5
†Gen 2:24
1 Cor 6:16
Eph 5:31

⁷"Then why did Moses say in the law that a man could give his wife a written notice of divorce and send her away?"* they asked.

19:7
†Deut 24:1
Matt 5:31

⁸ Jesus replied, "Moses permitted divorce only as a concession to your hard hearts, but it was not what God had originally intended. ⁹And I tell you this, whoever divorces his wife and marries someone else commits adultery—unless his wife has been unfaithful.*"

19:9
Matt 5:32
Luke 16:18
1 Cor 7:10-11

¹⁰ Jesus' disciples then said to him, "If this is the case, it is better not to marry!"

¹¹"Not everyone can accept this statement," Jesus said. "Only those whom God helps. ¹²Some are born as eunuchs, some have been made eunuchs by others, and some choose not to marry* for the sake of the Kingdom of Heaven. Let anyone accept this who can."

19:11
1 Cor 7:7-9, 17
19:12
1 Cor 7:32, 34

Jesus Blesses the Children (**174**/Mark 10:13-16; Luke 18:15-17)

¹³One day some parents brought their children to Jesus so he could lay his hands on them and pray for them. But the disciples scolded the parents for bothering him.

¹⁴ But Jesus said, "Let the children come to me. Don't stop them! For the Kingdom of Heaven belongs to those who are like these children." ¹⁵And he placed his hands on their heads and blessed them before he left.

19:14
Matt 18:2-3

19:4 Gen 1:27; 5:2.   **19:5** Gen 2:24.   **19:7** See Deut 24:1.   **19:9** Some manuscripts add *And anyone who marries a divorced woman commits adultery.* Compare Matt 5:32.   **19:12** Greek *and some make themselves eunuchs.*

19:3-12 John had been put in prison and killed, at least in part for his public opinions on marriage and divorce, so the Pharisees hoped to trap Jesus, too. They were trying to trick Jesus by having him choose sides in a theological controversy. Two schools of thought represented two opposing views of divorce. One group supported divorce for almost any reason. The other believed that divorce could be allowed only for marital unfaithfulness. This conflict hinged on how each group interpreted Deuteronomy 24:1-4. In his answer, however, Jesus focused on marriage rather than divorce. He pointed out that God intended marriage to be permanent and gave four reasons for the importance of marriage (19:4-6).

19:4-6 Today, many homosexuals want to commit to "marry" with the blessing of the church. Reasons for homosexual feelings and desires are complex and serious. Christians should not trivialize the situation or flippantly condemn the homosexual person. But Jesus made God's ideal very plain: At creation he approved one kind of marriage bond, man to woman. These become one flesh—one before God. See Romans 1:24-27 for further discussion.

Where does that leave homosexual marriage? At best, it is a human invention without any biblical precedent. God created man and woman. Heterosexual monogamy is God's plan for marriage—the best plan, the only one.

19:7, 8 This law is found in Deuteronomy 24:1-4. In Moses' day, as well as in Jesus' day, the practice of marriage fell far short of God's intention. The same is true today. Jesus said that Moses gave this law only because of the people's hard hearts—permanent marriage was God's intention. But because sinful human nature made divorce inevitable, Moses instituted some

laws to help its victims. These were civil laws designed especially to protect the women who, in that culture, were quite vulnerable when living alone. Because of Moses' law, a man could no longer just throw his wife out—he had to write a formal letter of dismissal. This was a radical step toward civil rights, for it made men think twice about divorce. God designed marriage to be indissoluble. Instead of looking for reasons to leave each other, husbands and wives should concentrate on how to stay together (19:3-9).

19:10-12 Although divorce was relatively easy in Old Testament times (19:7), it is not what God originally intended. Couples should decide against divorce from the start and build their marriage on mutual commitment. There are also many good reasons for not marrying, one being to have more time to work for God's Kingdom. Don't assume that God wants everyone to marry. For many it may be better if they don't. Be sure that you prayerfully seek God's will before you make the lifelong commitment of marriage.

19:12 A "eunuch" is an emasculated male—a man with no testicles. Jesus' point here is that some people have physical limitations that prevent their marrying, while others choose not to marry because, in their particular situation, they can serve God better as single people. Jesus was not teaching us to avoid marriage because it is inconvenient or takes away our freedom. That would be selfishness. A good reason to remain single is to use the time and freedom to serve God. Paul elaborates on this in 1 Corinthians 7.

19:13-15 The disciples must have forgotten what Jesus had said about children (18:4-6). Jesus wanted little children to come to him because he loves them and because they have a guileless trust in God. All people need childlike faith in God. The receptiveness of little children was a great contrast to the stubbornness of the religious leaders, who let their education and sophistication stand in the way of the simple faith needed to believe in Jesus.

Jesus Speaks to the Rich Young Man (175/Mark 10:17-31; Luke 18:18-30)

19:16
Matt 19:29
Luke 10:25

19:17
Lev 18:5
Luke 10:28

19:18
†Exod 20:12-16
†Deut 5:17-21

19:19
Exod 20:12
†Lev 19:18
Deut 5:16
Matt 5:43-44; 22:39
Luke 10:27
Rom 13:9

19:21
Acts 2:45; 4:34-37

19:23
Matt 13:22
1 Tim 6:9-10

19:26
Gen 18:14
Job 42:2
Jer 32:17
Zech 8:6

19:27
Matt 4:19

16Someone came to Jesus with this question: "Teacher,* what good deed must I do to have eternal life?"

17 "Why ask me about what is good?" Jesus replied. "There is only One who is good. But to answer your question—if you want to receive eternal life, keep* the commandments."

18"Which ones?" the man asked.

And Jesus replied: "'You must not murder. You must not commit adultery. You must not steal. You must not testify falsely. 19 Honor your father and mother. Love your neighbor as yourself.'* "

20"I've obeyed all these commandments," the young man replied. "What else must I do?"

21 Jesus told him, "If you want to be perfect, go and sell all your possessions and give the money to the poor, and you will have treasure in heaven. Then come, follow me."

22 But when the young man heard this, he went away sad, for he had many possessions.

23 Then Jesus said to his disciples, "I tell you the truth, it is very hard for a rich person to enter the Kingdom of Heaven. 24I'll say it again—it is easier for a camel to go through the eye of a needle than for a rich person to enter the Kingdom of God!"

25 The disciples were astounded. "Then who in the world can be saved?" they asked.

26 Jesus looked at them intently and said, "Humanly speaking, it is impossible. But with God everything is possible."

27 Then Peter said to him, "We've given up everything to follow you. What will we get?"

19:16 Some manuscripts read *Good Teacher.* **19:17** Some manuscripts read *continue to keep.* **19:18-19** Exod 20:12-16; Deut 5:16-20; Lev 19:18.

19:16 To this man seeking assurance of eternal life, Jesus pointed out that salvation does not come from good deeds unaccompanied by love for God. The man needed a whole new starting point. Instead of adding another commandment to keep or good deed to perform, the young man needed to submit humbly to the lordship of Christ.

19:17ff In response to the young man's question about what good deed he needed to do in order to be assured of eternal life, Jesus told him to keep God's Ten Commandments. Jesus then listed six of them, all referring to relationships with others. When the young man replied that he had kept the commandments, Jesus told him that he must do something more—sell everything and give the money to the poor. Jesus' statement exposed the man's weakness. In reality, his wealth was his god, his idol, and he would not give it up. Thus, he violated the first and greatest commandment (Exodus 20:3; Matthew 22:36-40).

19:21 When Jesus told this young man that he would "be perfect" if he gave everything he had to the poor, Jesus wasn't speaking in the temporal, human sense. He was explaining how to be justified and made whole or complete in God's sight.

19:21 Should all believers sell everything they own? No. We are responsible to care for our own needs and the needs of our families so as not to be a burden on others. We should, however, be willing to give up anything if God asks us to do so. This kind of attitude allows nothing to come between us and God and keeps us from using our God-given wealth selfishly. If you are relieved by the fact that Christ did not tell all his followers to sell all their possessions, then you may be too attached to what you have.

19:22 We cannot love God with all our heart and yet keep our money to ourselves. Loving him totally means using our money in ways that please him.

19:24-26 Because it is impossible for a camel to go through the eye of a needle, it appears impossible for a rich person to get into the Kingdom of Heaven. The disciples were astounded. They thought that if anyone could be saved, it would be the rich, whom their culture considered especially blessed by God. Jesus explained, however, that "with God everything is possible" (19:26). Even rich people can enter the Kingdom if God brings them in. Faith in Christ, not in self or riches, is what counts. On what are you counting for salvation?

19:27 In the Bible, God gives rewards to his people according to his justice. In the Old Testament, obedience often brought reward in this life (Deuteronomy 28), but obedience and immediate reward are not always linked. If they were, good people would always be rich, and suffering would always be a sign of sin. As believers, our reward is God's presence and power through his indwelling Holy Spirit. Later, in eternity, we will be rewarded for our faith and service. If material rewards in this life came to us for every faithful deed, we would be tempted to boast about our achievements and act out of wrong motivations.

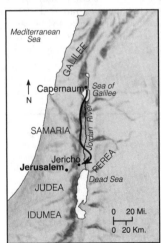

JESUS TRAVELS TOWARD JERUSALEM
Jesus left Galilee for the last time—heading toward Jerusalem and death. He again crossed the Jordan, spending some time in Perea before going on to Jericho.

28 Jesus replied, "I assure you that when the world is made new* and the Son of Man* sits upon his glorious throne, you who have been my followers will also sit on twelve thrones, judging the twelve tribes of Israel. 29And everyone who has given up houses or brothers or sisters or father or mother or children or property, for my sake, will receive a hundred times as much in return and will inherit eternal life. 30 But many who are the greatest now will be least important then, and those who seem least important now will be the greatest then.*

19:28
Luke 22:28-30
Rev 3:21

19:30
Matt 20:16
Mark 10:31
Luke 13:30

Jesus Tells the Parable of the Vineyard Workers (176)

20 "For the Kingdom of Heaven is like the landowner who went out early one morning to hire workers for his vineyard. 2He agreed to pay the normal daily wage* and sent them out to work.

20:1
Matt 21:28, 33

3 "At nine o'clock in the morning he was passing through the marketplace and saw some people standing around doing nothing. 4So he hired them, telling them he would pay them whatever was right at the end of the day. 5So they went to work in the vineyard. At noon and again at three o'clock he did the same thing.

6 "At five o'clock that afternoon he was in town again and saw some more people standing around. He asked them, 'Why haven't you been working today?'

7 "They replied, 'Because no one hired us.'

"The landowner told them, 'Then go out and join the others in my vineyard.'

8 "That evening he told the foreman to call the workers in and pay them, beginning with the last workers first. 9When those hired at five o'clock were paid, each received a full day's wage. 10When those hired first came to get their pay, they assumed they would receive more. But they, too, were paid a day's wage. 11When they received their pay, they protested to the owner, 12 'Those people worked only one hour, and yet you've paid them just as much as you paid us who worked all day in the scorching heat.'

20:8
Lev 19:13
Deut 24:15

13 "He answered one of them, 'Friend, I haven't been unfair! Didn't you agree to work all day for the usual wage? 14Take your money and go. I wanted to pay this last worker the same as you. 15 Is it against the law for me to do what I want with my money? Should you be jealous because I am kind to others?'

16 "So those who are last now will be first then, and those who are first will be last."

20:15
Deut 15:9
20:16
Matt 19:30
Mark 10:31
Luke 13:30

Jesus Predicts His Death the Third Time (177/Mark 10:32-34; Luke 18:31-34)

17As Jesus was going up to Jerusalem, he took the twelve disciples aside privately and told them what was going to happen to him. 18 "Listen," he said, "we're going up to Jerusalem, where the Son of Man* will be betrayed to the leading priests and the teachers of religious law. They will sentence him to die. 19 Then they will hand him over to the Romans* to be mocked, flogged with a whip, and crucified. But on the third day he will be raised from the dead."

20:18-19
Matt 16:21;
17:22-23
Luke 9:22
Acts 2:23

19:28a Or *in the regeneration.*   **19:28b** "Son of Man" is a title Jesus used for himself.   **19:30** Greek *But many who are first will be last; and the last, first.*   **20:2** Greek *a denarius,* the payment for a full day's labor; similarly in 20:9, 10, 13.   **20:18** "Son of Man" is a title Jesus used for himself.   **20:19** Greek *the Gentiles.*

19:29 Jesus assured the disciples that anyone who gives up something valuable for his sake will be repaid many times over in this life, although not necessarily in the same form. For example, a person may be rejected by his or her family for accepting Christ, but he or she will gain the larger family of believers.

19:30 Jesus turned the world's values upside down. Consider the most powerful or well-known people in our world—how many got where they are by being humble, self-effacing, and gentle? Not many! But in the life to come, the last will be first. Don't forfeit eternal rewards for temporary benefits. Be willing to make sacrifices now for greater rewards later. Be willing to accept human disapproval, while knowing that you have God's approval.

20:1ff Jesus further clarified the membership rules of the Kingdom of Heaven: Entrance is by God's grace alone. In this parable, God is the landowner and believers are the workers. This parable speaks especially to those who feel superior because of heritage or position, to those who feel superior because they have spent

so much time with Christ, and to new believers as reassurance of God's grace.

20:15 This parable is not about rewards but about salvation. It is a strong teaching about *grace,* God's generosity. We shouldn't begrudge those who turn to God in the last moments of life, because, in reality, *no one* deserves eternal life.

Many people we don't expect to see in the Kingdom will be there. The criminal who repented as he was dying (Luke 23:40-43) will be there along with people who have believed and served God for many years. Do you resent God's gracious acceptance of the despised, the outcast, and the sinners who have turned to him for forgiveness? Have you ever been jealous of what God has given to another person? Instead, focus on God's gracious benefits to you, and be thankful for what you have.

20:17-19 Jesus predicted his death and resurrection for the third time (see 16:21 and 17:22, 23 for the first two times). But the disciples still didn't accept and believe what he meant. They continued to argue over their positions in Christ's Kingdom (20:20-28).

Jesus Teaches about Serving Others (**178**/Mark 10:35-45)

20:21
Matt 19:28

20Then the mother of James and John, the sons of Zebedee, came to Jesus with her sons. She knelt respectfully to ask a favor. 21 "What is your request?" he asked.

She replied, "In your Kingdom, please let my two sons sit in places of honor next to you, one on your right and the other on your left."

20:22
Matt 26:39, 42
Mark 14:36
Luke 22:42
John 18:11

22 But Jesus answered by saying to them, "You don't know what you are asking! Are you able to drink from the bitter cup of suffering I am about to drink?"

"Oh yes," they replied, "we are able!"

20:23
Acts 12:2
Rev 1:9

23 Jesus told them, "You will indeed drink from my bitter cup. But I have no right to say who will sit on my right or my left. My Father has prepared those places for the ones he has chosen."

20:26
Matt 23:11
Mark 9:35
Luke 9:48

24When the ten other disciples heard what James and John had asked, they were indignant. 25 But Jesus called them together and said, "You know that the rulers in this world lord it over their people, and officials flaunt their authority over those under them. 26But among you it will be different. Whoever wants to be a leader among you must be your servant,

20:28
Isa 53:10
Phil 2:7
1 Tim 2:6
1 Pet 1:18-19

27and whoever wants to be first among you must become your slave. 28 For even the Son of Man came not to be served but to serve others and to give his life as a ransom for many."

Jesus Heals Two Blind Beggars (**179**/Mark 10:46-52; Luke 18:35-43)

29As Jesus and the disciples left the town of Jericho, a large crowd followed behind. 30Two blind men were sitting beside the road. When they heard that Jesus was coming that way, they began shouting, "Lord, Son of David, have mercy on us!"

31"Be quiet!" the crowd yelled at them.

But they only shouted louder, "Lord, Son of David, have mercy on us!"

32When Jesus heard them, he stopped and called, "What do you want me to do for you?"

33"Lord," they said, "we want to see!" 34Jesus felt sorry for them and touched their eyes. Instantly they could see! Then they followed him.

20:20 The mother of James and John came to Jesus and "knelt respectfully to ask a favor." She gave Jesus worship, but her real motive was to get something from him. Too often this happens in our churches and in our life. We play religious games, expecting God to give us something in return. True worship, however, adores and praises Christ for who he is and for what he has done.

20:20 The mother of James and John asked Jesus to give her sons special positions in his Kingdom. Parents naturally want to see their children promoted and honored, but this desire is dangerous if it causes them to stand in the way of God's specific will for their children. God may have different work in mind for them—perhaps not as glamorous but just as important. Thus, parents' desires for their children's advancement must be held in check as they pray that God's will be done in their children's lives.

20:20 According to 27:56, the mother of James and John was at the cross when Jesus was crucified. Some have suggested that she was the sister of Mary, the mother of Jesus. A close family relationship may have prompted her to make this request for her sons.

20:22 James, John, and their mother failed to grasp Jesus' previous teachings on rewards (19:16-30) and eternal life (20:1-16). They failed to understand the suffering they must face before living in the glory of God's Kingdom. The "cup" was the suffering and crucifixion that Christ faced. Both James and John would also face great suffering. James would be put to death for his faith, and John would be exiled.

20:23 Jesus was showing that he was under the authority of the Father, who alone makes the decisions about leadership in heaven. Such rewards are not granted as favors. They are for those who have maintained their commitment to Jesus in spite of severe trials.

20:24 The other disciples were upset with James and John for trying to grab the top positions. *All* the disciples wanted to be the greatest (18:1), but Jesus taught them that the greatest person in

God's Kingdom is the servant of all. Authority is given, not for self-importance, ambition, or respect, but for useful service to God and his creation.

20:27 Jesus described leadership from a new perspective. Instead of using people, we are to serve them. Jesus' mission was to serve others and to give his life away. A real leader has a servant's heart. Servant leaders appreciate others' worth and realize that they're not above any job. If you see something that needs to be done, don't wait to be asked. Take the initiative and do it like a faithful servant.

20:28 A "ransom" was the price paid to release a slave from bondage. Jesus often told his disciples that he must die, but here he told them why—to redeem all people from the bondage of sin and death. The disciples thought that as long as Jesus was alive, he could save them. But Jesus revealed that only his death would save them and the world.

20:29-34 Matthew records that there were two blind men, while Mark and Luke mention only one. This is probably the same event, but Mark and Luke singled out the more vocal of the two men.

20:30 The blind men called Jesus "Son of David" because the Jews knew that the Messiah would be a descendant of David (see Isaiah 9:6, 7; 11:1; Jeremiah 23:5, 6). These blind beggars could *see* that Jesus was the long-awaited Messiah, while the religious leaders who witnessed Jesus' miracles were blind to his identity, refusing to open their eyes to the truth. Seeing with your eyes doesn't guarantee seeing with your heart.

20:32, 33 Although Jesus was concerned about the coming events in Jerusalem, he demonstrated what he had just told the disciples about service (20:28) by stopping to care for the blind men.

Jesus Rides into Jerusalem on a Donkey
(**183**/Mark 11:1-11; Luke 19:28-44; John 12:12-19)

21 As Jesus and the disciples approached Jerusalem, they came to the town of Bethphage on the Mount of Olives. Jesus sent two of them on ahead. 2 "Go into the village over there," he said. "As soon as you enter it, you will see a donkey tied there, with its colt beside it. Untie them and bring them to me. 3If anyone asks what you are doing, just say, 'The Lord needs them,' and he will immediately let you take them."

4This took place to fulfill the prophecy that said,

5 "Tell the people of Jerusalem,*
'Look, your King is coming to you.
He is humble, riding on a donkey—
riding on a donkey's colt.'"*

6The two disciples did as Jesus commanded. 7They brought the donkey and the colt to him and threw their garments over the colt, and he sat on it.*

8Most of the crowd spread their garments on the road ahead of him, and others cut branches from the trees and spread them on the road. 9Jesus was in the center of the procession, and the people all around him were shouting,

"Praise God* for the Son of David!
Blessings on the one who comes in the name of the LORD!
Praise God in highest heaven!"*

10The entire city of Jerusalem was in an uproar as he entered. "Who is this?" they asked. 11And the crowds replied, "It's Jesus, the prophet from Nazareth in Galilee."

Jesus Clears the Temple Again (**184**/Mark 11:12-19; Luke 19:45-48)
12Jesus entered the Temple and began to drive out all the people buying and selling animals for sacrifice. He knocked over the tables of the money changers and the chairs of those selling doves. 13He said to them, "The Scriptures declare, 'My Temple will be called a house of prayer,' but you have turned it into a den of thieves!" *

14The blind and the lame came to him in the Temple, and he healed them. 15The leading priests and the teachers of religious law saw these wonderful miracles and heard even the children in the Temple shouting, "Praise God for the Son of David."

21:5
†Isa 62:11
†Zech 9:9

21:9
†Pss 118:25-26;
148:1
Luke 13:35

21:11
Luke 7:16, 39
John 1:21, 25;
6:14; 7:40; 9:17

21:13
†Isa 56:7
†Jer 7:11

21:14
Isa 35:5-6

21:15
Matt 21:9

21:5a Greek *Tell the daughter of Zion.* Isa 62:11.   **21:5b** Zech 9:9.   **21:7** Greek *over them, and he sat on them.*
21:9a Greek *Hosanna,* an exclamation of praise that literally means "save now"; also in 21:9b, 15.   **21:9b** Pss
118:25-26; 148:1.   **21:13** Isa 56:7; Jer 7:11.

21:2-5 Matthew mentions a donkey and a colt, while the other Gospels mention only the colt. This was the same event, but Matthew focuses on the prophecy in Zechariah 9:9, where a

PREPARATION FOR THE TRIUMPHAL ENTRY
On their way from Jericho, Jesus and the disciples neared Bethphage, on the slope of the Mount of Olives, just outside Jerusalem. Two disciples went into the village, as Jesus told them, to bring back a donkey and its colt. Jesus rode into Jerusalem on the colt, an unmistakable sign of his kingship.

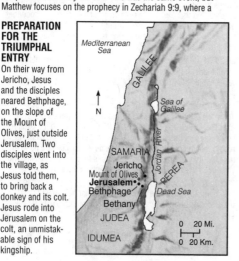

donkey and a colt are mentioned. He shows how Jesus' actions fulfilled the prophet's words, thus giving another indication that Jesus was indeed the Messiah. When Jesus entered Jerusalem on a donkey's colt, he affirmed his messianic royalty as well as his humility. On the practical side, what better way to lead an unbroken colt for its first ride down a crowded road than to have its mother with it?

21:8 This verse is one of the few places where the Gospels record that Jesus' glory is recognized on earth. Jesus boldly rode as the King of peace, and the crowd gladly joined him. But these same people would bow to political pressure and desert him in just a few days. Today we celebrate this event on Palm Sunday. That day should remind us to guard against superficial acclaim for Christ.

21:12 This is the second time Jesus cleared the Temple (see John 2:13-17). Merchants and money changers set up their booths in the Court of the Gentiles in the Temple, crowding out the Gentiles who had come from all over the civilized world to worship God. The merchants sold sacrificial animals at high prices, taking advantage of those who had come long distances. The money changers exchanged all international currency for the special Temple coins—the only money the merchants would accept. They often deceived foreigners who didn't know the exchange rates. Their commercialism in God's house frustrated people's attempts at worship. This, of course, greatly angered Jesus. Any practice that interferes with worshiping God should be stopped.

21:16
†Ps 8:2

But the leaders were indignant. ¹⁶They asked Jesus, "Do you hear what these children are saying?"

21:17
Mark 11:1
John 11:1, 18; 12:1

"Yes," Jesus replied. "Haven't you ever read the Scriptures? For they say, 'You have taught children and infants to give you praise.'*" ¹⁷Then he returned to Bethany, where he stayed overnight.

Jesus Says the Disciples Can Pray for Anything (**188**/Mark 11:20-26)

¹⁸In the morning, as Jesus was returning to Jerusalem, he was hungry, ¹⁹and he noticed a fig tree beside the road. He went over to see if there were any figs, but there were only leaves. Then he said to it, "May you never bear fruit again!" And immediately the fig tree withered up.

21:21
Matt 17:20
Luke 17:6
1 Cor 13:2
Jas 1:6

²⁰The disciples were amazed when they saw this and asked, "How did the fig tree wither so quickly?"

²¹Then Jesus told them, "I tell you the truth, if you have faith and don't doubt, you can do things like this and much more. You can even say to this mountain, 'May you be lifted up and thrown into the sea,' and it will happen. ²² You can pray for anything, and if you have faith, you will receive it."

21:22
Matt 7:7-11
John 14:13-14

Religious Leaders Challenge Jesus' Authority (**189**/Mark 11:27-33; Luke 20:1-8)

21:23
Acts 4:7

²³When Jesus returned to the Temple and began teaching, the leading priests and elders came up to him. They demanded, "By what authority are you doing all these things? Who gave you the right?"

²⁴ "I'll tell you by what authority I do these things if you answer one question," Jesus replied. ²⁵ "Did John's authority to baptize come from heaven, or was it merely human?"

They talked it over among themselves. "If we say it was from heaven, he will ask us why we didn't believe John. ²⁶But if we say it was merely human, we'll be mobbed because the people believe John was a prophet." ²⁷ So they finally replied, "We don't know."

21:26
Matt 11:9

And Jesus responded, "Then I won't tell you by what authority I do these things.

Jesus Tells the Parable of the Two Sons (**190**)

21:28
Luke 15:11

²⁸ "But what do you think about this? A man with two sons told the older boy, 'Son, go out and work in the vineyard today.' ²⁹The son answered, 'No, I won't go,' but later he changed his mind and went anyway. ³⁰ Then the father told the other son, 'You go,' and he said, 'Yes, sir, I will.' But he didn't go.

³¹ "Which of the two obeyed his father?"

They replied, "The first."*

21:16 Ps 8:2.   **21:29-31** Other manuscripts read *"The second."* In still other manuscripts the first son says "Yes" but does nothing, the second son says "No" but then repents and goes, and the answer to Jesus' question is that the second son obeyed his father.

21:19 Why did Jesus curse the fig tree? This was not a thoughtless, angry act but an acted-out parable. Jesus was showing his anger at religion without substance. Just as the fig tree looked good from a distance but was fruitless on close examination, so the Temple looked impressive at first glance, but its sacrifices and other activities were hollow because they were not done to worship God sincerely (see 21:43). If you only appear to have faith without putting it to work in your life, you are like the fig tree that withered and died because it bore no fruit. Genuine faith means bearing fruit for God's Kingdom. For more information about the fig tree, see the note on Mark 11:13-26.

21:21 Many have wondered about Jesus' statement that if we have faith and don't doubt, we can move mountains. Jesus, of course, was not suggesting that his followers use prayer as "magic" and perform capricious "mountain moving" acts. Instead, he was making a strong point about the disciples' (and our) lack of faith. What kinds of mountains do you face? Have you talked to God about them? How strong is your faith?

21:22 This verse is not a guarantee that we can get *anything* we want simply by asking Jesus and believing. God does not grant requests that would hurt us or others or that would violate his own nature or will. Jesus' statement is not a blank check. To be fulfilled, our requests must be in harmony with the principles of God's Kingdom. The stronger our belief, the more likely our

prayers will be in line with God's will, and then God will be happy to grant them.

21:23-27 The Pharisees demanded to know where Jesus got his authority. If Jesus said his authority came from God, they would accuse him of blasphemy. If he said that he was acting on his own authority, the crowds would be convinced that the Pharisees had the greater authority. But Jesus answered them with a seemingly unrelated question that exposed their real motives. They didn't really want an answer to their question; they only wanted to trap him. Jesus showed that the Pharisees wanted the truth only if it supported their own views and causes.

21:25 For more information on John the Baptist, see Matthew 3 and his Profile in John 1, p. 1749.

• **21:30** The son who said he would obey and then didn't represented many of the people of Israel in Jesus' day, particularly the religious leaders. They said they wanted to do God's will, but they constantly disobeyed. They were phony, just going through the motions. It is dangerous to pretend to obey God when our heart is far from him because God knows our true intentions. Our actions must match our words.

Then Jesus explained his meaning: "I tell you the truth, corrupt tax collectors and prostitutes will get into the Kingdom of God before you do. 32 For John the Baptist came and showed you the right way to live, but you didn't believe him, while tax collectors and prostitutes did. And even when you saw this happening, you refused to believe him and repent of your sins.

21:32
Matt 3:1-12
Luke 3:12-13;
7:29-30

Jesus Tells the Parable of the Evil Farmers (191/Mark 12:1-12; Luke 20:9-19)

33 "Now listen to another story. A certain landowner planted a vineyard, built a wall around it, dug a pit for pressing out the grape juice, and built a lookout tower. Then he leased the vineyard to tenant farmers and moved to another country. 34At the time of the grape harvest, he sent his servants to collect his share of the crop. 35 But the farmers grabbed his servants, beat one, killed one, and stoned another. 36 So the landowner sent a larger group of his servants to collect for him, but the results were the same.

21:33
Isa 5:1-2

21:35
Matt 23:34, 37

37 "Finally, the owner sent his son, thinking, 'Surely they will respect my son.'

38 "But when the tenant farmers saw his son coming, they said to one another, 'Here comes the heir to this estate. Come on, let's kill him and get the estate for ourselves!' 39So they grabbed him, dragged him out of the vineyard, and murdered him.

40 "When the owner of the vineyard returns," Jesus asked, "what do you think he will do to those farmers?"

41The religious leaders replied, "He will put the wicked men to a horrible death and lease the vineyard to others who will give him his share of the crop after each harvest."

42Then Jesus asked them, "Didn't you ever read this in the Scriptures?

21:41
Matt 8:11-12
Luke 21:24
Acts 13:46

21:42
†Ps 118:22-23
Isa 28:16
Acts 4:11
Eph 2:20
1 Pet 2:6-7

'The stone that the builders rejected
    has now become the cornerstone.
This is the LORD's doing,
    and it is wonderful to see.'*

43I tell you, the Kingdom of God will be taken away from you and given to a nation that will produce the proper fruit. 44Anyone who stumbles over that stone will be broken to pieces, and it will crush anyone it falls on.*"

45When the leading priests and Pharisees heard this parable, they realized he was telling the story against them—they were the wicked farmers. 46They wanted to arrest him, but they were afraid of the crowds, who considered Jesus to be a prophet.

21:44
Isa 8:14-15
Dan 2:34-35, 44-45

21:46
Matt 21:26

Jesus Tells the Parable of the Wedding Dinner (192)

22 Jesus also told them other parables. He said, 2 "The Kingdom of Heaven can be illustrated by the story of a king who prepared a great wedding feast for his son. 3 When the banquet was ready, he sent his servants to notify those who were invited. But they all refused to come!

4 "So he sent other servants to tell them, 'The feast has been prepared. The bulls and fattened cattle have been killed, and everything is ready. Come to the banquet!' 5But the guests he had invited ignored them and went their own way, one to his farm, another to his business. 6 Others seized his messengers and insulted them and killed them.

22:3
Matt 21:34

22:4
Matt 21:36

22:6
Matt 21:35

21:42 Ps 118:22-23.   **21:44** This verse is not included in some early manuscripts. Compare Luke 20:18.

• **21:33ff** The main elements in this parable are (1) the landowner—God, (2) the vineyard—Israel, (3) the tenant farmers—the Jewish religious leaders, (4) the landowner's servants—the prophets and priests who remained faithful to God and preached to Israel, (5) the son—Jesus (21:38), and (6) the other tenants—the Gentiles. Jesus was exposing the religious leaders' murderous plot (21:45).

21:37 In trying to reach us with his love, God finally sent his own Son. Jesus' perfect life, his words of truth, and his sacrifice of love are meant to cause us to listen to him and to follow him as Lord. If we ignore God's gracious gift of his Son, we reject God himself.

21:42 Jesus refers to himself as "the stone that the builders rejected." Although Jesus was rejected by many of his people,

he will become the cornerstone of his new building, the church (see Acts 4:11; 1 Peter 2:7).

21:44 Jesus used this metaphor to show that one truth can affect people in different ways, depending on how they relate to it (see Isaiah 8:14, 15; 28:16; Daniel 2:34, 44, 45). Ideally they will build on it; many, however, will trip over it. And at the Last Judgment God's enemies will be crushed by it. In the end, Christ, the "building block," will become the "crushing stone." He offers mercy and forgiveness *now* and promises judgment later. We should choose him now!

22:1-14 In this culture, two invitations were expected when banquets were given. The first asked the guests to attend; the second announced that all was ready. In this story the king invited his guests three times, and each time they rejected his invitation. God wants us to join him at his banquet, which will last for eternity. That's why he sends us invitations again and again. Have you accepted his invitation?

22:7
Luke 19:27

22:8
Acts 13:46

22:10
Matt 13:47-48

22:12
Matt 20:13; 26:50

22:13
Matt 8:12; 25:30

22:14
2 Pet 1:10
Rev 17:14

7"The king was furious, and he sent out his army to destroy the murderers and burn their town. 8And he said to his servants,' The wedding feast is ready, and the guests I invited aren't worthy of the honor. 9 Now go out to the street corners and invite everyone you see.' 10So the servants brought in everyone they could find, good and bad alike, and the banquet hall was filled with guests.

11 "But when the king came in to meet the guests, he noticed a man who wasn't wearing the proper clothes for a wedding. 12 'Friend,' he asked, 'how is it that you are here without wedding clothes?' But the man had no reply. 13Then the king said to his aides, 'Bind his hands and feet and throw him into the outer darkness, where there will be weeping and gnashing of teeth.'

14 "For many are called, but few are chosen."

Religious Leaders Question Jesus about Paying Taxes
(193/Mark 12:13-17; Luke 20:20-26)

22:17
Matt 17:25

15Then the Pharisees met together to plot how to trap Jesus into saying something for which he could be arrested. 16 They sent some of their disciples, along with the supporters of Herod, to meet with him. "Teacher," they said, "we know how honest you are. You teach the way of God truthfully. You are impartial and don't play favorites. 17Now tell us what you think about this: Is it right to pay taxes to Caesar or not?"

18 But Jesus knew their evil motives. "You hypocrites!" he said. "Why are you trying to trap me? 19 Here, show me the coin used for the tax." When they handed him a Roman coin,* 20 he asked, "Whose picture and title are stamped on it?"

22:21
Rom 13:7

21"Caesar's," they replied.

"Well, then," he said, "give to Caesar what belongs to Caesar, and give to God what belongs to God."

22 His reply amazed them, and they went away.

Religious Leaders Question Jesus about the Resurrection
(194/Mark 12:18-27; Luke 20:27-40)

22:23
Acts 23:8
1 Cor 15:12

22:24
†Deut 25:5-6

23That same day Jesus was approached by some Sadducees—religious leaders who say there is no resurrection from the dead. They posed this question: 24"Teacher, Moses said, 'If a man dies without children, his brother should marry the widow and have a child who will carry on the brother's name.'* 25 Well, suppose there were seven brothers. The oldest one married and then died without children, so his brother married the widow. 26But the second brother also died, and the third brother married her. This continued with all seven

22:19 Greek *a denarius*.   **22:24** Deut 25:5-6.

22:11, 12 It was customary for wedding guests to be given wedding clothes to wear to the banquet. It was unthinkable to refuse to wear these clothes. That would insult the host, who could only assume that the guest was arrogant and thought he didn't need these clothes, or that he did not want to take part in the wedding celebration. The wedding clothes picture the righteousness needed to enter God's Kingdom—the total acceptance in God's eyes that Christ gives every believer. Christ has provided these clothes of righteousness for everyone, but each person must choose to put them on in order to enter the King's banquet (eternal life). There is an open invitation, but we must be ready. For more on the imagery of clothes of righteousness and salvation, see Psalm 132:16; Isaiah 61:10; Zechariah 3:3-5; Revelation 3:4, 5; 19:7, 8.

22:15-17 The Pharisees, a religious group, opposed the Roman occupation of Palestine. The supporters of Herod, a political party, supported Herod Antipas and the policies instituted by Rome. Normally these two groups were bitter enemies, but here they united against Jesus. Thinking they had a foolproof plan to corner him, together their representatives asked Jesus about paying Roman taxes. If Jesus agreed that it was right to pay taxes to Caesar, the Pharisees would say he was opposed to God, the only King they recognized. If Jesus said the taxes should not be paid, the supporters of Herod would hand him over to Herod on the charge of rebellion. In this case the Pharisees were not motivated by love for God's laws, and Herod's supporters were not motivated by love for Roman justice. Jesus' answer exposed their evil motives and embarrassed them both.

22:17 The Jews were required to pay taxes to support the Roman government. They hated this taxation because the money went directly into Caesar's treasury, where some of it went to support the pagan temples and decadent lifestyle of the Roman aristocracy. Caesar's image on the coins was a constant reminder of Israel's subjection to Rome.

22:21 Jesus avoided this trap by showing that we have dual citizenship (1 Peter 2:17). Our citizenship in the nation requires that we pay money for the services and benefits we receive. Our citizenship in the Kingdom of Heaven requires that we pledge to God our ultimate obedience and commitment.

22:23ff After the Pharisees and supporters of Herod had failed to trap Jesus, the Sadducees smugly stepped in to try. They did not believe in the resurrection because the Pentateuch (Genesis—Deuteronomy) has no direct teaching on it. The Pharisees had never been able to come up with a convincing argument from the Pentateuch for the resurrection, and the Sadducees thought they had trapped Jesus for sure. But Jesus was about to show them otherwise (see 22:31, 32 for Jesus' answer).

22:24 The law said that when a woman's husband died without having a son, the man's brother had a responsibility to marry and care for the widow (Deuteronomy 25:5, 6). This law protected women who were left alone, because in that culture they usually had no other means to support themselves.

of them. 27Last of all, the woman also died. 28So tell us, whose wife will she be in the resurrection? For all seven were married to her."

29 Jesus replied, "Your mistake is that you don't know the Scriptures, and you don't know the power of God. 30 For when the dead rise, they will neither marry nor be given in marriage. In this respect they will be like the angels in heaven.

31 "But now, as to whether there will be a resurrection of the dead—haven't you ever read about this in the Scriptures? Long after Abraham, Isaac, and Jacob had died, God said,* 32 'I am the God of Abraham, the God of Isaac, and the God of Jacob.'* So he is the God of the living, not the dead."

33When the crowds heard him, they were astounded at his teaching.

Religious Leaders Question Jesus about the Greatest Commandment
(**195**/Mark 12:28-34)

34But when the Pharisees heard that he had silenced the Sadducees with his reply, they met together to question him again. 35One of them, an expert in religious law, tried to trap him with this question: 36"Teacher, which is the most important commandment in the law of Moses?"

37 Jesus replied, "'You must love the LORD your God with all your heart, all your soul, and all your mind.'* 38This is the first and greatest commandment. 39A second is equally important: 'Love your neighbor as yourself.'* 40 The entire law and all the demands of the prophets are based on these two commandments."

Religious Leaders Cannot Answer Jesus' Question
(**196**/Mark 12:35-37; Luke 20:41-44)

41Then, surrounded by the Pharisees, Jesus asked them a question: 42"What do you think about the Messiah? Whose son is he?"

They replied, "He is the son of David."

43 Jesus responded, "Then why does David, speaking under the inspiration of the Spirit, call the Messiah 'my Lord'? For David said,

44 'The LORD said to my Lord,
Sit in the place of honor at my right hand
    until I humble your enemies beneath your feet.'*

45Since David called the Messiah 'my Lord,' how can the Messiah be his son?"

46No one could answer him. And after that, no one dared to ask him any more questions.

22:31 Greek *read about this? God said.*   **22:32** Exod 3:6.   **22:37** Deut 6:5.   **22:39** Lev 19:18.   **22:44** Ps 110:1.

22:29
John 20:9

22:32
†Exod 3:6, 15-16
Acts 7:32

22:33
Matt 7:28; 13:54
Mark 11:18

22:35
Luke 10:25

22:37
†Deut 6:5

22:39
†Lev 19:18
Matt 5:43; 19:19
Mark 12:31
Luke 10:27
Rom 13:9

22:40
Matt 7:12
Luke 10:25-28
Rom 13:10

22:43
2 Sam 23:2
Acts 2:30
2 Pet 1:20-21

22:44
†Ps 110:1
Acts 2:34-35
Heb 1:13

22:46
Mark 12:34
Luke 20:40

22:29, 30 The Sadducees asked Jesus what marriage would be like in heaven. Jesus said it was more important to understand God's power than know what heaven will be like. In every generation and culture, ideas of eternal life tend to be based on images and experiences of present life. Jesus answered that these faulty ideas are caused by ignorance of God's Word. We must not make up our own ideas about eternity and heaven by thinking of it and God in human terms. We should concentrate more on our relationship with God than about what heaven will look like. Eventually we will find out, and it will be far beyond our greatest expectations.

22:31, 32 Because the Sadducees accepted only the Pentateuch as God's divine Word, Jesus answered them from the book of Exodus (3:6). God would not have said, "I *am* the God of Abraham, the God of Isaac, and the God of Jacob" if God thought of Abraham, Isaac, and Jacob as dead. From God's perspective, they are alive. Jesus' use of the present tense pointed to the resurrection and the eternal life that all believers enjoy in him.

22:34 We might think the Pharisees would have been glad to see the Sadducees silenced. The question that the Sadducees had always used to trap them was finally answered by Jesus. But the Pharisees were too proud to be impressed. Jesus'

answer gave them a theological victory over the Sadducees, but they were more interested in defeating Jesus than in learning the truth.

22:35-40 The Pharisees, who had classified over 600 laws, often tried to distinguish the more important from the less important. So one of them, an "expert in religious law," asked Jesus to identify the most important law. Jesus quoted from Deuteronomy 6:5 and Leviticus 19:18. By fulfilling these two commands, a person keeps all the others. They summarize the Ten Commandments and the other Old Testament moral laws.

22:37-40 Jesus said that if we truly love God and our neighbor, we will naturally keep the commandments. This is looking at God's law positively. Rather than worrying about all we should *not* do, we should concentrate on all we *can* do to show our love for God and others.

22:41-45 The Pharisees, Sadducees, and supporters of Herod had asked their questions. Then Jesus turned the tables and asked them a penetrating question—who they thought the Messiah was. The Pharisees knew that the Messiah would be a descendant of David, but they did not understand that he would be God himself. Jesus quoted from Psalm 110:1 to show that the Messiah would be greater than David. (Hebrews 1:13 uses the same text as proof of Christ's deity.) The most important question we will ever answer is what we believe about Christ. Other theological questions are irrelevant until we believe that Jesus is who he said he is.

Jesus Warns against the Religious Leaders (197/Mark 12:38-40; Luke 20:45-47)

23:2
Ezra 7:6, 25
Neh 8:1-4

23:4
Luke 11:46
Acts 15:20
Gal 6:13

23:5
Exod 13:9
Num 15:37-40
Deut 6:8

23:11
Matt 20:26-27
Mark 9:35;
10:43-45
Luke 9:48; 22:26

23:12
Job 22:29
Prov 29:23
Ezek 21:26
Luke 14:11; 18:14

23 Then Jesus said to the crowds and to his disciples, 2 "The teachers of religious law and the Pharisees are the official interpreters of the law of Moses.* 3So practice and obey whatever they tell you, but don't follow their example. For they don't practice what they teach. 4They crush people with unbearable religious demands and never lift a finger to ease the burden.

5 "Everything they do is for show. On their arms they wear extra wide prayer boxes with Scripture verses inside, and they wear robes with extra long tassels.* 6And they love to sit at the head table at banquets and in the seats of honor in the synagogues. 7They love to receive respectful greetings as they walk in the marketplaces, and to be called 'Rabbi.'*

8 "Don't let anyone call you 'Rabbi,' for you have only one teacher, and all of you are equal as brothers and sisters.* 9And don't address anyone here on earth as 'Father,' for only God in heaven is your spiritual Father. 10And don't let anyone call you ' Teacher,' for you have only one teacher, the Messiah. 11The greatest among you must be a servant. 12 But those who exalt themselves will be humbled, and those who humble themselves will be exalted.

Jesus Condemns the Religious Leaders (198)

23:13
Luke 11:52

13 "What sorrow awaits you teachers of religious law and you Pharisees. Hypocrites! For you shut the door of the Kingdom of Heaven in people's faces. You won't go in yourselves, and you don't let others enter either.*

23:2 Greek *and the Pharisees sit in the seat of Moses.*   **23:5** Greek *They enlarge their phylacteries and lengthen their tassels.*   **23:7** *Rabbi, from Aramaic, means "master" or "teacher."*   **23:8** Greek *brothers.*   **23:13** Some manuscripts add verse 14, *What sorrow awaits you teachers of religious law and you Pharisees. Hypocrites! You shamelessly cheat widows out of their property and then pretend to be pious by making long prayers in public. Because of this, you will be severely punished.* Compare Mark 12:40 and Luke 20:47.

THE SEVEN SORROWS

23:13	Not letting others enter the Kingdom of Heaven and not entering yourselves
23:15	Converting people away from God to be like yourselves
23:16-22	Blindly leading God's people to follow man-made traditions instead of God's Word
23:23, 24	Involving yourself in every last detail and ignoring what is really important: justice, mercy, and faith
23:25, 26	Keeping up appearances while your private world is corrupt
23:27, 28	Acting spiritual to cover up sin
23:29-36	Pretending to have learned from past history, but your present behavior shows you have learned nothing

Jesus mentioned seven ways to guarantee God's anger, when he told the religious leaders, " What sorrow awaits you." These seven statements were strong and unforgettable. They are still applicable anytime we become so involved in perfecting the practice of religion that we forget that God is also concerned with mercy, real love, and forgiveness.

● **23:2, 3** The Pharisees' traditions and their interpretations and applications of the laws had become as important to them as God's law itself. Their laws were not all bad—some were beneficial. Problems arose when the religious leaders (1) held that man-made rules were equal to God's laws, (2) told the people to obey these rules but did not do so themselves, or (3) obeyed the rules, not to honor God, but to make themselves look good. Usually Jesus did not condemn what the Pharisees taught but what they *were*—hypocrites.

● **23:5** These "prayer boxes" were leather boxes containing Scripture verses. Very religious people wore these boxes on their foreheads and arms in order to obey Deuteronomy 6:8 and Exodus 13:9, 16. But the prayer boxes had been made extra wide and had become more important for the status they gave than for the truth they contained.

● **23:5-7** Jesus again exposed the hypocritical attitudes of the religious leaders. They knew the Scriptures but did not live by them. They didn't care about *being* holy—just *looking* holy in order to receive people's admiration and praise. Today, like the Pharisees, many people say they know the Bible but do not let it change their lives. They say they follow Jesus, but they don't live by his standards of love. We must make sure that our actions match our beliefs.

23:5-7 People desire positions of leadership not only in business but also in the church. It is dangerous when love for position grows stronger than loyalty to God. This is what happened to the Pharisees and teachers of religious law. Jesus condemned leaders who serve themselves rather than others.

23:11, 12 Jesus challenged society's norms. To him, greatness comes from serving—giving of yourself to help God and others. Service keeps us aware of others' needs, and it stops us from focusing only on ourselves. Jesus came as a servant. What kind of greatness do you seek?

● **23:13, 14** Being a religious leader in Jerusalem was very different from being a pastor in a secular society today. Israel's history, culture, and daily life centered around its relationship with God. The religious leaders were the best known, most powerful, and most respected of all leaders. Jesus made these stinging accusations because the leaders' hunger for more power, money, and status had made them lose sight of God, and their blindness was spreading to the whole nation.

¹⁵ "What sorrow awaits you teachers of religious law and you Pharisees. Hypocrites! For you cross land and sea to make one convert, and then you turn that person into twice the child of hell* you yourselves are!

¹⁶ "Blind guides! What sorrow awaits you! For you say that it means nothing to swear 'by God's Temple,' but that it is binding to swear 'by the gold in the Temple.' ¹⁷ Blind fools! Which is more important—the gold or the Temple that makes the gold sacred? ¹⁸And you say that to swear 'by the altar' is not binding, but to swear 'by the gifts on the altar' is binding. ¹⁹ How blind! For which is more important—the gift on the altar or the altar that makes the gift sacred? ²⁰When you swear 'by the altar,' you are swearing by it and by everything on it. ²¹And when you swear 'by the Temple,' you are swearing by it and by God, who lives in it. ²²And when you swear 'by heaven,' you are swearing by the throne of God and by God, who sits on the throne.

²³ "What sorrow awaits you teachers of religious law and you Pharisees. Hypocrites! For you are careful to tithe even the tiniest income from your herb gardens,* but you ignore the more important aspects of the law—justice, mercy, and faith. You should tithe, yes, but do not neglect the more important things. ²⁴ Blind guides! You strain your water so you won't accidentally swallow a gnat, but you swallow a camel!*

²⁵ "What sorrow awaits you teachers of religious law and you Pharisees. Hypocrites! For you are so careful to clean the outside of the cup and the dish, but inside you are filthy—full of greed and self-indulgence! ²⁶ You blind Pharisee! First wash the inside of the cup and the dish,* and then the outside will become clean, too.

²⁷ "What sorrow awaits you teachers of religious law and you Pharisees. Hypocrites! For you are like whitewashed tombs—beautiful on the outside but filled on the inside with dead people's bones and all sorts of impurity. ²⁸ Outwardly you look like righteous people, but inwardly your hearts are filled with hypocrisy and lawlessness.

²⁹ "What sorrow awaits you teachers of religious law and you Pharisees. Hypocrites! For you build tombs for the prophets your ancestors killed, and you decorate the monuments of the godly people your ancestors destroyed. ³⁰ Then you say, 'If we had lived in the days of our ancestors, we would never have joined them in killing the prophets.'

³¹ "But in saying that, you testify against yourselves that you are indeed the descendants of those who murdered the prophets. ³² Go ahead and finish what your ancestors started. ³³Snakes! Sons of vipers! How will you escape the judgment of hell?

³⁴ "Therefore, I am sending you prophets and wise men and teachers of religious law. But you will kill some by crucifixion, and you will flog others with whips in your synagogues, chasing them from city to city. ³⁵As a result, you will be held responsible for the murder of all godly people of all time—from the murder of righteous Abel to the murder of Zechariah son of Barachiah, whom you killed in the Temple between the sanctuary and the altar. ³⁶ I tell you the truth, this judgment will fall on this very generation.

23:15 Greek *of Gehenna;* also in 23:33.   **23:23** Greek *tithe the mint, the dill, and the cumin.*   **23:24** See Lev 11:4, 23, where gnats and camels are both forbidden as food.   **23:26** Some manuscripts do not include *and the dish.*

23:16
Isa 9:16
Matt 5:33-35; 15:14
Rom 2:19

23:19
Exod 29:37

23:21
1 Kgs 8:13
Ps 26:8

23:22
Ps 11:4
Isa 66:1
Matt 5:34
Acts 7:49

23:23
Lev 27:30
Hos 6:6
Mic 6:8
Zech 7:9
Luke 11:42

23:24
Matt 23:16

23:25
Mark 7:4

23:27
Luke 11:44
Acts 23:3

23:28
Luke 16:15

23:31
Acts 7:52

23:33
Matt 3:7; 12:34
Luke 3:7

23:34
Matt 10:23
Acts 7:52; 22:19
2 Cor 11:23-25
1 Thes 2:15

23:35
Gen 4:8
2 Chr 24:20-21
Zech 1:1
Heb 11:4

• **23:15** The Pharisees' converts were attracted to religion, not to God. By getting caught up in the details of their additional laws and regulations, they completely missed God, to whom the laws pointed. A religion of works puts pressure on people to surpass others in what they know and do. Thus, a hypocritical teacher was likely to have students who were even more hypocritical. We must make sure we are not creating Pharisees by emphasizing outward obedience at the expense of inner renewal.

• **23:23, 24** It's possible to obey the details of the laws but still be disobedient in our general behavior. For example, we could be very precise and faithful about giving 10 percent of our money to God but refuse to give one minute of our time in helping others. Tithing is important, but giving a tithe does not exempt us from fulfilling God's other directives.

• **23:24** The Pharisees strained their water so they wouldn't accidentally swallow a gnat—an unclean insect according to the law. Meticulous about the details of ceremonial cleanliness, they nevertheless had lost their perspective on inner purity—in essence, they would then swallow a camel and not even notice. They were ceremonially clean on the outside but had corrupt hearts.

• **23:25-28** Jesus condemned the Pharisees and religious leaders for outwardly appearing upright and holy but inwardly remaining full of corruption and greed. Living our Christianity merely as a show for others is like washing only the outside of a cup. When we are clean on the inside, our cleanliness on the outside won't be a sham.

• **23:34-36** These prophets, wise men, and teachers were probably leaders in the early church who were persecuted, scourged, and killed, as Jesus predicted. The people of Jesus' generation said they would not act as their fathers did in killing the prophets whom God sent to them (23:30), but they were about to kill the Messiah himself and his faithful followers. Thus, they would become guilty of all the righteous blood shed through the centuries.

23:35 Jesus summarized the history of Old Testament martyrdom. Abel was the first martyr (Genesis 4); Zechariah was the last mentioned in the Hebrew Bible, which ended with 2 Chronicles. Zechariah is a classic example of a man of God who was killed by those who claimed to be God's people (see 2 Chronicles 24:20, 21).

Jesus Grieves over Jerusalem Again (199)

37 "O Jerusalem, Jerusalem, the city that kills the prophets and stones God's messengers! How often I have wanted to gather your children together as a hen protects her chicks beneath her wings, but you wouldn't let me. 38And now, look, your house is abandoned and desolate.* 39 For I tell you this, you will never see me again until you say, 'Blessings on the one who comes in the name of the LORD!'* "

23:39
†Ps 118:26
Matt 21:9
Mark 11:10
Luke 19:38

7. Jesus teaches on the Mount of Olives

Jesus Tells about the Future (201/Mark 13:1-23; Luke 21:5-24)

24 As Jesus was leaving the Temple grounds, his disciples pointed out to him the various Temple buildings. 2But he responded, "Do you see all these buildings? I tell you the truth, they will be completely demolished. Not one stone will be left on top of another!"

24:2
Luke 19:44

3Later, Jesus sat on the Mount of Olives. His disciples came to him privately and said, "Tell us, when will all this happen? What sign will signal your return and the end of the world?*"

24:3
Matt 13:39; 28:20
Luke 17:30

4Jesus told them, "Don't let anyone mislead you, 5for many will come in my name, claiming, 'I am the Messiah.' They will deceive many. 6And you will hear of wars and threats of wars, but don't panic. Yes, these things must take place, but the end won't follow immediately. 7 Nation will go to war against nation, and kingdom against kingdom. There will be famines and earthquakes in many parts of the world. 8 But all this is only the first of the birth pains, with more to come.

24:4
Mark 13:5

24:5
Matt 24:11, 23-24
John 5:43
1 Jn 2:18

24:6
Dan 2:28-29

24:7
Isa 19:2

9 "Then you will be arrested, persecuted, and killed. You will be hated all over the world because you are my followers.* 10And many will turn away from me and betray and hate each other. 11And many false prophets will appear and will deceive many people. 12 Sin will be rampant everywhere, and the love of many will grow cold. 13 But the one who endures to

24:9-14
Matt 10:17-22

24:9
John 16:2

24:11
Matt 24:5, 24

23:38 Some manuscripts do not include *and desolate.*   **23:39** Ps 118:26.   **24:3** Or *the age?*   **24:9** Greek *on account of my name.*

23:37 Jesus wanted to gather his people together as a hen protects her chicks under her wings, but they wouldn't let him. Jesus also wants to protect us if we will just come to him. Many times we hurt and don't know where to turn. We reject Christ's help because we don't think he can give us what we need. But who knows our needs better than our Creator? Those who turn to Jesus will find that he helps and comforts as no one else can.

23:37 Jerusalem was the capital city of God's chosen people, the ancestral home of David, Israel's greatest king, and the location of the Temple, the earthly dwelling place of God. It was intended to be the center of worship of the true God and a symbol of justice to all people. But Jerusalem had become blind to God and insensitive to human need. Here we see the depth of Jesus' feelings for lost people and for his beloved city, which would soon be destroyed.

24:1, 2 Although no one knows exactly what this Temple looked like, it must have been beautiful. Herod had helped the Jews remodel and beautify it, no doubt to stay on friendly terms with his subjects. Next to the inner Temple, where the sacred objects were kept and the sacrifices offered, there was a large area called the Court of the Gentiles (where the money changers and merchants had their booths). Outside these courts were long porches. Solomon's Colonnade was 1,562 feet long, decorated with 160 columns stretching along its 921-foot length. Gazing at this glorious and massive structure, the disciples found Jesus' words about its destruction difficult to believe. But the Temple was indeed destroyed only 40 years later when the Romans sacked Jerusalem in A.D. 70.

• **24:3ff** Jesus was sitting on the Mount of Olives, the very place where the prophet Zechariah had predicted that the Messiah would stand when he came to establish his Kingdom (Zechariah 14:4). It was a fitting place for the disciples to ask Jesus when he would come in power and what they could expect then. Jesus' reply emphasized the events that would take place before the end of the age. He pointed out that his disciples should be less concerned with knowing the exact date and more concerned with being prepared—living God's way consistently so that no matter when Jesus came, they would be ready.

24:4 The disciples asked Jesus for the sign of his coming and of the end of the age. Jesus' first response was "Don't let anyone mislead you." The fact is that whenever we look for signs, we become very susceptible to being deceived. There are many "false prophets" (24:11, 24) around with counterfeit signs of spiritual power and authority. The only sure way to keep from being deceived is to focus on Christ and his words. Don't look for special signs, and don't spend time looking at other people. Look at Christ.

24:9-13 You may not be facing intense persecution now, but Christians in other parts of the world are. As you hear about Christians suffering for their faith, remember that they are your brothers and sisters in Christ. Pray for them. Ask God what you can do to help them in their troubles. When one part of the body suffers, the *whole* body suffers. But when all the parts join together to ease the suffering, the whole body benefits (1 Corinthians 12:26).

24:11 The Old Testament frequently mentions false prophets (see 2 Kings 3:13; Isaiah 44:25; Jeremiah 23:16; Ezekiel 13:2, 3; Micah 3:5; Zechariah 13:2). False prophets claimed to receive messages from God, but they preached a "health and wealth" message. They said what the people wanted to hear, even when the nation was not following God as it should. There were false prophets in Jesus' day, and we have them today. They are the popular leaders who tell people what they want to hear, such as "God wants you to be rich," "Do whatever your desires tell you," or "There is no such thing as sin or hell." Jesus said false teachers would come, and he warned his disciples, as he warns us, not to listen to their dangerous words.

24:12 With false teaching and loose morals comes a particularly destructive disease—the loss of true love for God and others. Sin cools your love for God and others by turning your focus on yourself. You cannot truly love if you think only of yourself.

the end will be saved. ¹⁴And the Good News about the Kingdom will be preached through-out the whole world, so that all nations* will hear it; and then the end will come.

¹⁵ "The day is coming when you will see what Daniel the prophet spoke about—the sacri-legious object that causes desecration* standing in the Holy Place." (Reader, pay attention!) ¹⁶ "Then those in Judea must flee to the hills. ¹⁷A person out on the deck of a roof must not go down into the house to pack. ¹⁸A person out in the field must not return even to get a coat. ¹⁹ How terrible it will be for pregnant women and for nursing mothers in those days. ²⁰And pray that your flight will not be in winter or on the Sabbath. ²¹ For there will be greater anguish than at any time since the world began. And it will never be so great again. ²²In fact, unless that time of calamity is shortened, not a single person will survive. But it will be short-ened for the sake of God's chosen ones.

²³ "Then if anyone tells you, 'Look, here is the Messiah,' or 'There he is,' don't believe it. ²⁴For false messiahs and false prophets will rise up and perform great signs and wonders so as to deceive, if possible, even God's chosen ones. ²⁵ See, I have warned you about this ahead of time.

Jesus Tells about His Return (**202**/Mark 13:24-31; Luke 21:25-33)
²⁶ "So if someone tells you, 'Look, the Messiah is out in the desert,' don't bother to go and look. Or, 'Look, he is hiding here,' don't believe it! ²⁷For as the lightning flashes in the east and shines to the west, so it will be when the Son of Man* comes. ²⁸ Just as the gathering of vultures shows there is a carcass nearby, so these signs indicate that the end is near.*

²⁹ "Immediately after the anguish of those days,

the sun will be darkened,
    the moon will give no light,
the stars will fall from the sky,
    and the powers in the heavens will be shaken.*

³⁰And then at last, the sign that the Son of Man is coming will appear in the heavens, and there will be deep mourning among all the peoples of the earth. And they will see the Son of Man coming on the clouds of heaven with power and great glory.* ³¹And he will send out his angels with the mighty blast of a trumpet, and they will gather his chosen ones from all over the world*—from the farthest ends of the earth and heaven.

³² "Now learn a lesson from the fig tree. When its branches bud and its leaves begin to sprout, you know that summer is near. ³³ In the same way, when you see all these things, you can know his return is very near, right at the door. ³⁴ I tell you the truth, this generation* will not pass from the scene until all these things take place. ³⁵ Heaven and earth will disappear, but my words will never disappear.

24:14	Matt 28:19 / Rev 3:10; 16:14
24:15	Dan 9:27; 11:31; 12:11
24:17	Luke 17:31
24:21	Dan 12:1 / Joel 2:2 / Rev 3:10; 7:14
24:23-24	Luke 17:21-23 / 2 Thes 2:9-10 / 1 Jn 4:1-3 / Rev 13:13-14
24:26-27	Luke 17:23-24
24:28	Luke 17:37 / Rev 19:17
24:29	Isa 13:10; 34:4 / Ezek 32:7 / Joel 2:10, 31; 3:15 / Rev 6:12-13
24:30	†Dan 7:13 / Zech 12:10-14 / Rev 1:7
24:31	1 Cor 15:52 / 1 Thes 4:16 / Rev 8:2; 11:15
24:33	Jas 5:9
24:34	Matt 16:28
24:35	Matt 5:18 / Luke 16:17

24:14 Or *all peoples.*   **24:15** Greek *the abomination of desolation.* See Dan 9:27; 11:31; 12:11.   **24:27** "Son of Man" is a title Jesus used for himself.   **24:28** Greek *Wherever the carcass is, the vultures gather.*   **24:29** See Isa 13:10; 34:4; Joel 2:10.   **24:30** See Dan 7:13.   **24:31** Greek *from the four winds.*   **24:34** Or *this age,* or *this nation.*

24:14 Jesus said that before he returns, the Good News about the Kingdom (the message of salvation) would be preached throughout the world. This was the disciples' mission—and it is ours today. Jesus talked about the end times and final judgment to show his followers the urgency of spreading the Good News of salvation to everyone.

24:15, 16 What was "the sacrilegious object that causes desecration" mentioned by both Daniel and Jesus? Rather than one specific object, event, or person, it could be seen as any deliberate attempt to mock and deny the reality of God's presence. Daniel's prediction came true in 168 B.C. when Antiochus Epiphanes sacrificed a pig to Zeus on the sacred Temple altar (Daniel 9:27; 11:30, 31). Jesus' words were remembered in A.D. 70 when Titus placed an idol on the site of the burned Temple after destroying Jerusalem. In the end times the Antichrist will set up an image of himself and order everyone to worship it (2 Thessalonians 2:4; Revelation 13:14, 15). These are all abominations to God.

24:21, 22 Jesus, talking about the end times, telescoped near future and far future events, as did the Old Testament prophets. Many of these persecutions have already occurred; more are yet to come. But God is in control of even the length of persecutions. He will not forget his people. This is all we need to know about the future to motivate us to live rightly now.

24:23, 24 Jesus' warnings about false teachers still hold true. Upon close examination it becomes clear that many nice-sounding messages don't agree with God's message in the Bible. Only a solid foundation in God's Word can equip us to perceive the errors and distortions in false teaching.

24:24-28 In times of persecution even strong believers will find it difficult to be loyal. To keep from being deceived by false messiahs, we must understand that Jesus' return will be unmis-takable (Mark 13:26); no one will doubt that it is he. If you have to be told that the Messiah has come, then he hasn't (24:27). Christ's coming will be obvious to everyone.

24:30 The nations of the earth will mourn because unbelievers will suddenly realize they have chosen the wrong side. Everything they have scoffed about will be happening, and it will be too late for them.

Jesus Tells about Remaining Watchful (203/Mark 13:32-37; Luke 21:34-38)

24:36
Acts 1:7
1 Thes 5:1-2

24:37-39
Gen 6:9–7:24

36 "However, no one knows the day or hour when these things will happen, not even the angels in heaven or the Son himself.* Only the Father knows.

37 "When the Son of Man returns, it will be like it was in Noah's day. 38In those days before the flood, the people were enjoying banquets and parties and weddings right up to the time Noah entered his boat. 39People didn't realize what was going to happen until the flood came and swept them all away. That is the way it will be when the Son of Man comes.

24:40-41
Luke 17:34-35

40 "Two men will be working together in the field; one will be taken, the other left. 41Two women will be grinding flour at the mill; one will be taken, the other left.

24:42
Matt 25:13
Luke 12:40
1 Thes 5:6
Rev 3:3; 16:15

42 "So you, too, must keep watch! For you don't know what day your Lord is coming. 43 Understand this: If a homeowner knew exactly when a burglar was coming, he would keep watch and not permit his house to be broken into. 44 You also must be ready all the time, for the Son of Man will come when least expected.

45 "A faithful, sensible servant is one to whom the master can give the responsibility of managing his other household servants and feeding them. 46 If the master returns and finds that the servant has done a good job, there will be a reward. 47I tell you the truth, the master will put that servant in charge of all he owns. 48 But what if the servant is evil and thinks, 'My master won't be back for a while,' 49 and he begins beating the other servants, partying, and

24:51
Matt 8:12; 25:30

getting drunk? 50The master will return unannounced and unexpected, 51 and he will cut the servant to pieces and assign him a place with the hypocrites. In that place there will be weeping and gnashing of teeth.

Jesus Tells the Parable of the Ten Bridesmaids (204)

25:1
Luke 12:35-38

25 "Then the Kingdom of Heaven will be like ten bridesmaids* who took their lamps and went to meet the bridegroom. 2 Five of them were foolish, and five were wise.

25:5
1 Thes 5:6

3The five who were foolish didn't take enough olive oil for their lamps, 4but the other five were wise enough to take along extra oil. 5When the bridegroom was delayed, they all became drowsy and fell asleep.

6 "At midnight they were roused by the shout, 'Look, the bridegroom is coming! Come out and meet him!'

25:8
Luke 12:35-40

7 "All the bridesmaids got up and prepared their lamps. 8Then the five foolish ones asked the others, 'Please give us some of your oil because our lamps are going out.'

9 "But the others replied, ' We don't have enough for all of us. Go to a shop and buy some for yourselves.'

25:10
Luke 13:24-25
Rev 19:9

10 "But while they were gone to buy oil, the bridegroom came. Then those who were ready went in with him to the marriage feast, and the door was locked. 11Later, when the other five

25:13
Matt 24:42, 44
Mark 13:35
Luke 12:40

bridesmaids returned, they stood outside, calling, 'Lord! Lord! Open the door for us!'

12 "But he called back, 'Believe me, I don't know you!'

13 "So you, too, must keep watch! For you do not know the day or hour of my return.

24:36 Some manuscripts do not include *or the Son himself.*   **25:1** Or *virgins;* also in 25:7, 11.

24:36 It is good that we don't know exactly when Christ will return. If we knew the precise date, we might be tempted to be lazy in our work for Christ. Worse yet, we might plan to keep sinning and then turn to God right at the end. Heaven is not our only goal; we have work to do here. And we must keep on doing it until death or until we see the unmistakable return of our Savior.

24:40-42 Christ's second coming will be swift and sudden. There will be no opportunity for last-minute repentance or bargaining. The choice we have already made will determine our eternal destiny.

24:44 Jesus' purpose in telling about his return is not to stimulate predictions and calculations about the date but to warn us to be prepared. Will you be ready? The only safe choice is to obey him *today* (24:46).

24:45-47 Jesus asks us to spend the time of waiting taking care of his people and doing his work here on earth, both within the church and outside it. This is the best way to prepare for Christ's return.

24:51 "Weeping and gnashing of teeth" is a phrase used to describe despair. God's coming judgment is as certain as Jesus' return to earth.

• **25:1ff** Jesus told the following parables to clarify further what it means to be ready for his return and how to live until he comes. In the story of the 10 bridesmaids (25:1-13), we are taught that every person is responsible for his or her own spiritual condition. The story of the three servants (25:14-30) shows the necessity of using well what God has entrusted to us. The parable of the sheep and goats (25:31-46) stresses the importance of serving others in need. No parable by itself *completely* describes our preparation. Instead, each paints one part of the whole picture.

25:1ff This parable is about a wedding. On the wedding day the bridegroom went to the bride's house for the ceremony; then the bride and groom, along with a great procession, returned to the groom's house, where a feast took place, often lasting a full week.

These 10 bridesmaids were waiting to join the procession, and they hoped to take part in the marriage feast. But when the groom didn't come at the expected time, five of them were out of lamp oil. By the time they had purchased extra oil, it was too late to join the feast.

When Jesus returns to take his people to heaven, we must be ready. Spiritual preparation cannot be bought or borrowed at the last minute. Our relationship with God must be our own.

Jesus Tells the Parable of the Loaned Money (205)

14 "Again, the Kingdom of Heaven can be illustrated by the story of a man going on a long trip. He called together his servants and entrusted his money to them while he was gone. 15 He gave five bags of silver* to one, two bags of silver to another, and one bag of silver to the last—dividing it in proportion to their abilities. He then left on his trip.

25:15
Matt 18:24-25
Rom 12:3, 6

16 "The servant who received the five bags of silver began to invest the money and earned five more. 17The servant with two bags of silver also went to work and earned two more. 18But the servant who received the one bag of silver dug a hole in the ground and hid the master's money.

19 "After a long time their master returned from his trip and called them to give an account of how they had used his money. 20The servant to whom he had entrusted the five bags of silver came forward with five more and said, 'Master, you gave me five bags of silver to invest, and I have earned five more.'

25:19
Matt 18:23

21 "The master was full of praise. ' Well done, my good and faithful servant. You have been faithful in handling this small amount, so now I will give you many more responsibilities. Let's celebrate together!*'

25:21
Matt 24:45-46
Luke 16:10

22 "The servant who had received the two bags of silver came forward and said, 'Master, you gave me two bags of silver to invest, and I have earned two more.'

23 "The master said, 'Well done, my good and faithful servant. You have been faithful in handling this small amount, so now I will give you many more responsibilities. Let's celebrate together!'

24 "Then the servant with the one bag of silver came and said, 'Master, I knew you were a harsh man, harvesting crops you didn't plant and gathering crops you didn't cultivate. 25I was afraid I would lose your money, so I hid it in the earth. Look, here is your money back.'

26 "But the master replied, 'You wicked and lazy servant! If you knew I harvested crops I didn't plant and gathered crops I didn't cultivate, 27why didn't you deposit my money in the bank? At least I could have gotten some interest on it.'

28 "Then he ordered,' Take the money from this servant, and give it to the one with the ten bags of silver. 29 To those who use well what they are given, even more will be given, and they will have an abundance. But from those who do nothing, even what little they have will be taken away. 30Now throw this useless servant into outer darkness, where there will be weeping and gnashing of teeth.'

25:29
Matt 13:12
Mark 4:25
Luke 8:18
25:30
Matt 8:12
Luke 13:28

Jesus Tells about the Final Judgment (206)

31"But when the Son of Man* comes in his glory, and all the angels with him, then he will sit upon his glorious throne. 32All the nations* will be gathered in his presence, and he will separate the people as a shepherd separates the sheep from the goats. 33 He will place the sheep at his right hand and the goats at his left.

25:31
Dan 7:13
Zech 14:5
Rev 20:11
25:32
Ezek 34:17, 20
Rev 20:12
25:33
Luke 12:32

25:15 Greek *talents;* also throughout the story. A talent is equal to 75 pounds or 34 kilograms. **25:21** Greek *Enter into the joy of your master* [or *your Lord*]; also in 25:23. **25:31** "Son of Man" is a title Jesus used for himself. **25:32** Or *peoples.*

25:15 The master divided the money among his servants according to their abilities. No one received more or less than he could handle. If he failed in his assignment, his excuse could not be that he was overwhelmed. Failure would indicate only laziness or hatred toward the master. The bags of silver represent any kind of resource we are given. God gives us time, gifts, and other resources according to our abilities, and he expects us to invest them wisely until he returns. We are responsible to use well what God has given us. The issue is not how much we have but how well we use what we have.

25:21 Jesus is coming back—we know this is true. Does this mean we must quit our jobs in order to serve God? No, it means we are to use our time, talents, and treasures diligently in order to serve God completely in whatever we do. For a few people, this may mean changing professions. For most of us, it means doing our daily work out of love for God.

25:24-30 This last man was thinking only of himself. He hoped to play it safe and protect himself from his hard master, but he was judged for his self-centeredness. We must not make excuses to avoid doing what God calls us to do. If God truly is our Master, we must obey willingly. Our time, abilities, and money aren't

ours in the first place—we are caretakers, not owners. When we ignore, squander, or abuse what we are given, we are rebellious and deserve to be punished.

• **25:29, 30** This parable describes the consequences of two attitudes toward Christ's return. The person who diligently prepares for it by investing his or her time and talents to serve God will be rewarded. The person who has no heart for the work of the Kingdom will be punished. God rewards faithfulness. Those who bear no fruit for God's Kingdom cannot expect to be treated the same as those who are faithful.

• **25:31-46** God will separate his obedient followers from pretenders and unbelievers. The real evidence of our belief is the way we act. To treat all persons we encounter as if they were Jesus is no easy task. What we do for others demonstrates what we really think about Jesus' words to us: Feed the hungry, give the homeless a place to stay, look after the sick. How well do your actions separate you from pretenders and unbelievers?

• **25:32** Jesus used sheep and goats to picture the division between believers and unbelievers. Sheep and goats often grazed together but were separated when it came time to shear the sheep. Ezekiel 34:17-24 also refers to the separation of sheep and goats.

25:34
Luke 22:30
1 Cor 15:50
Gal 5:21

25:35-36
Isa 58:7
Heb 13:3
Jas 2:15-16

25:40
Prov 19:17
Matt 10:40, 42

25:41
Matt 7:23
Mark 9:48
2 Pet 2:4
Rev 20:10

25:45
Prov 14:31; 17:5

25:46
Dan 12:2
John 3:15, 36; 5:29
Acts 13:46-48
Rom 2:7-8
Gal 6:8

26:2
Exod 12:1-27

26:3
Ps 2:2
John 11:47-53
Acts 4:6

34 "Then the King will say to those on his right, 'Come, you who are blessed by my Father, inherit the Kingdom prepared for you from the creation of the world. 35 For I was hungry, and you fed me. I was thirsty, and you gave me a drink. I was a stranger, and you invited me into your home. 36I was naked, and you gave me clothing. I was sick, and you cared for me. I was in prison, and you visited me.'

37 "Then these righteous ones will reply, 'Lord, when did we ever see you hungry and feed you? Or thirsty and give you something to drink? 38Or a stranger and show you hospitality? Or naked and give you clothing? 39When did we ever see you sick or in prison and visit you?'

40 "And the King will say, 'I tell you the truth, when you did it to one of the least of these my brothers and sisters,* you were doing it to me!'

41 "Then the King will turn to those on the left and say, 'Away with you, you cursed ones, into the eternal fire prepared for the devil and his demons.* 42 For I was hungry, and you didn't feed me. I was thirsty, and you didn't give me a drink. 43 I was a stranger, and you didn't invite me into your home. I was naked, and you didn't give me clothing. I was sick and in prison, and you didn't visit me.'

44 "Then they will reply, 'Lord, when did we ever see you hungry or thirsty or a stranger or naked or sick or in prison, and not help you?'

45 "And he will answer, 'I tell you the truth, when you refused to help the least of these my brothers and sisters, you were refusing to help me.'

46 "And they will go away into eternal punishment, but the righteous will go into eternal life."

C. DEATH AND RESURRECTION OF JESUS, THE KING (26:1—28:20)

After facing much opposition for his teaching, Jesus is betrayed by Judas, denied by the disciples, crucified, and he dies. Three days later he rises from the dead and appears to the disciples, confirming that he is indeed King over life and death. The long-awaited King has brought in his Kingdom, but it is different than expected, for he reigns in our heart until the day he comes again to establish a new and perfect world.

Religious Leaders Plot to Kill Jesus (207/Mark 14:1-2; Luke 22:1-2)

26 When Jesus had finished saying all these things, he said to his disciples, 2 "As you know, Passover begins in two days, and the Son of Man* will be handed over to be crucified."

3At that same time the leading priests and elders were meeting at the residence of Caiaphas, the high priest, 4plotting how to capture Jesus secretly and kill him. 5"But not during the Passover celebration," they agreed, "or the people may riot."

25:40 Greek *my brothers.*   **25:41** Greek *his angels.*   **26:2** "Son of Man" is a title Jesus used for himself.

• **25:34-40** This parable describes acts of mercy we all can do every day. These acts do not depend on wealth, ability, or intelligence; they are simple acts freely given and freely received. We have no excuse to neglect those who have deep needs, and we cannot hand over this responsibility to the church or government. Jesus demands our personal involvement in caring for others' needs (Isaiah 58:7).

• **25:40** There has been much discussion about the identity of the "brothers and sisters." Some have said they are the Jews; others say they are all Christians; still others say they are suffering people everywhere. Such a debate is much like the lawyer's earlier question to Jesus, "Who is my neighbor?" (Luke 10:29). The point of this parable is not the *who*, but the *what*—the importance of serving where service is needed. The focus of this parable is that we should love every person and serve anyone we can. Such love for others glorifies God by reflecting our love for him.

25:46 Eternal punishment takes place in hell (the lake of fire, or Gehenna), the place of punishment after death for all those who refuse to repent. In the Hebrew, three words were used in connection with eternal punishment.

(1) *Sheol*, or "the grave," was used in the Hebrew Old Testament to mean the place of the dead, generally thought to be under the earth. (In the Hebrew, this word occurs in Job 24:19; Psalm 16:10; Isaiah 38:10.)

(2) *Hades* is the Greek word for the underworld, the realm

of the dead. It is the word used in the New Testament for Sheol. (In the Greek, this word occurs in Matthew 16:18; Revelation 1:18; 20:13, 14.)

(3) *Gehenna*, or hell, was named after the valley of Ben-Hinnom near Jerusalem, where children were sacrificed by fire to the pagan gods (see 2 Kings 23:10; 2 Chronicles 28:3). This is the place of eternal fire (Matthew 5:22; 10:28; Mark 9:43; Luke 12:5; James 3:6; Revelation 19:20) prepared for the devil, his angels, and all those who do not believe in God (25:46; Revelation 20:9, 10). This is the final and eternal state of the wicked after the resurrection and the Last Judgment.

When Jesus warns against unbelief, he is trying to save us from agonizing, eternal punishment.

26:3 Caiaphas was the ruling high priest during Jesus' ministry. He was the son-in-law of Annas, the previous high priest. The Roman government had taken over the process of appointing all political and religious leaders. Caiaphas served for 18 years, longer than most high priests, suggesting that he was gifted at cooperating with the Romans. He was the first to recommend Jesus' death in order to "save" the nation (John 11:49, 50).

26:3-5 This was a deliberate plot to kill Jesus. Without this plot, there would have been no groundswell of popular opinion against him. In fact, because of Jesus' popularity, the religious leaders were afraid to arrest him during the Passover. They did not want their actions to incite a riot.

A Woman Anoints Jesus with Perfume (182/Mark 14:3-9; John 12:1-11)

6Meanwhile, Jesus was in Bethany at the home of Simon, a man who had previously had leprosy. 7While he was eating,* a woman came in with a beautiful alabaster jar of expensive perfume and poured it over his head.

8The disciples were indignant when they saw this. "What a waste!" they said. 9"It could have been sold for a high price and the money given to the poor."

10 But Jesus, aware of this, replied, "Why criticize this woman for doing such a good thing to me? 11You will always have the poor among you, but you will not always have me. 12She has poured this perfume on me to prepare my body for burial. 13I tell you the truth, wherever the Good News is preached throughout the world, this woman's deed will be remembered and discussed."

26:11
Deut 15:11

Judas Agrees to Betray Jesus (208/Mark 14:10-11; Luke 22:3-6)

14Then Judas Iscariot, one of the twelve disciples, went to the leading priests 15and asked, "How much will you pay me to betray Jesus to you?" And they gave him thirty pieces of silver. 16From that time on, Judas began looking for an opportunity to betray Jesus.

26:14-16
John 11:57
26:15
Exod 21:32
Zech 11:12

Disciples Prepare for the Passover (209/Mark 14:12-16; Luke 22:7-13)

17On the first day of the Festival of Unleavened Bread, the disciples came to Jesus and asked, "Where do you want us to prepare the Passover meal for you?"

18 "As you go into the city," he told them, "you will see a certain man. Tell him, ' The Teacher says: My time has come, and I will eat the Passover meal with my disciples at your house.' " 19So the disciples did as Jesus told them and prepared the Passover meal there.

26:17
Exod 12:18-20
Deut 16:5-8

Jesus and the Disciples Share the Last Supper
(211/Mark 14:17-25; Luke 22:14-30; John 13:21-30)

20When it was evening, Jesus sat down at the table* with the twelve disciples.* 21While they were eating, he said, "I tell you the truth, one of you will betray me."

26:7 Or *reclining.* **26:20a** Or *Jesus reclined.* **26:20b** Some manuscripts read *the Twelve.*

- **26:6-13** Matthew and Mark put this event just before the Last Supper, while John has it just before the Triumphal Entry. Of the three, John places this event in the most likely chronological order. We must remember that the main purpose of the Gospel writers was to give an accurate record of Jesus' message, not to present an exact chronological account of his life. Matthew and Mark may have chosen to place this event here to contrast the complete devotion of Mary with the betrayal of Judas, the next event they record in their Gospels.
- **26:7** This woman was Mary, the sister of Martha and Lazarus, who lived in Bethany (John 12:1-3). Alabaster jars were carved from a translucent gypsum. These jars were used to hold perfumed oil.

VISIT IN BETHANY
Chronologically, the events of Matthew 26:6-13 precede the events of 21:1ff. In 20:29, Jesus left Jericho, heading toward Jerusalem. Then he arrived in Bethany, where a woman anointed him. From there he went toward Bethphage, where two of his disciples got the colt that he would ride into Jerusalem.

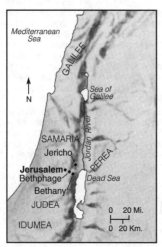

- **26:8** All the disciples were indignant, but John's Gospel singles out Judas Iscariot as especially so (John 12:4).
- **26:11** Here Jesus brought back to mind Deuteronomy 15:11: "There will always be some in the land who are poor." This statement does not justify ignoring the needs of the poor. Scripture continually exhorts us to care for the needy. The passage in Deuteronomy continues: "That is why I am commanding you to share freely with the poor and with other Israelites in need." Rather, by saying this, Jesus highlighted the special sacrifice Mary made for him.
- **26:14, 15** Why would Judas want to betray Jesus? Judas, like the other disciples, expected Jesus to start a political rebellion and overthrow Rome. As treasurer, Judas certainly assumed (as did the other disciples—see Mark 10:35-37) that he would be given an important position in Jesus' new government. But when Jesus praised Mary for pouring out perfume worth a year's salary, Judas may have realized that Jesus' Kingdom was not physical or political but spiritual. Judas's greedy desire for money and status could not be realized if he followed Jesus, so he betrayed Jesus in exchange for money and favor from the religious leaders.
- **26:15** Matthew alone records the exact amount of money Judas accepted to betray Jesus—30 silver coins, the price of a slave (Exodus 21:32). The religious leaders had planned to wait until after the Passover to take Jesus, but with Judas's unexpected offer, they accelerated their plans.

26:17 The Passover took place on one night and at one meal, but the Festival of Unleavened Bread, which was celebrated with it, continued for a week. The people removed all yeast from their homes in commemoration of their ancestors' exodus from Egypt, when they did not have time to let the bread dough rise. Thousands of people poured into Jerusalem from all over the Roman Empire for this festival. For more information on how the Passover was celebrated, see the notes on Mark 14:1 and in Exodus 12.

²² Greatly distressed, each one asked in turn, "Am I the one, Lord?"

26:23
Ps 41:9

²³ He replied, "One of you who has just eaten from this bowl with me will betray me. ²⁴ For the Son of Man must die, as the Scriptures declared long ago. But how terrible it will be for the one who betrays him. It would be far better for that man if he had never been born!"

26:24
Ps 22:7-8, 16-18
Isa 53:8-9
Luke 24:25-27, 46
1 Pet 1:10-11

²⁵ Judas, the one who would betray him, also asked, "Rabbi, am I the one?"

And Jesus told him, "You have said it."

²⁶As they were eating, Jesus took some bread and blessed it. Then he broke it in pieces and gave it to the disciples, saying, "Take this and eat it, for this is my body."

26:28
Exod 24:8
Jer 31:31
Zech 9:11
Heb 9:20

²⁷And he took a cup of wine and gave thanks to God for it. He gave it to them and said, "Each of you drink from it, ²⁸for this is my blood, which confirms the covenant* between

26:28 Some manuscripts read *the new covenant.*

MARY **LAZARUS'S SISTER**

Hospitality is an art. Making sure a guest is welcomed, warmed, and well fed requires creativity, organization, and teamwork. Their ability to accomplish these goals makes Mary and her sister, Martha, one of the best hospitality teams in the Bible. Their frequent guest was Jesus Christ.

For Mary, hospitality meant giving more attention to the guest himself than to the needs he might have. She would rather talk than cook. She was more interested in her guest's words than in the cleanliness of her home or the timeliness of her meals. She let her older sister, Martha, take care of those details. Mary's approach to events shows her to be mainly a "responder." She did little preparation—her role was participation. Unlike her sister, who had to learn to stop and listen, Mary needed to learn that action is often appropriate and necessary.

We first meet Mary during a visit Jesus paid to her home. She simply sat at his feet and listened. When Martha became irritated at her sister's lack of help, Jesus stated that Mary's choice to enjoy his company was the most appropriate response at the time. Our last glimpse of Mary shows her to have become a woman of thoughtful and worshipful action. Again she was at Jesus' feet, washing them with perfume and wiping them with her hair. She seemed to understand, better even than the disciples, why Jesus was going to die. Jesus said her act of worship would be told everywhere, along with the gospel, as an example of costly service.

What kind of hospitality does Jesus receive from your life? Are you so busy planning and running your life that you neglect precious time with him? Or do you respond to him by listening to his Word, then finding ways to worship him with your life? It is that kind of hospitality he longs for from each of us.

Strengths and accomplishments	• Perhaps the only person who understood and accepted Jesus' coming death, taking time to anoint his body while he was still living • Learned when to listen and when to act
Lessons from her life	• The busyness of serving God can become a barrier to knowing him personally • Small acts of obedience and service have widespread effects
Vital statistics	• Where: Bethany • Relatives: Sister: Martha. Brother: Lazarus.
Key verses	"'She has poured this perfume on me to prepare my body for burial. I tell you the truth, wherever the Good News is preached throughout the world, this woman's deed will be remembered and discussed'" (Matthew 26:12-13).

Mary's story is told in Matthew 26:6-13; Mark 14:3-9; Luke 10:38-42; John 11:17-45; 12:1-11.

26:23 In Jesus' time, some food was eaten from a common bowl into which everyone dipped their hand.

26:26 Each name we use for this sacrament brings out a different dimension to it. It is the *Lord's Supper* because it commemorates the Passover meal Jesus ate with his disciples; it is the *Eucharist* (thanksgiving) because in it we thank God for Christ's work for us; it is *Communion* because through it we commune with God and with other believers. As we eat the bread and drink the wine, we should be quietly reflective as we recall Jesus' death and his promise to come again, grateful for God's wonderful gift to us, and joyful as we meet with Christ and the body of believers.

26:28 How does Jesus' blood relate to the new covenant? People under the old covenant (those who lived before Jesus) could approach God only through a priest and an animal sacrifice. Now all people can come directly to God through faith because Jesus' death has made us acceptable in God's eyes (Romans 3:21-24).

The old covenant was a shadow of the new (Jeremiah 31:31; Hebrews 8:1ff), pointing forward to the day when Jesus himself would be the final and ultimate sacrifice for sin. Rather than an unblemished lamb slain on the altar, the perfect Lamb of God was slain on the cross, a sinless sacrifice, so that our sins could be forgiven once and for all. All those who believe in Christ receive that forgiveness.

God and his people. It is poured out as a sacrifice to forgive the sins of many. ²⁹Mark my words—I will not drink wine again until the day I drink it new with you in my Father's Kingdom."

26:29
Acts 10:41

³⁰ Then they sang a hymn and went out to the Mount of Olives.

26:30
Pss 113–118

Jesus Again Predicts Peter's Denial (222/Mark 14:26-31)

³¹On the way, Jesus told them, "Tonight all of you will desert me. For the Scriptures say,

26:31
†Zech 13:7
John 16:32

'God will strike* the Shepherd,
    and the sheep of the flock will be scattered.'

³² But after I have been raised from the dead, I will go ahead of you to Galilee and meet you there."

26:32
Matt 28:7

³³ Peter declared, "Even if everyone else deserts you, I will never desert you."

26:34
Matt 26:69-75
Mark 14:66-72
Luke 22:56-62
John 18:25-27

³⁴Jesus replied, "I tell you the truth, Peter—this very night, before the rooster crows, you will deny three times that you even know me."

³⁵"No!" Peter insisted. "Even if I have to die with you, I will never deny you!" And all the other disciples vowed the same.

26:35
John 13:37

Jesus Agonizes in the Garden (223/Mark 14:32-42; Luke 22:39-46)

³⁶Then Jesus went with them to the olive grove called Gethsemane, and he said, "Sit here while I go over there to pray." ³⁷ He took Peter and Zebedee's two sons, James and John, and he became anguished and distressed. ³⁸He told them, "My soul is crushed with grief to the point of death. Stay here and keep watch with me."

26:36
John 18:1

26:38
†Pss 42:6; 43:5
John 12:27

³⁹ He went on a little farther and bowed with his face to the ground, praying, "My Father! If it is possible, let this cup of suffering be taken away from me. Yet I want your will to be done, not mine."

26:39
Matt 20:22
John 5:30; 6:38
Heb 5:7-8

26:31 Greek *I will strike*. Zech 13:7.

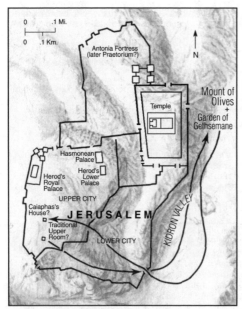

THE PASSOVER MEAL AND GETHSEMANE Jesus, who would soon be the final Passover Lamb, ate the traditional Passover meal with his disciples in the upper room of a house in Jerusalem. During the meal they partook of the bread and wine, which would be the elements of future Communion celebrations, and then went out to the Garden of Gethsemane on the Mount of Olives.

26:29 Again Jesus assured his disciples of victory over death and of their future with him. The next few hours would bring apparent defeat, but soon they would experience the power of the Holy Spirit and witness the great spread of the Good News. And one day they would all be together again in God's new Kingdom.

26:30 It is possible that the hymn the disciples sang was from Psalms 115–118, the traditional psalms sung as part of the Passover meal.

• **26:35** All the disciples declared that they would die before denying Jesus. A few hours later, however, they all scattered. Talk is cheap. It is easy to say we are devoted to Christ, but our claims are meaningful only when they are tested in the crucible of persecution. How strong is your faith? Is it strong enough to stand up under intense trial?

26:37, 38 Jesus was in great anguish over his approaching physical pain, separation from the Father, and death for the sins of the world. The divine course was set, but he, in his human nature, still struggled (Hebrews 5:7-9). Because of the anguish Jesus experienced, he can relate to our suffering. Jesus' strength to obey came from his relationship with God the Father, who is also the source of our strength (John 17:11, 15, 16, 21, 26).

26:39 Jesus was not rebelling against his Father's will when he asked that the cup of suffering and separation be taken away. In fact, he reaffirmed his desire to do God's will by saying, "Yet I want your will to be done, not mine." His prayer reveals to us his terrible suffering. His agony was worse than death because he paid for *all* sin by being separated from God. The sinless Son of God took our sins upon himself to save us from suffering and separation.

26:39 In times of suffering people sometimes wish they knew the future, or they wish they could understand the reason for their anguish. Jesus knew what lay ahead of him, and he knew the reason. Even so, his struggle was intense—more wrenching than any struggle we will ever have to face. What does it take to be able to say, "I want your will to be done"? It takes firm trust in God's plans; it takes prayer and obedience each step of the way.

26:41
Matt 6:13

40 Then he returned to the disciples and found them asleep. He said to Peter, "Couldn't you watch with me even one hour? 41Keep watch and pray, so that you will not give in to temptation. For the spirit is willing, but the body is weak!"

42 Then Jesus left them a second time and prayed, "My Father! If this cup cannot be taken away* unless I drink it, your will be done." 43When he returned to them again, he found them sleeping, for they couldn't keep their eyes open.

26:45
John 12:23-27;
13:1; 17:1

44 So he went to pray a third time, saying the same things again. 45Then he came to the disciples and said, "Go ahead and sleep. Have your rest. But look—the time has come. The Son of Man is betrayed into the hands of sinners. 46Up, let's be going. Look, my betrayer is here!"

Jesus Is Betrayed and Arrested (**224**/Mark 14:43-52; Luke 22:47-53; John 18:1-11)
47 And even as Jesus said this, Judas, one of the twelve disciples, arrived with a crowd of men armed with swords and clubs. They had been sent by the leading priests and elders of the people. 48 The traitor, Judas, had given them a prearranged signal: "You will know which one to arrest when I greet him with a kiss." 49So Judas came straight to Jesus. "Greetings, Rabbi!" he exclaimed and gave him the kiss.

26:52
Gen 9:6
Rev 13:10

26:53
2 Kgs 6:16-17
Ps 91:11
Dan 7:10

26:54
Ps 22:7-8, 16-18
Isa 53:8-9
Luke 24:25-27, 46
1 Pet 1:10-11

50 Jesus said, "My friend, go ahead and do what you have come for."
Then the others grabbed Jesus and arrested him. 51But one of the men with Jesus pulled out his sword and struck the high priest's slave, slashing off his ear.
52 "Put away your sword," Jesus told him. "Those who use the sword will die by the sword. 53 Don't you realize that I could ask my Father for thousands* of angels to protect us, and he would send them instantly? 54But if I did, how would the Scriptures be fulfilled that describe what must happen now?"

26:56
Isa 53:7
Zech 13:7
Matt 26:31

55 Then Jesus said to the crowd, "Am I some dangerous revolutionary, that you come with swords and clubs to arrest me? Why didn't you arrest me in the Temple? I was there teaching every day. 56 But this is all happening to fulfill the words of the prophets as recorded in the Scriptures." At that point, all the disciples deserted him and fled.

Caiaphas Questions Jesus (**226**/Mark 14:53-65)

26:58
Mark 14:66
Luke 22:55
John 18:15

57 Then the people who had arrested Jesus led him to the home of Caiaphas, the high priest, where the teachers of religious law and the elders had gathered. 58Meanwhile, Peter

26:42 Greek *If this cannot pass.*   **26:53** Greek *twelve legions.*

BETRAYED!

Delilah betrayed Samson to the Philistines.	Judges 16:16-21
Absalom betrayed David, his father	2 Samuel 15:10-16
Jehu betrayed Joram and killed him	2 Kings 9:14-27
Officials betrayed Joash and killed him.	2 Kings 12:20, 21
Judas betrayed Jesus	Matthew 26:46-56

Scripture records a number of occasions on which a person or group was betrayed. The tragedies caused by these violations of trust are a strong lesson about the importance of keeping our commitments.

26:40, 41 Jesus used Peter's drowsiness to warn him about the kinds of temptation he would soon face. The way to overcome temptation is to keep alert and pray. Keeping alert means being aware of the possibilities of temptation, sensitive to the subtleties, and spiritually equipped to fight it. Because temptation strikes where we are most vulnerable, we can't resist it alone. Prayer is essential because God's strength can shore up our defenses and defeat Satan's power.

• **26:48** Judas had told the crowd to arrest the man he kissed. This was not an arrest by Roman soldiers under Roman law but an arrest by the religious leaders. Judas pointed Jesus out, not because Jesus was hard to recognize, but because Judas had agreed to be the formal accuser in case a trial was called. Judas was able to lead the group to one of Jesus' retreats, where no onlookers would interfere with the arrest.

26:51-53 The man who cut off the servant's ear was Peter (John 18:10). Peter was trying to prevent what he saw as *defeat*. He didn't realize that Jesus had to die in order to gain *victory*. But

Jesus demonstrated perfect commitment to his Father's will. His Kingdom would not be advanced with swords but with faith and obedience. Luke 22:51 records that Jesus then touched the servant's ear and healed him.

26:55 Although the religious leaders could have arrested Jesus at any time, they came at night because they were afraid of the crowds that followed him each day (see 26:5).

• **26:56** A few hours earlier, this band of men had said they would rather die than desert their Lord (see the note on 26:35).

26:57 Earlier in the evening, Jesus had been questioned by Annas (the former high priest and the father-in-law of Caiaphas). Annas then sent Jesus to Caiaphas's home to be questioned (John 18:12-24). Because of their haste to complete the trial and see Jesus die before the Sabbath, less than 24 hours away, the religious leaders met in Caiaphas's home at night instead of waiting for daylight and meeting in the Temple.

followed him at a distance and came to the high priest's courtyard. He went in and sat with the guards and waited to see how it would all end.

[59] Inside, the leading priests and the entire high council* were trying to find witnesses who would lie about Jesus, so they could put him to death. [60] But even though they found many who agreed to give false witness, they could not use anyone's testimony. Finally, two men came forward [61] who declared, "This man said, 'I am able to destroy the Temple of God and rebuild it in three days.'"

[62] Then the high priest stood up and said to Jesus, "Well, aren't you going to answer these charges? What do you have to say for yourself?" [63] But Jesus remained silent. Then the high priest said to him, "I demand in the name of the living God—tell us if you are the Messiah, the Son of God."

[64] Jesus replied, "You have said it. And in the future you will see the Son of Man seated in the place of power at God's right hand* and coming on the clouds of heaven."*

[65] Then the high priest tore his clothing to show his horror and said, "Blasphemy! Why do we need other witnesses? You have all heard his blasphemy. [66] What is your verdict?"

"Guilty!" they shouted. "He deserves to die!"

[67] Then they began to spit in Jesus' face and beat him with their fists. And some slapped him, [68] jeering, "Prophesy to us, you Messiah! Who hit you that time?"

Peter Denies Knowing Jesus (227/Mark 14:66-72; Luke 22:54-65; John 18:25-27)
[69] Meanwhile, Peter was sitting outside in the courtyard. A servant girl came over and said to him, "You were one of those with Jesus the Galilean."

[70] But Peter denied it in front of everyone. "I don't know what you're talking about," he said.

[71] Later, out by the gate, another servant girl noticed him and said to those standing around, "This man was with Jesus of Nazareth.*"

26:59 Greek *the Sanhedrin.* **26:64a** Greek *seated at the right hand of the power.* See Ps 110:1. **26:64b** See Dan 7:13. **26:71** Or *Jesus the Nazarene.*

Marginal cross-references:
26:60 Deut 19:15; Ps 27:12
26:61 Matt 27:40; John 2:19; Acts 6:14
26:63 Matt 16:16-18
26:64 Ps 110:1; †Dan 7:13; Matt 24:30; Rev 1:7
26:65-66 Lev 24:16; John 19:7
26:67 Isa 50:6; 53:5

26:59 The high council was the most powerful religious and political body of the Jewish people. Although the Romans controlled Israel's government, they gave the people power to handle religious disputes and some civil disputes, so the high council made many of the local decisions affecting daily life. But a death sentence had to be approved by the Romans (John 18:31).

26:60, 61 The high council tried to find witnesses who would distort some of Jesus' teachings. Finally, they found two witnesses who distorted Jesus' words about the Temple (see John 2:19). They claimed that Jesus had said he could destroy the Temple—a blasphemous boast. Actually Jesus had said, "Destroy this temple, and in three days I will raise it up" (John 2:19). Jesus, of course, had been talking about his body, not the building. Ironically, the religious leaders were about to destroy Jesus' body just as he had said, and three days later he would rise from the dead.

26:64 Jesus declared his royalty in no uncertain terms. In calling himself the Son of Man, Jesus was claiming to be the Messiah, as his listeners well knew. He knew this declaration would be his undoing, but he did not panic. He was calm, courageous, and determined.

26:65, 66 The high priest accused Jesus of blasphemy—calling himself God. To the Jews, this was a great crime, punishable by death (Leviticus 24:16). The religious leaders refused even to consider that Jesus' words might be true. They had decided to kill Jesus, and in so doing, they sealed their own fate as well as his. Like the members of the high council, you must decide whether Jesus' words are blasphemy or truth. Your decision has eternal implications.

• **26:69ff** There were three stages to Peter's denial. First, he acted confused and tried to divert attention from himself by changing the subject. Second, using an oath he denied that he knew Jesus. Third, he swore that he did not know Jesus. Believers who deny Christ often begin doing so subtly by pretending not to know him. When opportunities to discuss religious issues come up, they walk away or pretend they don't know the answers. With only a little more pressure, they can be induced to deny flatly their relationship with Christ. If you find yourself subtly diverting conversation so you don't have to talk about Christ, watch out. You may be on the road to denying him.

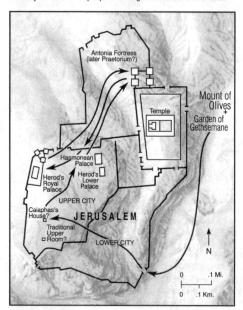

JESUS' TRIAL After Judas singled Jesus out for arrest, the mob took Jesus first to Caiaphas, the high priest. This trial, a mockery of justice, ended at daybreak with their decision to kill him; but the Jews needed Rome's permission for the death sentence. Jesus was taken to Pilate (who was probably in the Praetorium), then to Herod (Luke 23:5–12), and back to Pilate, who sentenced him to die.

72Again Peter denied it, this time with an oath. "I don't even know the man," he said.

73A little later some of the other bystanders came over to Peter and said, "You must be one of them; we can tell by your Galilean accent."

26:75
Matt 26:34
Mark 14:30
Luke 22:34
John 13:38

74Peter swore, "A curse on me if I'm lying—I don't know the man!" And immediately the rooster crowed.

75Suddenly, Jesus' words flashed through Peter's mind: "Before the rooster crows, you will deny three times that you even know me." And he went away, weeping bitterly.

The Council of Religious Leaders Condemns Jesus (**228**/Mark 15:1; Luke 22:66-71)

27:1-2
Mark 15:1
Luke 23:1-2
John 18:28

27 Very early in the morning the leading priests and the elders of the people met again to lay plans for putting Jesus to death. 2Then they bound him, led him away, and took him to Pilate, the Roman governor.

Jesus' first words to Simon Peter were "Come, follow me" (Mark 1:17). His last words to him were "Follow me" (John 21:22). Every step of the way between those two challenges, Peter never failed to follow—even though he often stumbled.

When Jesus entered Peter's life, this plain fisherman became a new person with new goals and new priorities. He did not become a perfect person, however, and he never stopped being Simon Peter. We may wonder what Jesus saw in Simon that made him greet this potential disciple with a new name: Peter—the "rock." Impulsive Peter certainly didn't act like a rock much of the time. But when Jesus chose his followers, he wasn't looking for models; he was looking for real people. He chose people who could be changed by his love, and then he sent them out to communicate that his acceptance was available to anyone—even to those who often fail.

We may wonder what Jesus sees in us when he calls us to follow him. But we know Jesus accepted Peter, and, in spite of his failures, Peter went on to do great things for God. Are you willing to keep following Jesus, even when you fail?

Strengths and accomplishments	• Became the recognized leader among Jesus' disciples—one of the inner group of three • Was the first great voice of the gospel during and after Pentecost • Probably knew Mark and gave him information for the Gospel of Mark • Wrote 1 and 2 Peter
Weaknesses and mistakes	• Often spoke without thinking; was brash and impulsive • During Jesus' trial, denied three times that he even knew Jesus • Later found it hard to treat Gentile Christians as equals
Lessons from his life	• Enthusiasm has to be backed up by faith and understanding, or it fails • God's faithfulness can compensate for our greatest unfaithfulness • It is better to be a follower who sometimes fails than one who fails to follow
Vital statistics	• Occupations: Fisherman, disciple • Relatives: Father: John. Brother: Andrew. • Contemporaries: Jesus, Pilate, Herod
Key verse	"Now I say to you that you are Peter (which means 'rock'), and upon this rock I will build my church, and all the powers of hell will not conquer it" (Matthew 16:18).

Peter's story is told in the Gospels and the book of Acts. He is mentioned in Galatians 1:18 and 2:7-14; and he wrote the books of 1 and 2 Peter.

• **26:72-74** That Peter denied that he knew Jesus, using an oath and swearing, does not mean he used foul language. This was the kind of swearing that a person does in a court of law. Peter was swearing that he did not know Jesus and was invoking a curse on himself if his words were untrue. In effect he was saying, "May God strike me dead if I am lying."

27:1, 2 The religious leaders had to persuade the Roman government to sentence Jesus to death because they did not have the authority to do it themselves. The Romans had taken away the religious leaders' authority to inflict capital punishment. Politically, it looked better for the religious leaders anyway if someone else was responsible for killing Jesus. They wanted the death to appear Roman sponsored so the crowds couldn't blame them. The Jewish leaders had arrested Jesus on theological grounds—blasphemy. Because this charge would be thrown out of a Roman court, how-

ever, they had to come up with a political reason for Jesus' death. Their strategy was to show Jesus as a rebel who claimed to be a king and thus a threat to Caesar.

27:2 Pilate was the Roman governor for the regions of Samaria and Judea from A.D. 26 to 36. Jerusalem was located in Judea. Pilate took special pleasure in demonstrating his authority over the Jews; for example, he impounded money from the Temple treasuries to build an aqueduct. Pilate was not popular, but the religious leaders had no other way to get rid of Jesus than to go to him. Ironically, when Jesus, a Jew, came before him for trial, Pilate found him innocent. He could not find a single fault in Jesus, nor could he contrive one.

Judas Hangs Himself (229)

3 When Judas, who had betrayed him, realized that Jesus had been condemned to die, he was filled with remorse. So he took the thirty pieces of silver back to the leading priests and the elders. 4"I have sinned," he declared, "for I have betrayed an innocent man."

"What do we care?" they retorted. "That's your problem."

5 Then Judas threw the silver coins down in the Temple and went out and hanged himself. 6The leading priests picked up the coins. "It wouldn't be right to put this money in the Temple treasury," they said, "since it was payment for murder."* 7After some discussion they finally decided to buy the potter's field, and they made it into a cemetery for foreigners. 8That is why the field is still called the Field of Blood. 9 This fulfilled the prophecy of Jeremiah that says,

"They took* the thirty pieces of silver—
   the price at which he was valued by the people of Israel,
10 and purchased the potter's field,
   as the LORD directed.*"

27:3
Matt 26:14-15

27:5-10
Acts 1:18-19

27:9-10
†Jer 32:6-9
†Zech 11:12-13

Jesus Stands Trial before Pilate (230/Mark 15:2-5; Luke 23:1-5; John 18:28-38)

11Now Jesus was standing before Pilate, the Roman governor. "Are you the king of the Jews?" the governor asked him.

Jesus replied, "You have said it."

12But when the leading priests and the elders made their accusations against him, Jesus remained silent. 13"Don't you hear all these charges they are bringing against you?" Pilate demanded. 14 But Jesus made no response to any of the charges, much to the governor's surprise.

27:12
Isa 53:7
Matt 26:63
John 19:9
1 Pet 2:22

27:14
Mark 14:61

Pilate Hands Jesus Over to Be Crucified
(232/Mark 15:6-15; Luke 23:13-25; John 18:39–19:16)

15Now it was the governor's custom each year during the Passover celebration to release one prisoner to the crowd—anyone they wanted. 16This year there was a notorious prisoner, a man named Barabbas.* 17As the crowds gathered before Pilate's house that morning, he asked them, "Which one do you want me to release to you—Barabbas, or Jesus who is called the Messiah?" 18(He knew very well that the religious leaders had arrested Jesus out of envy.)

19Just then, as Pilate was sitting on the judgment seat, his wife sent him this message: "Leave that innocent man alone. I suffered through a terrible nightmare about him last night."

27:19
Job 33:14-16

27:6 Greek *since it is the price for blood.* **27:9** Or *I took.* **27:9-10** Greek *as the LORD directed me.* Zech 11:12-13;
Jer 32:6-9. **27:16** Some manuscripts read *Jesus Barabbas;* also in 27:17.

27:3, 4 Jesus' formal accuser (see 26:48 note) wanted to drop his charges, but the religious leaders refused to halt the trial. When he betrayed Jesus, perhaps Judas was trying to force Jesus' hand to get him to lead a revolt against Rome. This did not work, of course. Whatever his reason, Judas changed his mind, but it was too late. Many of the plans we set into motion cannot be reversed. It is best to think of the potential consequences before we launch into an action we may later regret.

27:4 The priests' job was to teach people about God and act as intercessors for them, helping administer the sacrifices to cover their sins. Judas returned to the priests, exclaiming that he had sinned. Rather than helping him find forgiveness, however, the priests said, "That's your problem." Not only had they rejected the Messiah, they had rejected their role as priests.

• **27:5** According to Matthew, Judas hanged himself. Acts 1:18, however, says that he fell and burst open. The best explanation is that the limb from which he was hanging broke, and the resulting fall split open his body.

27:6 These leading priests felt no guilt in giving Judas money to betray an innocent man, but when Judas returned the money, the priests couldn't accept it because it was wrong to accept payment for murder! Their hatred for Jesus had caused them to lose all sense of right and wrong.

27:9, 10 This prophecy is found specifically in Zechariah 11:12, 13 but may also have been taken from Jeremiah 18:1-4; 19:1-11;

or 32:6-15. In Old Testament times, Jeremiah was considered the collector of some of the prophets' writings, so perhaps his name is cited rather than Zechariah.

27:12 Standing before Pilate, the religious leaders accused Jesus of a different crime than the ones for which they had arrested him. They arrested him for blasphemy (claiming to be God), but that charge would mean nothing to the Romans. So the religious leaders had to accuse Jesus of crimes that would have concerned the Roman government, such as encouraging the people not to pay taxes, claiming to be a king, and causing riots. These accusations were not true, but the religious leaders were determined to kill Jesus, and they broke several commandments in order to do so.

27:14 Jesus' silence fulfilled the words of the prophet (Isaiah 53:7). Pilate was amazed that Jesus didn't try to defend himself. He recognized the obvious plot against Jesus and wanted to let him go, but Pilate was already under pressure from Rome to keep peace in his territory. The last thing he needed was a rebellion over this quiet and seemingly insignificant man.

27:15, 16 Barabbas had taken part in a rebellion against the Roman government (Mark 15:7). Although an enemy to Rome, he may have been a hero to the Jews. Ironically, Barabbas was guilty of the crime for which Jesus was accused.

27:19 For a leader who was supposed to administer justice, Pilate proved to be more concerned about political expediency

27:20
Acts 3:14

20 Meanwhile, the leading priests and the elders persuaded the crowd to ask for Barabbas to be released and for Jesus to be put to death. 21So the governor asked again, "Which of these two do you want me to release to you?"

The crowd shouted back, "Barabbas!"

27:22
Matt 1:16

22 Pilate responded, "Then what should I do with Jesus who is called the Messiah?"

They shouted back, "Crucify him!"

23"Why?" Pilate demanded. "What crime has he committed?"

But the mob roared even louder, "Crucify him!"

27:24
Deut 21:5-9
Ps 26:6

24Pilate saw that he wasn't getting anywhere and that a riot was developing. So he sent for a bowl of water and washed his hands before the crowd, saying, "I am innocent of this man's blood. The responsibility is yours!"

27:25
Acts 5:28
27:26
Isa 53:5
John 19:1

25And all the people yelled back, "We will take responsibility for his death—we and our children!"*

26So Pilate released Barabbas to them. He ordered Jesus flogged with a lead-tipped whip, then turned him over to the Roman soldiers to be crucified.

Roman Soldiers Mock Jesus (**233**/Mark 15:16-20)

27:29
Ps 22:8
Isa 53:3
John 19:2-3

27Some of the governor's soldiers took Jesus into their headquarters* and called out the entire regiment. 28They stripped him and put a scarlet robe on him. 29They wove thorn branches into a crown and put it on his head, and they placed a reed stick in his right hand as a scepter. Then they knelt before him in mockery and taunted, "Hail! King of the Jews!"

27:30
Isa 50:6
27:31
Isa 53:7

30And they spit on him and grabbed the stick and struck him on the head with it. 31When they were finally tired of mocking him, they took off the robe and put his own clothes on him again. Then they led him away to be crucified.

27:25 Greek *"His blood be on us and on our children."*   **27:27** Or *into the Praetorium.*

THE SEVEN LAST WORDS OF JESUS ON THE CROSS

"Father, forgive them, for they don't know what they are doing." . . . . Luke 23:34

"I assure you, today you will be with me in paradise." . . . . Luke 23:43

Speaking to Mary and John: "Dear woman, here is your son. . . . Here is your mother." . . . . John 19:26, 27

"My God, my God, why have you abandoned me?" . . . . Matthew 27:46; Mark 15:34

"I am thirsty." . . . . John 19:28

"It is finished!" . . . . John 19:30

"Father, I entrust my spirit into your hands!" . . . . Luke 23:46

The statements that Jesus made from the cross have been treasured by all who have followed him as Lord. They demonstrate both his humanity and his divinity. They also capture the last moments of all that Jesus went through to gain our forgiveness.

---

than about doing what was right. He had several opportunities to make the right decision. His conscience told him Jesus was innocent; Roman law said an innocent man should not be put to death; and his wife had a nightmare that caused her to encourage her husband to let Jesus go. Pilate had no good excuse to condemn Jesus, but he was afraid of the crowd.

27:21 Crowds are fickle. They loved Jesus on Sunday because they thought he was going to inaugurate his Kingdom. Then they hated him on Friday when his power appeared broken. In the face of the mass uprising against Jesus, his friends were afraid to speak up.

27:24 At first Pilate hesitated to give the religious leaders permission to crucify Jesus. He perceived that they were simply jealous of a teacher who was more popular with the people than they were. But when the Jews threatened to report Pilate to Caesar (John 19:12), Pilate became afraid. Historical records indicate that the Jews had already threatened to lodge a formal complaint against Pilate for his stubborn flouting of their traditions—and such a complaint would most likely have led to his recall by Rome. His job was in jeopardy. The Roman government could not afford to put large numbers of troops in all the

regions under their control, so one of Pilate's main duties was to do whatever was necessary to maintain peace.

27:24 In making no decision, Pilate made the decision to let the crowds crucify Jesus. Although he washed his hands, the guilt remained. Washing your hands of a tough situation doesn't cancel your guilt. It merely gives you a false sense of peace. Don't make excuses—take responsibility for the decisions you make.

27:27 A regiment was a division of the Roman legion, containing about 200 men.

Jesus Is Led Away to Be Crucified (**234**/Mark 15:21-24; Luke 23:26-31; John 19:17)
32Along the way, they came across a man named Simon, who was from Cyrene,* and the soldiers forced him to carry Jesus' cross. 33And they went out to a place called Golgotha (which
means "Place of the Skull"). 34The soldiers gave him wine mixed with bitter gall, but when he
had tasted it, he refused to drink it.

27:34
Ps 69:21

Jesus Is Placed on the Cross (**235**/Mark 15:25-32; Luke 23:32-43; John 19:18-27)
35After they had nailed him to the cross, the soldiers gambled for his clothes by throwing
dice.* 36Then they sat around and kept guard as he hung there. 37A sign was fastened
above Jesus' head, announcing the charge against him. It read: "This is Jesus, the King
of the Jews." 38Two revolutionaries* were crucified with him, one on his right and one on
his left.

27:35
†Ps 22:18

27:38
Isa 53:12

39The people passing by shouted abuse, shaking their heads in mockery. 40"Look at you
now!" they yelled at him. "You said you were going to destroy the Temple and rebuild it in
three days. Well then, if you are the Son of God, save yourself and come down from the
cross!"

27:39
Pss 22:7; 109:25
Lam 2:15

27:40
Matt 26:61
John 2:19-20

41The leading priests, the teachers of religious law, and the elders also mocked Jesus.
42"He saved others," they scoffed, "but he can't save himself! So he is the King of Israel, is he?
Let him come down from the cross right now, and we will believe in him! 43He trusted God,
so let God rescue him now if he wants him! For he said, 'I am the Son of God.'" 44Even the revolutionaries who were crucified with him ridiculed him in the same way.

Jesus Dies on the Cross (**236**/Mark 15:33-41; Luke 23:44-49; John 19:28-37)
45At noon, darkness fell across the whole land until three o'clock. 46At about three o'clock,
Jesus called out with a loud voice, *"Eli, Eli,* lema sabachthani?"* which means "My God, my
God, why have you abandoned me?"*

27:45
Amos 8:9

27:46
†Ps 22:1

27:32 *Cyrene* was a city in northern Africa.   **27:35** Greek *by casting lots.* A few late manuscripts add *This fulfilled the
word of the prophet: "They divided my garments among themselves and cast lots for my robe."* See Ps 22:18.
27:38 Or *criminals;* also in 27:44.   **27:46a** Some manuscripts read *Eloi, Eloi.*   **27:46b** Ps 22:1.

THE WAY OF THE CROSS   The Roman soldiers took Jesus
into their headquarters at the Praetorium and mocked him, dress-
ing him in a scarlet robe and a crown of thorns. They then led
him to the crucifixion site outside the city. He was so weakened
by his beatings that he could not carry his cross, and a man from
Cyrene was forced to carry it to Golgotha.

27:32   Condemned prisoners had to carry their own crosses to
the execution site. Jesus, weakened from the beatings he had
received, was physically unable to carry his cross any farther.
Thus, a bystander, Simon, was forced to do so. Simon was from
Cyrene, in northern Africa, and was probably one of the thousands
of Jews visiting Jerusalem for the Passover.

27:33   Some scholars say Golgotha ("Place of the Skull") derives
its name from its appearance. Golgotha may have been a regular
place of execution in a prominent public place outside the city.
Executions held there would serve as a deterrent to criminals.

27:34   Wine mixed with gall was offered to Jesus to help reduce
his pain, but Jesus refused to drink it. Gall is generally understood
to be a narcotic that was used to deaden pain. Jesus would suffer
fully conscious and with a clear mind.

27:35   The soldiers customarily took the clothing of those they
crucified. These soldiers threw dice and divided Jesus' clothing
among themselves, fulfilling the prophecy made by David. Much
of Psalm 22 parallels Jesus' crucifixion.

27:40   This accusation was used against Jesus in his trial by
the high council (26:61). It is ironic that Jesus was in the very
process of fulfilling his own prophecy. Because Jesus is the Son
of God, who always obeys the will of the Father, he did not come
down from the cross.

27:44   Later one of these criminals repented. Jesus promised
that the repentant criminal would join him in paradise (Luke
23:39-43).

27:45   We do not know how this darkness occurred, but it is
clear that God caused it. Nature testified to the gravity of Jesus'
death, while Jesus' friends and enemies alike fell silent in the
encircling gloom. The darkness on that Friday afternoon was
both physical and spiritual.

27:46   Jesus was not questioning God; he was quoting the first
line of Psalm 22—a deep expression of the anguish he felt when
he took on the sins of the world, which caused him to be separated from his Father. *This* was what Jesus dreaded as he prayed

27:48
Ps 69:21
John 19:29-30

27:51
Exod 26:31-33
Heb 10:19-20

27:52
Ezek 37:12

27:55-56
Luke 8:2-3

27:60
Matt 28:2
Mark 16:3-4
Luke 24:2
John 20:1

⁴⁷Some of the bystanders misunderstood and thought he was calling for the prophet Elijah. ⁴⁸One of them ran and filled a sponge with sour wine, holding it up to him on a reed stick so he could drink. ⁴⁹But the rest said, "Wait! Let's see whether Elijah comes to save him."*

⁵⁰Then Jesus shouted out again, and he released his spirit. ⁵¹At that moment the curtain in the sanctuary of the Temple was torn in two, from top to bottom. The earth shook, rocks split apart, ⁵²and tombs opened. The bodies of many godly men and women who had died were raised from the dead. ⁵³They left the cemetery after Jesus' resurrection, went into the holy city of Jerusalem, and appeared to many people.

⁵⁴The Roman officer* and the other soldiers at the crucifixion were terrified by the earthquake and all that had happened. They said, "This man truly was the Son of God!"

⁵⁵And many women who had come from Galilee with Jesus to care for him were watching from a distance. ⁵⁶Among them were Mary Magdalene, Mary (the mother of James and Joseph), and the mother of James and John, the sons of Zebedee.

Jesus Is Laid in the Tomb (**237**/Mark 15:42-47; Luke 23:50-56; John 19:38-42)

⁵⁷As evening approached, Joseph, a rich man from Arimathea who had become a follower of Jesus, ⁵⁸went to Pilate and asked for Jesus' body. And Pilate issued an order to release it to him. ⁵⁹Joseph took the body and wrapped it in a long sheet of clean linen cloth. ⁶⁰He placed it in his own new tomb, which had been carved out of the rock. Then he rolled a great stone across the entrance and left. ⁶¹Both Mary Magdalene and the other Mary were sitting across from the tomb and watching.

27:49 Some manuscripts add *And another took a spear and pierced his side, and out flowed water and blood.* Compare John 19:34.   27:54 Greek *The centurion.*

**HOW JESUS'
TRIAL WAS
ILLEGAL**

1. Even before the trial began, it had been determined that Jesus must die (Mark 14:1; John 11:50). There was no "innocent until proven guilty" approach.

2. False witnesses were sought to testify against Jesus (Matthew 26:59). Usually the religious leaders went through an elaborate system of screening witnesses to ensure justice.

3. No defense for Jesus was sought or allowed (Luke 22:67-71).

4. The trial was conducted at night (Mark 14:53-65; 15:1), which was illegal according to the religious leaders' own laws.

5. The high priest put Jesus under oath, but then incriminated him for what he said (Matthew 26:63-66).

6. Cases involving such serious charges were to be tried only in the high council's regular meeting place, not in the high priest's home (Mark 14:53-65).

The religious leaders were not interested in giving Jesus a fair trial. In their minds, Jesus had to die. This blind obsession led them to pervert the justice they were appointed to protect. Above are many examples of the actions taken by the religious leaders that were illegal according to their own laws.

---

to God in the garden to take the cup from him (26:39). The physical agony was horrible, but even worse was the period of spiritual separation from God. Jesus suffered this double death so that we would never have to experience eternal separation from God.

27:47 The bystanders misinterpreted Jesus' words and thought he was calling for Elijah. Because Elijah ascended into heaven without dying (2 Kings 2:11), they thought he would return again to rescue them from great trouble (Malachi 4:5). At their annual Passover meal, each family set an extra place for Elijah in expectation of his return.

• **27:51** The Temple had three main parts: the courts, the Holy Place (where only the priests could enter), and the Most Holy Place (where only the high priest could enter, and only once a year, to atone for the sins of the nation—Leviticus 16:1-35). The curtain separating the Holy Place from the Most Holy Place was torn in two at Christ's death, symbolizing that the barrier between God and humanity was removed. Now all people are free to approach God because of Christ's sacrifice for our sins (see Hebrews 9:1-14; 10:19-22).

• **27:52, 53** Christ's death was accompanied by at least four

miraculous events: darkness, the tearing in two of the curtain in the Temple, an earthquake, and dead people rising from their tombs. Jesus' death, therefore, could not have gone unnoticed. Everyone knew something significant had happened.

27:57, 58 Joseph of Arimathea was a secret disciple of Jesus. He was a religious leader, an honored member of the high council (Mark 15:43). Joseph courageously asked to take Jesus' body from the cross and to bury it. The disciples who publicly followed Jesus had fled, but this Jewish leader, who followed Jesus in secret, came forward and did what was right.

27:60 The tomb where Jesus was laid was probably a man-made cave cut out of one of the many limestone hills in the area. These caves were often large enough to walk into.

Guards Are Posted at the Tomb (238)

62 The next day, on the Sabbath,* the leading priests and Pharisees went to see Pilate. 63 They told him, "Sir, we remember what that deceiver once said while he was still alive: 'After three days I will rise from the dead.' 64 So we request that you seal the tomb until the third day. This will prevent his disciples from coming and stealing his body and then telling everyone he was raised from the dead! If that happens, we'll be worse off than we were at first."

65 Pilate replied, "Take guards and secure it the best you can." 66 So they sealed the tomb and posted guards to protect it.

27:63
Matt 12:40; 16:21; 17:23; 20:19
Mark 8:31; 9:31; 10:34
Luke 9:22; 18:33
27:64
Matt 28:13
27:66
Dan 6:17

Jesus Rises from the Dead (239/Mark 16:1-8; Luke 24:1-12; John 20:1-10)

28 Early on Sunday morning,* as the new day was dawning, Mary Magdalene and the other Mary went out to visit the tomb.

2 Suddenly there was a great earthquake! For an angel of the Lord came down from heaven, rolled aside the stone, and sat on it. 3 His face shone like lightning, and his clothing was as white as snow. 4 The guards shook with fear when they saw him, and they fell into a dead faint.

5 Then the angel spoke to the women. "Don't be afraid!" he said. "I know you are looking for Jesus, who was crucified. 6 He isn't here! He is risen from the dead, just as he said would happen. Come, see where his body was lying. 7 And now, go quickly and tell his disciples that he has risen from the dead, and he is going ahead of you to Galilee. You will see him there. Remember what I have told you."

28:3
Dan 7:9; 10:5-6
28:6
Matt 12:40; 16:21; 17:23; 20:19
Mark 8:31; 9:31; 10:34
Luke 9:22; 18:33; 24:7
28:7
Matt 26:32
Mark 14:28; 16:7

Jesus Appears to the Women (241)

8 The women ran quickly from the tomb. They were very frightened but also filled with great joy, and they rushed to give the disciples the angel's message. 9 And as they went, Jesus met them and greeted them. And they ran to him, grasped his feet, and worshiped him. 10 Then Jesus said to them, "Don't be afraid! Go tell my brothers to leave for Galilee, and they will see me there."

28:10
John 20:17
Rom 8:29
Heb 2:11-13, 17

Religious Leaders Bribe the Guards (242)

11 As the women were on their way, some of the guards went into the city and told the leading priests what had happened. 12 A meeting with the elders was called, and they decided to give

27:62 Or *On the next day, which is after the Preparation.* **28:1** Greek *After the Sabbath, on the first day of the week.*

- **27:64-66** The religious leaders took Jesus' resurrection claims more seriously than the disciples did. The disciples didn't remember Jesus' teaching about his resurrection (20:17-19); but the religious leaders remembered and took steps they thought would prevent it (or at least a fabrication of it). Because of his claims, they were almost as afraid of Jesus after his death as when he was alive. They tried to take every precaution that his body would remain in the tomb. Because the tomb was hewn out of rock in the side of a hill, there was only one entrance. The tomb was sealed by stringing a cord across the stone that was rolled over the entrance. The cord was sealed at each end with clay. But the religious leaders took a further precaution, asking that guards be placed at the tomb's entrance. The Pharisees failed to understand that no rock, seal, guard, or army could prevent the Son of God from rising again.

28:1 The other Mary was not Jesus' mother. She could have been the wife of Clopas (John 19:25). Or, she may have been Jesus' aunt, the mother of James and John (Matthew 27:56).

- **28:2** The stone was not rolled aside so Jesus could get out, but so others could get in and see that Jesus had indeed risen from the dead, just as he had promised.

- **28:5-7** The angel who announced the good news of the Resurrection to the women gave them four messages: (1) *Don't be afraid.* The reality of the Resurrection brings joy, not fear. When you are afraid, remember the empty tomb. (2) *He isn't here.* Jesus is not dead and is not to be looked for among the dead. He is alive, with his people. (3) *Come, see.* The women could check the evidence themselves. The tomb was empty then, and it is empty today. The Resurrection is a historical fact. (4) *Go*

quickly and tell. They were to spread the joy of the Resurrection. We, too, are to spread the great news about Jesus' resurrection.

- **28:6** Jesus' resurrection is the key to the Christian faith. Why? (1) Just as he promised, Jesus rose from the dead. We can be confident, therefore, that he will accomplish all he has promised. (2) Jesus' bodily resurrection shows us that the living Christ is ruler of God's eternal Kingdom, not a false prophet or impostor. (3) We can be certain of our resurrection because he was resurrected. Death is not the end—there is future life. (4) The power that brought Jesus back to life is available to us to bring our spiritually dead selves back to life. (5) The Resurrection is the basis for the church's witness to the world. Jesus is more than just a human leader; he is the Son of God.

28:10 By "brothers," Jesus probably meant his disciples. This showed that he had forgiven them, even after they had denied and deserted him. Jesus told the women to pass a message on to the disciples—that he would meet them in Galilee, as he had previously told them (Mark 14:28). But the disciples, afraid of the religious leaders, stayed hidden behind locked doors in Jerusalem (John 20:19). So Jesus met them first there (Luke 24:36) and then later in Galilee (John 21).

- **28:11-15** Jesus' resurrection was already causing a great stir in Jerusalem. A group of women was moving quickly through the streets, looking for the disciples to tell them the amazing news that Jesus was alive. At the same time, a group of religious leaders was plotting how to cover up the Resurrection.
  Today there is still a great stir over the Resurrection, and there are still only two choices: to believe that Jesus rose from the dead, or to be closed to the truth—denying it, ignoring it, or trying to explain it away.

28:13
Matt 27:64

the soldiers a large bribe. ¹³They told the soldiers, "You must say, 'Jesus' disciples came during the night while we were sleeping, and they stole his body.' ¹⁴If the governor hears about it, we'll stand up for you so you won't get in trouble." ¹⁵So the guards accepted the bribe and said what they were told to say. Their story spread widely among the Jews, and they still tell it today.

Jesus Gives the Great Commission (**248**/Mark 16:15-18)

28:18
John 3:35; 13:3;
17:2
Eph 1:20-22
Phil 2:9-10

28:19
Luke 24:47
Acts 1:8; 2:38

¹⁶Then the eleven disciples left for Galilee, going to the mountain where Jesus had told them to go. ¹⁷ When they saw him, they worshiped him—but some of them doubted!
¹⁸ Jesus came and told his disciples, "I have been given all authority in heaven and on earth. ¹⁹ Therefore, go and make disciples of all the nations,* baptizing them in the name of the Father and the Son and the Holy Spirit. ²⁰Teach these new disciples to obey all the commands I have given you. And be sure of this: I am with you always, even to the end of the age."

28:19 Or *all peoples.*

• **28:18** God gave Jesus authority over heaven and earth. On the basis of that authority, Jesus told his disciples to make more disciples as they preached, baptized, and taught. With this same authority, Jesus still commands us to tell others the Good News and make them disciples for the Kingdom.

• **28:18-20** When someone is dying or leaving us, his or her last words are very important. Jesus left the disciples with these last words of instruction: They were under his authority; they were to make more disciples; they were to baptize and teach these new disciples to obey Christ; Christ would be with them always. Whereas in previous missions Jesus had sent his disciples only to the Jews (10:5, 6), their mission from now on would be worldwide. Jesus is Lord of the earth, and he died for the sins of people from all nations.

We are to go—whether it is next door or to another country—and make disciples. It is not an option but a command to all who call Jesus "Lord." We are not all evangelists in the formal sense, but we have all received gifts that we can use to help fulfill the great commission. As we obey, we have comfort in the knowledge that Jesus is always with us.

28:19 Jesus' words affirm the reality of the Trinity. Some people accuse theologians of making up the concept of the Trinity and reading it into Scripture. As we see here, the concept comes

directly from Jesus himself. He did not say baptize them in the *names,* but in the *name* of the Father, Son, and Holy Spirit. The word *Trinity* does not occur in Scripture, but it well describes the three-in-one nature of the Father, Son, and Holy Spirit.

28:19 The disciples were to baptize people because baptism unites believers with Jesus Christ in their death to sin and their resurrection to new life. Baptism symbolizes submission to Christ, a willingness to live God's way, and identification with God's covenant people.

• **28:20** How is Jesus "with" us? Jesus was with the disciples physically until he ascended into heaven and then spiritually through the Holy Spirit (Acts 1:4). The Holy Spirit would be Jesus' presence that would never leave them (John 14:26). Jesus continues to be with us today through his Spirit.

• **28:20** The Old Testament prophecies and genealogies in the book of Matthew present Jesus' credentials for being King of the world—not a military or political leader, as the disciples had originally hoped, but a spiritual King who can overcome all evil and rule in the heart of every person. If we refuse to serve the King faithfully, we are disloyal subjects, fit only to be banished from the Kingdom. We must make Jesus King of our life and worship him as our Savior, King, and Lord.

STUDY QUESTIONS

Thirteen lessons for individual or group study

HOW TO USE THIS BIBLE STUDY

It's always exciting to get more than you expect. And that's what you'll find in this Bible study guide—much more than you expect. Our goal was to write thoughtful, practical, dependable, and application-oriented studies of God's word.

This study guide contains the complete text of the selected Bible book. The commentary is accurate, complete, and loaded with unique charts, maps, and profiles of Bible people.

With the Bible text, extensive notes and features, and questions to guide discussion, Life Application Bible Studies have everything you need in one place.

The lessons in this Bible study guide will work for large classes as well as small-group studies. To get everyone involved in your discussions, encourage participants to answer the questions before each meeting.

Each lesson is divided into five easy-to-lead sections. The section called "Reflect" introduces you and the members of your group to a specific area of life touched by the lesson. "Read" shows which chapters to read and which notes and other features to use. Additional questions help you understand the passage. "Realize" brings into focus the biblical principle to be learned with questions, a special insight, or both. "Respond" helps you make connections with your own situation and personal needs. The questions are designed to help you find areas in your life where you can apply the biblical truths. "Resolve" helps you map out action plans for that day.

Begin and end each lesson with prayer, asking for the Holy Spirit's guidance, direction, and wisdom.

Recommended time allotments for each section of a lesson are as follows:

Segment	60 minutes	90 minutes
Reflect on your life	*5 minutes*	*10 minutes*
Read the passage	*10 minutes*	*15 minutes*
Realize the principle	*15 minutes*	*20 minutes*
Respond to the message	*20 minutes*	*30 minutes*
Resolve to take action	*10 minutes*	*15 minutes*

All five sections work together to help a person learn the lessons, live out the principles, and obey the commands taught in the Bible.

Also, at the end of each lesson, there is a section entitled "More for studying other themes in this section." These questions will help you lead the group in studying other parts of each section not covered in depth by the main lesson.

But don't just listen to God's word. You must do what it says. Otherwise, you are only fooling yourselves. For if you listen to the word and don't obey, it is like glancing at your face in a mirror. You see yourself, walk away, and forget what you look like. But if you look carefully into the perfect law that sets you free, and if you do what it says and don't forget what you heard, then God will bless you for doing it (James 1:22-25).

LESSON 1
FAMILY TREE
MATTHEW 1:1-17

REFLECT
on your life

1 Briefly describe a time when you met someone you considered very important.

_____

_____

_____

_____

_____

2 How did this meeting affect you positively or negatively?

_____

_____

_____

_____

_____

READ
the passage

Read the introductory material to Matthew, Matthew 1:1-17, and the following notes:

❒ 1:1   ❒ 1:1-17   ❒ 1:16

3 What is the main purpose of the Gospel of Matthew?

_____

_____

_____

4 How far is it from Jerusalem to Caesarea Philippi? What town or city is about that far from where you live? (Use the map "Key Places in Matthew" in the introductory material.)

_____

_____

_____

5 There are four women besides Mary mentioned in Jesus' genealogy. Why do you think they were included in this list of fathers?

_____

_____

_____

_____

_____

REALIZE
the principle

6 Why was it important for Matthew to include a list of Jesus' ancestors in his Gospel?

_____

_____

_____

The purpose of the Gospels is to give us a clear picture of Jesus so we can get to know him better. They tell us who he is, what he came to do, and what he wants us to do. Matthew's unique snapshot gives us a picture of Jesus the King. By the time you reach the end of the Gospel of Matthew, your knowledge of Jesus should be deeper, your picture of him should be clearer, and your understanding of what he wants you to be and do should be more mature. In the end, if you are willing, you will know him better, too.

7 Roughly how many times have you read the Gospel of Matthew all the way through?   ❐ Never   ❐ Once   ❐ A couple of times   ❐ Quite a few times
❐ Many times

RESPOND
to the message

8 Which of the five Megathemes (from the introductory material) are you most interested in understanding better?

_____

_____

_____

9 Briefly describe how you would like your understanding of Jesus to change.

_____

_____

_____

_____

_____

_____

10 In what specific ways do you think you would be different if you knew Jesus better than you do right now?

_____

_____

_____

_____

_____

_____

RESOLVE
to take action

11 What will you do this week to get to know Jesus better?

_____

_____

_____

_____

_____

12 Throughout the coming week, pray that God will enable you to benefit from your study of Matthew by helping you to understand yourself and Jesus better.

MORE
for studying
other themes
in this section

A Which of the Old Testament people in Jesus' family tree do you recognize? What do you know about them? Which people would you like to learn more about?

B Use the timeline and the Blueprint outline in the introduction to figure out the length of time covered in each of the main sections of Matthew. How did Jesus spend most of his time during his ministry? What does his example say about our priorities? How might you adjust your priorities?

C Several titles and names for Jesus are used in the introductory material. Which one means the most to you? Why?

D What was the world's political situation at the time of Jesus' birth? What longings did this create in God's people? How did God address those longings? What longings or desires does our world's present situation create in you? Which of God's provisions meets your desires most?

LESSON 2
DECISIONS, DECISIONS
MATTHEW 1:18–4:25

R
REFLECT
on your life

1 What are some small decisions in life?

_____

_____

_____

_____

_____

2 What are some big decisions in life?

_____

_____

_____

_____

_____

R
READ
the passage

Read Matthew 1:18–4:25, Joseph's profile, Herod's profile, and the following notes:

❐ 1:18 ❐ 1:19 ❐ 1:24 ❐ 2:3 ❐ 2:4-6 ❐ 2:8 ❐ 2:13

❐ 2:16 ❐ 4:1 ❐ 4:1ff ❐ 4:1-10 ❐ 4:3, 4 ❐ 4:6 ❐ 4:8-10

3 What helped Joseph make his significant decisions (1:18-21, 24-25; 2:13-15, 19-23)?

_____

_____

_____

_____

4 How did Herod make decisions (2:3-8)?

_____

_____

_____

_____

5 How did Jesus handle the tempting choices offered by Satan (4:1-11)?

_____

_____

_____

6 How was God involved in the choices of the people in this passage?

_____

_____

_____

REALIZE
the principle

7 What was so tempting about the offers the devil made to Jesus?

_____

_____

_____

_____

8 How can temptations hinder us from making good decisions?

_____

_____

_____

Herod made many wrong choices. Although he built fortresses and palaces, he destroyed lives. And other people paid dearly for his bad choices. In contrast, Jesus made the right choices. Even though the devil tempted him directly and tried to lure him with offers of fame, power, and authority, Jesus chose correctly in every decision. Likewise, Joseph had only one desire whenever he was faced with decisions: to do what God wanted. Whatever God desired was Joseph's desire. We learn from these examples that every opportunity to make a wrong choice is also an opportunity to make a right choice. The right choice will always honor God. How often do you consider God in your day-to-day choices?

9 Why should Christians include God in their decision making?

_____

_____

_____

10 What kinds of choices require Christians to actively seek God's guidance?

_____

_____

_____

11 Why do people leave God out of small decisions?

_____

_____

_____

12 Why do people leave God out of big decisions?

_____

_____

_____

_____

13 How can you include God in more of your decisions?

_____

_____

_____

_____

14 With what day-to-day choices do you need to seek God's help more often?

_____

_____

_____

_____

15 For what big decision will you seek God's wisdom this week?

_____

_____

_____

_____

A What were some of Joseph's strengths or virtues (1:18–2:23)? How did he handle difficult or unexpected circumstances? What does this challenge you to do when you face difficult or unexpected circumstances?

MORE
for studying
other themes
in this section

B Why is the Virgin Birth (1:18) important to the Christian faith? What makes it important to you personally?

C What role did angels play in the birth and early life of Jesus (1:18-21; 2:12-13, 19-22)? What role do angels play today? How might an awareness of their role boost your confidence in God's ability and willingness to look out for you?

D Why did the wise men seek Jesus (2:1-2)? How did they express their devotion to him (2:9-11)? How can we express devotion to Jesus?

E Why did John the Baptist call people to repent (3:1-2)? Of what do you need to repent?

F John the Baptist said harsh things to the Pharisees and Sadducees who came to see him (3:7-10). When is it good to use harsh language with people? How can you be sure to use harsh language only when it is necessary?

G How was the Trinity evident at Jesus' baptism (3:16-17)? How does God make himself known today?

H Why do you think Peter and Andrew chose to leave their nets and follow Jesus when he asked them to (4:18-20)? What have you been challenged to leave in order to follow Jesus?

I What were the main aspects of Jesus' early ministry (4:23-25)? How are these same ministries carried on today? What is your role in God's work here on earth?

LESSON 3
TRUE HAPPINESS
MATTHEW 5:1-48

REFLECT
on your life

1 Complete this sentence in as many ways as you can: Happiness is . . .

_____

_____

_____

_____

2 To what do people typically turn for happiness today?

_____

_____

_____

READ
the passage

Read Matthew 5:1-48, the chart "Key Lessons from the Sermon on the Mount," and the following notes:

❏ 5:1ff   ❏ 5:1, 2   ❏ 5:3-5   ❏ 5:3-12   ❏ 5:11, 12

3 Listed below are the attitudes that make a person blessed in God's eyes (5:3-12). What do you think it means to . . .

realize your need for God? _____

_____

mourn? _____

_____

be humble? _____

_____

hunger and thirst for justice? _____

_____

be merciful? _____

_____

have a pure heart? _____

_____

work for peace? _____

_____

be persecuted for doing right? _____

_____

4 How are the Beatitudes related to each other?

_____

_____

_____

REALIZE
the principle

5 What response to this part of the Sermon on the Mount do you think would
have pleased Jesus the most?

_____

_____

_____

Although Jesus' disciples had left everything to follow him, they still had little
idea of what he wanted them to do. With this list of Beatitudes, Jesus began their
initiation. His description of the person whom God blesses surely cut across
the disciples' natural experience, as it does ours. We don't expect happiness
to come from being poor, pure, or caught in the cross fire while making peace.
Yet those who follow and obey Christ are more than happy—they are *blessed*.
They are blessed because they have a hope and joy that isn't based on feeling
or circumstance. Following Jesus means living by standards entirely different
from public opinion. Rather than making us eminently popular and famous, it
often means facing opposition and misunderstanding. Yet all of this makes us
blessed.

6 In what ways is a person who lives out the Beatitudes blessed?

_____

_____

_____

7 How can a person exhibit the Beatitudes in his/her life?

_____

_____

_____

R
RESPOND
to the message

8 What natural tendencies go against the qualities that make a person blessed?

_____

_____

_____

9 What qualities that Jesus mentioned in the Beatitudes are already a part of your life?

_____

_____

_____

10 What Beatitudes are most lacking in your life?

_____

_____

_____

_____

11 What changes in your lifestyle or priorities would help you conform more to Jesus' description of the blessed person?

_____

_____

_____

_____

R
RESOLVE
to take action

12 Which Beatitude do you want to be more evident in your life?

_____

_____

_____

13 In what ways can you live out this Beatitude?

_____

_____

_____

14 This week, pray that God will help you to value what he values. Use the chart "Key Lessons from the Sermon on the Mount" to shape your prayer.

A Describe what you imagine the scene was like when Jesus delivered the Sermon on the Mount. What characteristics of good teaching did Jesus demonstrate (5:1-48)? How do you think you would have reacted to the things Jesus said? What response do his words evoke in you now?

MORE for studying other themes in this section

B Describe in one sentence what Jesus taught about the following subjects (5:1-48): the identity of believers in the world; God's law; anger; lust; divorce; the dependability of our words; revenge; relating to enemies. Which of these areas are you challenged to change? What change do you need to make?

C Why should Christ's disciples be happy when they are persecuted (5:11-12)? When are you persecuted? How can you be happy?

D What was Jesus referring to when he said that salt and light have a powerful effect on the world (5:13-16)? What can you do to have a significant effect on your world?

E What did Jesus mean by saying he wasn't abolishing the law but fulfilling it (5:17-20)? What steps can we take to avoid misusing or misapplying God's word?

F What is your understanding of Jesus' statement "You are to be perfect, even as your Father in heaven is perfect" (5:48)? How is God helping us toward this goal? What should you be doing in the process?

G As Jesus moved from subject to subject in this sermon, what phrase did he keep repeating (5:21, 27, 31, 33, 38, 43)? What points did he emphasize with the repetition? Which of these points hits the area of greatest need in your life now? What can you do about this need?

LESSON 4
HIDDEN IN PLAIN SIGHT
MATTHEW 6:1-34

REFLECT
on your life

1 What is a show-off . . .

in sports? _____

_____

at your place of work? _____

_____

at church? _____

_____

2 Why do people show off?

_____

_____

_____

3 In what ways do Christians sometimes show off?

_____

_____

_____

READ
the passage

Read Matthew 6:1-34 and the following notes:

❏ 6:2 ❏ 6:3 ❏ 6:3, 4 ❏ 6:5, 6 ❏ 6:16 ❏ 6:20 ❏ 6:22, 23
❏ 6:33

4 What did Jesus tell his disciples to avoid (6:1)?

_____

_____

_____

5 Summarize in a sentence what Jesus taught about showing off in each of the following areas:

Giving (6:2-4) _____

_____

_____

Prayer (6:5-8) _____

_____

_____

Fasting (6:16-18) _____

_____

_____

6 Why would Jesus express so much concern about the outward actions of his followers?

_____

_____

REALIZE
the principle

Tax deductions, appreciation by others, power, prestige, obedience to Christ, care for others—the reasons for doing good are frequently mixed. The same action can be done with any number of different motives. Actions tend to be public, but motives are almost always hidden. Jesus expects his disciples to keep their motives focused on him. Christians cannot keep people from noticing what they do. The mistake Jesus wants us to avoid is doing good so others will notice. Asking ourselves one question will help keep our motives clear: Are we willing to obey Christ when no one else notices? Life will present us with many opportunities to test our answer.

7 Which of the three areas Jesus mentioned do you think a follower of his would find most difficult keeping private? Why?

_____

_____

_____

_____

8 In what situations is it good to let your acts of devotion be seen by others in order to set an example or be a Christian witness?

_____

_____

_____

9 What role do motives play in where and how we choose to give, pray, or fast?

_____

_____

_____

RESPOND
to the message

10 If you were taking classes in giving, praying, and fasting, what grade would you give yourself for the last three months? (Give separate grades for actions and motives.)

	Actions	Motives
Giving	_____	_____
Praying	_____	_____
Fasting	_____	_____

11 Which act of devotion do you find easiest to keep private?

_____

_____

12 Which act of devotion do you find the most difficult to keep private?

_____

_____

_____

RESOLVE
to take action

13 What are some specific steps you could take this week to make sure you are doing your acts of devotion with proper motives?

Giving _____

_____

Praying _____

_____

Fasting _____

_____

14 Each day ask Christ to help you have godly motives in all you do.

A What does Jesus' teaching about prayer have to say about praying in front of groups (6:5-13)? In what ways can public prayers be made appropriate or inappropriate? How can you be sure to follow Christ's guidelines when you pray in front of others?

MORE
for studying other themes in this section

B If the Lord's Prayer is meant to be a model for our prayers, what specific areas ought we to keep in mind when we pray (6:9-13)?

C When will God withhold forgiveness from us (6:14-15)? Whom have you not forgiven? How can you take a step toward forgiving this person?

D What is the difference between *planning* for tomorrow and *worrying* about tomorrow (6:25-34)? For what do you need to plan? What aspects of the future do you need to entrust to God?

LESSON 5
ROCK SOLID
MATTHEW 7:1-29

REFLECT
on your life

1 What's the worst storm you've ever experienced?

_____

_____

_____

2 What's scary about storms?

_____

_____

_____

_____

READ
the passage

Read Matthew 7:1-29 and the following notes:

❏ 7:21   ❏ 7:21-23   ❏ 7:22   ❏ 7:24   ❏ 7:26, 27   ❏ 7:29

3 Who will enter the Kingdom of Heaven (7:21-23)?

_____

_____

_____

4 What is the main difference between the wise and foolish builders (7:24-27)?

_____

_____

_____

5 If Jesus and his teachings are like a rock, then what things are like sand?

_____

_____

_____

_____

6 Why is a good foundation so crucial for weathering storms?

_____

_____

_____

_____

*REALIZE
the principle*

Jesus told his disciples that choosing whether or not to follow his instructions was much like choosing where to build a house. A life of submission to Christ and his teaching is like a house built on a solid foundation, able to withstand the storms of life. A life built on anything apart from God's word is like a house built on sand, completely unable to withstand trials. In giving us his word, Jesus offers us a solid foundation on which to build our life. What are you building your life on?

7 What is so attractive about building a life on a foundation of sand?

_____

_____

_____

8 What are some of the hazards of ignoring God's instructions?

_____

_____

_____

9 What does it take to build a life on solid rock?

_____

_____

_____

_____

10 Why do people ignore God's instructions?

RESPOND
to the message

_____

_____

_____

_____

_____

11 How can we avoid the mistake of the foolish builder?

_____

_____

_____

_____

_____

12 How does it feel to know that you are responsible to obey everything Jesus taught?

_____

_____

_____

_____

13 If you could ask Jesus to clarify one expectation he has for your life, what would that be?

_____

_____

_____

_____

14 Skim through the Sermon on the Mount, beginning at Matthew 5:1. For what areas of your life do these instructions provide a solid foundation?

RESOLVE
to take action

_____

_____

_____

_____

15 What can you do this week to build your life on Christ?

_____

_____

_____

_____

_____

A What is the difference between judging and thinking critically (7:1-6)? How can we avoid judging without being naive or blind to the facts? About whom is it difficult for you to be objective? What can you do to be fair in your assessment of this person?

MORE
for studying
other themes
in this section

B What are the pearls we should not share with people who won't listen to God's message (7:6)? How can we practice discernment in what we say to others about God?

C Why is it good to do for others what you would like them to do for you (7:12)? What is golden about the Golden Rule? Toward whom do you need to practice the Golden Rule more consistently?

D The crowds were amazed at Jesus' teachings (7:28-29). What impresses you about Jesus' teachings? How do his teachings affect your attitudes and actions?

LESSON 6
FULL PRICE
MATTHEW 8:1–10:42

REFLECT
on your life

1 What items do people commonly buy with coupons or try to get at a discount?

_____

_____

_____

_____

_____

2 When are people willing to pay full price for something?

_____

_____

_____

_____

_____

READ
the passage

Read Matthew 8:1–10:42, the chart "Counting the Cost of Following Christ," and the following notes:

❒ 8:19, 20   ❒ 8:21, 22   ❒ 10:17, 18   ❒ 10:19, 20   ❒ 10:22   ❒ 10:25

❒ 10:29-31   ❒ 10:34   ❒ 10:34-39   ❒ 10:38   ❒ 10:39

3 What costs might a person have to pay to follow Jesus (8:18-22; 10:17-42)?

_____

_____

_____

_____

4 Why might these costs involve opposition or conflict (10:17-39)?

_____

_____

_____

5 How was the crowd's understanding of Christ still quite naive (8:18-22)?

_____

_____

_____

REALIZE
the principle

Many people wanted to follow Jesus, but they weren't always prepared to pay the price. That's why Jesus challenged those who wanted to follow him to count the cost, because it would involve living with discomfort, self-sacrifice, and even rejection. Jesus meets each of us with the call, "Follow me." His request is simple and direct. But following Jesus is not like joining a wholesale club. He requires more commitment from us than that. He wants us to have him at the very center of our life, submitting all our values, relationships, and belongings to his authority. We must count these costs before committing to follow him.

6 What did it cost the disciples to follow Christ?

_____

_____

_____

7 What made it worth the price?

_____

_____

_____

8 What might it cost a person to follow Jesus today?

_____

_____

_____

_____

RESPOND
to the message

9 What costs keep people from following Christ?

_____

_____

_____

_____

_____

10 What costs have you had to pay to follow Christ?

_____

_____

_____

_____

_____

11 What costs have you been unwilling to pay in following Christ?

_____

_____

_____

_____

12 How could your plans for the future change if you became willing to pay any price to follow Christ?

_____

_____

_____

_____

R
RESOLVE
to take action

13 The next time you have to pay a price for doing what God desires of you, what do you want to remember?

_____

_____

_____

_____

A Why did Jesus tell the paralyzed man that he was forgiven before he healed the man's physical condition (9:2-8)? What does Jesus want to heal most in every person? How can Christians reflect that concern in the way they carry out God's work in the world?

MORE
for studying
other themes
in this section

B Where did Jesus go that caused the religious leaders to question his actions (9:10-11)? Why did Jesus go there (9:12-13)? Where and to whom can you go in following Jesus' example?

C Why didn't Jesus' disciples fast (9:14-17)? What are some good reasons for fasting? How could you use fasting as a spiritual discipline?

D What impossible situation did Jesus use his power to change (9:18-26)? Why did he step in to do something? With what impossible situation can you ask Jesus to help you?

E What is one need for which God specifically asks us to pray (9:36-38)? How can you fulfill this request in your own times of prayer?

F What special traveling instructions did Jesus give his disciples when he sent them out to perform miracles in his name (10:1-15)? What is timeless about these instructions? What areas of your life do his instructions affect?

G What did Jesus mean when he said, "If you cling to your life, you will lose it; but if you give up your life for me, you will find it" (10:39)? When we decide to follow Christ, what do we lose? What do we find? How can you remember that the benefits of your faith outweigh the sacrifices Christ asks you to make?

LESSON 7
THE FOUR SOILS
MATTHEW 11:1–13:58

REFLECT
on your life

1 What is the most successful gardening experience you've ever had?

_____

_____

_____

2 What enabled your garden to do so well?

_____

_____

_____

_____

READ
the passage

Read Matthew 11:1–13:58 and the following notes:

❑ 13:2, 3   ❑ 13:8   ❑ 13:9, 10   ❑ 13:22   ❑ 13:23

3 In the parable of the four soils, what happened to the seed the farmer planted (13:4-8)?

_____

_____

_____

4 Why did only some of the seed produce a crop?

_____

_____

_____

5 What four common responses do people have to God's word (13:19-23)?

_____

_____

_____

6 Why does God's word make a lasting difference in the lives of some people but not in the lives of others?

_____

_____

_____

_____

The people who heard Jesus speak responded to his message in many different ways. Some scoffed. Some followed him as long as it was easy. Some, like Judas, followed for a little while but then were lured away by the concerns of this world. And some followed to the end. These four basic actions cover the range of response God's word has always received. There are many forces working against a person's full commitment to God's word: The devil, shallow conviction, worry, and money can all lure us away from following God's truth. Our challenge is to understand God's word and put it into practice in our life.

REALIZE
the principle

7 We know that the gospel is true. So why doesn't everyone respond to it positively?

_____

_____

_____

8 What steps can a person take to be like the good soil in receiving God's message?

_____

_____

_____

9 How could a person who is like one of the first three kinds of soil become like the good soil?

_____

_____

_____

RESPOND
to the message

10 What can we do to stop the devil from snatching away God's message before it takes root in a person's heart?

_____

_____

_____

11 What kinds of trouble or persecution test the strength of a Christian's conviction?

_____

_____

12 What worries in this life can choke out faith in Christ?

_____

_____

_____

13 What practical steps can you take to ensure that God's message takes root in your life?

_____

_____

_____

_____

RESOLVE
to take action

14 What troubles or worries have threatened your receptiveness to God recently?

_____

_____

_____

15 What biblical truth or promise do you need to remember during times of uncertainty?

_____

_____

_____

16 As you think of people who are close to you, visualize their lives as different kinds of soil. For whom will you pray? Ask God to do whatever is necessary to plow up their field into good soil.

_____

_____

A What was John the Baptist's relationship to Jesus (11:1-19)? What prompted him to send his disciples to ask Jesus a question? What is your relationship to Jesus? What would you like to ask him?

MORE
for studying
other themes
in this section

B How did John prepare the way for others to hear about Jesus (11:7-15)? How can you prepare the way for your friends, co-workers, and neighbors to hear about Jesus?

C How did insensitivity to God's message hurt the people of Korazin, Bethsaida, and Capernaum (11:20-24)? How can you be sure to maintain your sensitivity to God's word?

D In what way are those who are childlike wiser than some who are highly educated (11:25-26)? How can you become wise like a child?

E From where does Jesus' authority come (11:27)? How does his authority affect your life?

F From what burden or burdens does Jesus free us (11:28-30)? What makes Jesus' burden light by comparison? What burden do you carry that Jesus could lighten for you?

G What arguments did Jesus use to refute the accusation that his disciples were violating the Sabbath (12:1-8)? How can we make sure we don't put rules ahead of people?

H With whom did Jesus interact as he traveled (12:1-50)? How did Jesus respond to each one? Whom have you met over the last six months? How can you present Christ in a unique way to each one?

I How did Jesus anger the Pharisees (12:9-14)? What did they want to do to him? Why might people get angry at someone doing good? What does this reaction help you keep in mind?

J What can people tell about us by the language we use (12:33-37)? What does your choice of words say about you and the changes you need to make in your life?

K Who is Jesus' real family (12:46-50)? Whom does this include among the people you know? In what way does Christ draw you together?

L How did the hardness of people's hearts affect the way Jesus taught (13:13-15)? What can we do to avoid becoming hardened to God's word?

M What hindered the people of Jesus' hometown from accepting his identity (13:53-58)? What keeps people from accepting Christ today? What can we do to remove these barriers?

LESSON 8
AWESOME POWER
MATTHEW 14:1–15:39

1 What kinds of power do you see displayed in society?

REFLECT
on your life

_____

_____

_____

_____

2 What kind of power do you need for daily living?

_____

_____

_____

_____

READ
the passage

Read Matthew 14:1–15:39, the maps "Jesus Walks on the Sea" and "Ministry in Phoenicia," and the following notes:

❒ 14:14 ❒ 14:19-21 ❒ 14:21 ❒ 14:28 ❒ 14:30, 31 ❒ 14:35, 36 ❒ 14:36

❒ 15:23 ❒ 15:24 ❒ 15:29-31 ❒ 15:32ff ❒ 15:33

3 Fill in this chart about the five miracles recorded in Matthew 14–15:

	What was the miracle?	Over what did Jesus demonstrate power?
14:13-21	_____	_____
14:22-32	_____	_____
15:21-28	_____	_____
15:29-31	_____	_____
15:32-39	_____	_____

4 What often moved Jesus to perform miracles (14:14; 15:28, 32)?

_____

_____

_____

5 What did the people whom Jesus helped learn about him?

_____

_____

_____

REALIZE
the principle

6 What do these miracles show that Jesus can do for us?

_____

_____

_____

The disciples saw Jesus perform many miracles. In the events of this passage alone, they witnessed five. Among other things, they learned of Jesus' power through these miracles. He showed that he was ready and able to provide for them (14:13-21; 15:32-39), help them through difficult circumstances (14:22-32), free them from demonic forces (15:21-28), and heal them (15:29-31). Because Jesus lives and is God, his power is available to us today, too. God is able and willing to care for us with his mighty power!

7 Why might Jesus not use his power to heal or rescue us?

_____

_____

_____

8 What assurance do we have that God will . . .

provide for us? _____

_____

RESPOND
to the message

help us through difficult circumstances? _____

_____

protect us? _____

_____

heal us? _____

_____

9 Over what does Jesus have power today?

_____

_____

10 Why do people often lack confidence in God's ability?

_____

_____

11 How can we have faith in God's ability to help us without having unrealistic expectations?

_____

_____

_____

12 If you had been with the disciples in the boat the night Jesus walked on water, might you have joined Peter and gone over the side, or would you most likely have waited in the boat with the others? Explain.

_____

_____

_____

_____

13 For what situations do you need to ask Christ for help?

_____

_____

_____

RESOLVE
to take action

14 How can you pray differently this week, demonstrating faith in God and his power?

_____

_____

_____

15 What immediate worry or concern can you entrust to God's care?

_____

_____

_____

A Why did Jesus retreat to a remote area (14:13)? When is it helpful for you to retreat for private prayer and reflection?

B What do you think the crowds talked about after Jesus miraculously fed them (14:19-21; 15:36-38)? How do people respond today when they are the recipients of God's goodness? What can you do to show that you are grateful?

C How did the people of Jesus' day avoid the responsibility of caring for their parents (15:3-6)? What are your responsibilities toward your parents and family? What often gets in the way of fulfilling your responsibilities to these people? How can you serve them better?

D What is important about a person's inner condition (15:16-20)? How can you nurture this part of your life?

E Why did Jesus first refuse to help the Gentile woman (15:24-26)? Why did he then help her (15:27-28)? What does this tell you about how you should pray?

MORE
for studying
other themes
in this section

LESSON 9
JUST DO IT
MATTHEW 16:1–18:35

REFLECT
on your life

1 Who are the two or three best teachers you ever had?

_____

_____

_____

2 What made each person a great teacher?

_____

_____

_____

_____

_____

_____

READ
the passage

Read Matthew 16:1–18:35 and the following notes:

❐ 16:13-17   ❐ 16:18   ❐ 16:20   ❐ 16:21   ❐ 16:22   ❐ 16:26   ❐ 17:5
❐ 17:9   ❐ 17:22, 23

3 Who is Jesus (16:13-20)?

_____

_____

_____

_____

4 What difficulties did the disciples have with Jesus' true identity (16:5-12, 21-22; 17:4-8)?

_____

_____

_____

5 How was Jesus' transfiguration an important part of the disciples' training (17:1-13)?

_____

_____

The disciples were first attracted to Jesus by his teaching. Even today many people admire Jesus as a teacher but reject the idea that he is God. But there are two big problems with believing that Jesus is merely a great teacher. The first is that if we truly believed that, we would follow his teachings. In reality, most people who call Jesus great do very little to follow what he said. The second problem is that Jesus claimed to be the Son of God. Could he qualify as a great teacher if he were not who he claimed to be? So to say he was a great man yet not the Son of God doesn't make sense. Who do you say Jesus is? As Jesus made clear to his disciples, admiring him but not submitting to him is the same as not recognizing his true identity.

REALIZE
the principle

6 What difference does a person's belief about Jesus' identity make in his/her life?

_____

_____

_____

7 Who do people today often say Jesus is?

_____

_____

_____

RESPOND
to the message

8 Who do you say Jesus is?

_____

_____

_____

9 How has your understanding of Jesus' identity changed over time?

_____

_____

_____

_____

10 At what times do you struggle with Jesus' authority over your life?

_____

_____

_____

11 In what areas and situations do you need to submit more to Christ's authority?

_____

_____

_____

12 What area of your life will you submit more to the authority of Christ this week?

R
RESOLVE
to take action

_____

_____

_____

13 What does Christ want you to do in this area that you are not doing?

_____

_____

_____

_____

14 What will be your first step in submitting to Christ?

_____

_____

_____

_____

A Why wouldn't Jesus give some kind of sign to the people who were hounding him for evidence to support his divine claims (16:4)? What kind of signs do people often demand from God today? What evidence do they already have? What can you say to people who want God to prove his existence with a sign?

MORE
for studying
other themes
in this section

B How is yeast like wrong ideas and deceptive teaching (16:6, 11-12)? What false teaching do we need to beware of today?

C What does it mean to deny ourselves and follow Christ (16:24-28)? What must we deny to follow Christ? What "cross" must we take up? What changes has following Christ brought to your life? What have you lost and gained?

D What did the disciples try to do in their own strength (17:14-21)? What do we often try to do in our own strength today? How can we exercise faith in these areas of our life?

E What kind of tax did Peter pay for himself and Jesus (17:24-27)? In this instance, why did Jesus have them pay it? What did Jesus teach by his example?

F Why is it important not to tempt others to sin (18:7-9)? What steps can you take to avoid tempting others?

G What does it mean to welcome a little child on Christ's behalf (18:5)? With what children do you regularly come in contact? How could you welcome them in Christ's name?

H How do we know children are important to God (18:10-14)? In what ways do adults sometimes despise children? How can we be sure to treat children as God values them?

I How are we to respond when someone sins against us (18:15-17)? Who has wronged you? What could you do or say to this person that would help you respond as God wants you to?

J In the parable of the unforgiving debtor (18:21-35), why should the wicked servant have forgiven his borrower? Of what debt has God forgiven you? How does this compare to the debts owed you? How will you let Christ work in your life so that you can forgive those who have offended you?

LESSON 10
INSIDE AND OUT
MATTHEW 19:1–23:39

REFLECT
on your life

1 What kind of image does a typical politician try to project in running for office?

_____

_____

_____

_____

2 How have you found this image to be different from what the person is really like?

_____

_____

_____

_____

READ
the passage

Read Matthew 19:1–23:39, the chart "The Seven Sorrows," and the following notes:

❏ 21:30   ❏ 21:33ff   ❏ 23:2, 3   ❏ 23:5   ❏ 23:5-7   ❏ 23:13, 14   ❏ 23:15

❏ 23:23, 24   ❏ 23:24   ❏ 23:25-28   ❏ 23:34-36

3 In what ways were the religious leaders hypocritical (21:23-27, 33-46; 22:15-22; 23:1-36)?

_____

_____

_____

4 What did Jesus warn people about concerning the religious leaders (23:1-12)?

_____

_____

_____

5 Why did Jesus speak so harshly to the religious leaders (23:13-36)?

_____

_____

6 What hope did Jesus offer to those who were guilty of religious hypocrisy (19:20-21, 25-26; 20:25-28; 21:28-32; 22:29, 36-40)?

_____

_____

_____

_____

7 How did the Pharisees appear outwardly?

_____

_____

_____

REALIZE
the principle

8 What were the Pharisees like inwardly?

_____

_____

_____

_____

The Pharisees and experts in the law were hypocrites. While they knew a lot, they did not do what they taught. Jesus did not criticize them for what they taught but for how they lived. While believing in mercy, they did not practice it. While believing in devotion to God, they were actually devoted to fame and public praise. While believing in the law, they actually worked harder at keeping their traditions, often at the expense of what God really wanted. Perhaps these areas were blind spots for them; perhaps they were deliberate inconsistencies. In any case, we must beware of the human tendency to say one thing and do another. It takes conscious thought and effort to make sure we live according to the ideals we claim to uphold.

9 Why do people act hypocritically?

_____

_____

_____

10 What is the cure for hypocrisy?

_____

_____

_____

R
RESPOND
to the message

11 Which of the hypocrisies Jesus pointed out do you find to be an ongoing struggle in your own life (see the chart "The Seven Sorrows")?

_____

_____

_____

12 What inconsistencies have you found between your faith and your lifestyle?

_____

_____

_____

13 How might Jesus challenge you to change?

_____

_____

_____

_____

R
RESOLVE
to take action

14 In what area of your life do you need more consistency between what you project on the outside and what you are on the inside?

_____

_____

_____

_____

15 How can you become more genuine?

_____

_____

_____

_____

A What issues concerning marriage and divorce did Jesus clarify (19:3-12)? How do Jesus' words clash with the view most people have of marriage today? What can you do to preserve the integrity of marriage?

MORE
for studying
other themes
in this section

B In what way is it good to be like a child (19:13-15)? What areas of your life does this affect? What makes it difficult to be childlike toward God? How can you be more childlike in your faith?

C What basic human traits did the disciples display in rebuking the parents who brought their children to Jesus (19:13-15)? What conflicting priorities did this bring out? How did Jesus challenge his disciples to rethink their priorities? How can we bring our attitude toward children more in line with Jesus' view of them?

D In what ways can money draw us away from God (19:23-26)? What can you do to keep money from becoming more important to you than God?

E What important spiritual principle about grace did Jesus illustrate in his parable of the vineyard workers (20:1-16)? How has God shown his grace to you? How might you show your gratitude to him?

F What interpersonal conflict arose when the mother of James and John asked Jesus to give her sons special treatment (20:20-28)? Why do people expect special treatment? What is a better outlook to have?

G On the way out of Jericho, how did Jesus show his compassion toward the blind men sitting beside the road (20:29-34)? What means do you have for showing compassion?

H Who cheered Jesus at the Triumphal Entry (21:9-11)? What did many of those people say about him later (27:15-26)? Why did they change their minds? In what ways is our own loyalty to Christ fickle? How can we strengthen our devotion to him?

I What did Jesus show and teach about prayer (21:18-22)? How could you improve your prayer habits? When will you begin to make this change?

J In the parable of the wedding dinner (22:1-14), what response did the king seek from his guests? What holds people back from accepting God's invitation? How does this parable offer us hope?

LESSON 11
IT'S THE LEAST I COULD DO
MATTHEW 24:1–25:46

REFLECT
on your life

1 Imagine losing your job and not being able to find another one—no matter how hard you try—for more than two years. How might this affect you and your family?

_____

_____

_____

_____

_____

_____

2 How would you feel?

_____

_____

_____

_____

READ
the passage

Read Matthew 24:1–25:46 and the following notes:

❐ 24:3ff ❐ 25:1ff ❐ 25:29, 30 ❐ 25:31-46 ❐ 25:32 ❐ 25:34-40 ❐ 25:40

3 What do those who know God do for needy, weak, and helpless people (25:35-36)?

_____

_____

_____

_____

4 How will God reward his people (25:34, 46)?

_____

_____

_____

_____

5 In Matthew 24–25, Jesus warned his followers to be ready for his return. In what different ways did he want his disciples to be watchful (24:4, 42-43; 25:13)?

_____

_____

_____

_____

6 What will matter most when we stand before God at the Last Judgment?

_____

_____

_____

_____

REALIZE
the principle

Jesus' disciples knew they were following Israel's king. Though they didn't fully understand yet that Jesus would have to die and be raised to life, they expected him eventually to take his throne. How could they best serve their King? Through a parable, Jesus answered this question: by serving others. Of course, the weight of God's judgment will not rest on our acts of generosity to others, but an absence of generosity certainly shows a lack of understanding Jesus. The only way to be sure we are giving our King proper respect is to treat all people as if they were our King. Opportunities to serve hungry people, thirsty people, strangers, poor people, sick people, and prisoners are opportunities to serve Jesus, our King.

7 Who are the needy people of the world?

_____

_____

_____

_____

RESPOND
to the message

8 Who are the people with needs in your community?

_____

_____

_____

_____

9 Who are the needy people in your extended family?

_____

_____

_____

_____

10 What opportunities do you have for serving people with special needs?

_____

_____

_____

_____

_____

RESOLVE
to take action

11 Which needy people can you help this week?

_____

_____

_____

_____

_____

12 When and how will you help them?

_____

_____

_____

_____

_____

A What will make people think Christ has returned (24:4-8)? Why will people believe impostors' claims to be the returning Messiah? What is the best way to avoid being deceived by such impostors?

MORE
for studying
other themes
in this section

B What is one important milestone that must be passed before Christ returns (24:14)? What is your part in reaching this milestone?

C What errors did the following people make: the wicked servant (24:48-49); the foolish bridesmaids (25:3); the lazy servant (25:24-27)? What qualities mark the life of a pleasing servant?

D Why did the man in Jesus' parable of the loaned money give different amounts of gold to each of his servants (25:14-30)? What has God entrusted to you? How can you invest it?

E What are we responsible to do with what God has given us (25:20-23)? If Christ came for the accounting today, how anxious would you be about meeting him? What changes would make you more ready for his return?

LESSON 12
A GREAT VALUE
MATTHEW 26:1–27:14

R
REFLECT
on your life

1 What objects of value do you see around you?

_____

_____

_____

_____

_____

2 What object has the least value?

_____

_____

_____

3 How do people decide what is valuable to them and what isn't?

_____

_____

_____

_____

_____

R
READ
the passage

Read Matthew 26:1–27:14, the profile of Lazarus's sister Mary, and the following notes:

❏ 26:6-13 ❏ 26:7 ❏ 26:8 ❏ 26:11 ❏ 26:14, 15 ❏ 26:15 ❏ 26:35

❏ 26:48 ❏ 26:56 ❏ 26:69ff ❏ 26:72-74 ❏ 27:5

4 What was important to Lazarus's sister Mary (26:6-13)?

_____

_____

_____

5 What was important to Judas (26:14-16, 20-25, 47-50)?

_____

_____

_____

_____

6 What was important to Peter (26:31-54, 69-75)?

_____

_____

_____

7 How do our values affect the way we live?

_____

_____

REALIZE
the principle

_____

Mary, Judas, and Peter were all disciples of Jesus. Yet from their actions, we can tell that each had different values. Mary valued Jesus above all else, so she thought nothing of using expensive perfume to honor him. Judas loved money, so he thought nothing of betraying the Son of God to a band of murderers. And Peter, otherwise loyal, cared very much about his reputation, which caused him to deny his association with Jesus when pressed to identify with him. We face similar experiences today. From time to time we will be forced to choose between God and things or God and our reputation. We will hold on to the one we value most and sacrifice the other. Mary's example is the one we should follow.

8 Why is it difficult to let go of our possessions and reputation to serve God?

_____

_____

_____

_____

9 Why does God deserve to be valued above all else?

_____

_____

_____

RESPOND
to the message

10 What objects of value do people commonly hold on to?

_____

_____

_____

_____

11 In what way do you place a higher value on things and reputation than on God . . .

at home? _____

_____

at work? _____

_____

at church? _____

_____

in your private life? _____

_____

12 What stands between you and true devotion to Christ?

_____

_____

_____

RESOLVE
to take action

13 What can you do this week to demonstrate your devotion to God?

_____

_____

_____

_____

14 What will help you remember to cling to God above all else each day?

_____

_____

_____

_____

A What motivated Judas to betray Jesus (26:14-16)? What weakness tends to drag you down? What can you do to compensate for or overcome this weakness?

MORE
for studying
other themes
in this section

B Where does the practice of celebrating Communion come from (26:26-29)? What should a Christian do to prepare for Communion? How can you celebrate Communion in a way that affects your daily life?

C What failure did Peter think he would avoid (26:31-35)? What does this tell us about our own weaknesses? How can we lean on God's grace in times of weakness?

D How does the prayer-time experience of Jesus and the disciples in the garden compare to your own practice of prayer (26:36-46)?

E Why did Jesus not defend himself at his various trials (26:62, 63; 27:12-14)? In what way did his deeds speak for him? In what situations should you let your deeds speak for you?

LESSON 13
ALIVE!
MATTHEW 27:15–28:20

REFLECT
on your life

1 What is one of your favorite Easter traditions?

_____

_____

_____

2 What is one interesting or unusual Easter custom that you celebrate with your family?

_____

_____

_____

_____

_____

READ
the passage

Read Matthew 27:15–28:20 and the following notes:

❏ 27:51   ❏ 27:52, 53   ❏ 27:64-66   ❏ 28:2   ❏ 28:5-7   ❏ 28:6   ❏ 28:11-15
❏ 28:18   ❏ 28:18-20   ❏ 28:20

3 How did Jesus' disciples find out about his resurrection (28:8-11)?

_____

_____

_____

_____

4 Why did the religious leaders make up a story to explain away the Resurrection (28:11-15)?

_____

_____

_____

_____

5 How did Jesus' followers respond when they realized that he had risen from the dead (28:16-17)?

_____

_____

_____

_____

6 How did the Resurrection change the disciples' lives (28:18-20)?

_____

_____

_____

_____

7 Note below the three parts of Jesus' final words to his disciples in Matthew 28:18-20. What is the importance of each section?

Statement: _____

_____

Command: _____

_____

Promise: _____

_____

REALIZE
the principle

When Jesus was arrested, his disciples fled. They didn't show their faces in public again until after Jesus had risen and appeared to Mary, Mary Magdalene, and others. Once these cowardly men fully realized who Jesus was and what he had done, they were changed forever. Jesus' resurrection did not merely intrigue them or become a footnote in history—it was the turning point for the disciples and for us. With the Resurrection, Jesus sealed our forgiveness, brought us power for living, and gave us a new commission. Now it's our turn to give back to him all we can.

8 Why is the resurrection of Christ important?

_____

_____

_____

_____

9 How does the fact that Jesus is alive affect your life?

RESPOND
to the message

_____

_____

_____

_____

10 What would be an appropriate way to thank Jesus for taking away your sins?

_____

_____

_____

_____

11 Jesus is alive today. What implications does this have for . . .

the way you pray? _____

_____

_____

your confidence in God? _____

_____

_____

your worries? _____

_____

_____

your purpose in life? _____

_____

_____

_____

12 This week make it your goal to talk to the living Jesus each day. For what will you thank him?

_____

_____

_____

13 For what will you ask his forgiveness?

_____

_____

_____

14 What requests will you bring to him?

_____

_____

_____

15 For what will you praise him?

_____

_____

_____

A Who stirred up the crowd against Jesus (27:11-26)? Why is religion such an emotional topic? What can we do to minimize people's defensiveness about their religious views? With whom can you take these steps in talking about Jesus?

MORE
for studying
other themes
in this section

B What were Jesus' last words on the cross (27:45-50)? Why were those words significant? What do those words reveal about what Christ accomplished for you on the cross? How can you express your thanks?

C Throughout these last events of Christ's life, which person(s) would you like to have been beside (Judas, Peter, James, John, other disciples, Mary, Mary Magdalene, chief priests, Pharisees, Sadducees, elders, Pilate, Simon from Cyrene, Roman soldiers, thieves on the cross)? Why?

D What Christian hymn about the Crucifixion is most meaningful to you? Why?

E What Christian hymn about the Resurrection is most meaningful to you? Why?